AYODHYA

AYODHYA

AYODHYA

A BATTLEGROUND

HEMANT SHARMA

Published by
Rupa Publications India Pvt. Ltd 2020
7/16, Ansari Road, Daryaganj
New Delhi 110002

Sales Centres:
Allahabad Bengaluru Chennai
Hyderabad Jaipur Kathmandu
Kolkata Mumbai

Copyright © Hemant Sharma 2020

The views and opinions expressed in this book are the author's own and the facts are as reported by him which have been verified to the extent possible, and the publishers are not in any way liable for the same.

All rights reserved.
No part of this publication may be reproduced, transmitted, or stored in a retrieval system, in any form or by any means, electronic, mechanical, photocopying, recording or otherwise, without the prior permission of the publisher.

ISBN: 978-93-90356-63-8

First impression 2020

10 9 8 7 6 5 4 3 2 1

Printed at Nutech Print Services, Faridabad

The moral right of the author has been asserted.

This book is sold subject to the condition that it shall not, by way of trade or otherwise, be lent, resold, hired out, or otherwise circulated, without the publisher's prior consent, in any form of binding or cover other than that in which it is published.

CONTENTS

Rest Is Not for Me	vii
1. Demolition	1
2. Power Politics Behind the Game of Demolition	37
3. Kar Seva	78
4. Laying the Foundation	118
5. Liberation of Ram Lalla	141
6. The Benevolent Appears	169
7. Ayodhya Beneath the Land	201
8. Struggle	218
9. Chronology of Events	247
10. This Too Is Important	267
Epilogue	293
Acknowledgements	299

REST IS NOT FOR ME

I have a personal, cultural, religious and emotional relationship with Ayodhya. My father and grandfather lived there and so Ayodhya is a part of my culture and the values I grew up with. It is always on my mind. Ayodhya holds such a level of faith and respect for me and my family that my grandmother never called it Ayodhya. She always referred to it as 'Ayodhya ji'.

Being so connected to it, I have observed events in Ayodhya and the changes wrought upon it almost like a moving film. I have fearlessly written about whatever I have witnessed and felt, with utmost honesty. This book is an attempt to jot down all the happenings that I have been a witness to. Disregarding any bias, I have put down all that I saw.

It will be an overstatement to say that this book is a hundred per cent true documentation of all the events that unfolded. But it has been my resolve to write on every aspect that can become evidence of Ayodhya's truth. Reporting on the happenings at the time is just one aspect. I have also tried to bring out the politics and the intent of the political leaders behind it. It is almost like conducting a 'postmortem' on the happenings. I have tried to do this objectively as well. This book also contains insights into the archaeological history of Ayodhya. This history lay hidden somewhere inside Ayodhya. You may agree or not, but the fact remains that archaeological research has only helped in digging out the real truth behind the Ayodhya dispute. This enquiry carries the truth behind happenings in different time periods. Ayodhya is not only a centre of politics; it is the centre of Hindu faith. So what happened at this centre from time to time? How did the believers of faith win? How did they change or transform along this journey? How was it that the power of faith did not falter even during challenging times? A vignette of these brings out the research done by archeologists and valid proof revealed by history. The task was a tough one but I have tried to put

Ayodhya's truth in the context of the past, present and future in such a way that it reads as an authentic document.

Ayodhya has been known for its three controversial domes for a long time. But these three domes are not Ayodhya's exactness. After the Babri demolition, only the remains of these domes are left now. But there is more to the truth about Ayodhya. This truth is deeply embedded into India's heritage, tradition, cultural history and religious values. Ayodhya is still. Ayodhya is inactive. There is incompatibility even in the river flowing through Ayodhya. Drowned in devotion, Ayodhya's character is patient, quiet and absolute. Ayodhya is a symbol of vengeance against religious intolerance. Ayodhya is a symbol of India's injured self-respect. Ayodhya is a resolution to remain attached to its cultural heritage at any cost. Ayodhya is revenge for an ideology that was born out of hate and violence and that does not accept the Indian ideals of acceptance, liberal thoughts and religious tolerance.

Ayodhya means invincible. We all know the meaning of 'yuddh' or war. 'Yodhya' means the one worthy of a 'yuddh' or war. Humans only go to war with someone they feel they can conquer. So Ayodhya signifies 'that which cannot be conquered'. But Ayodhya's true meaning has become irrelevant because the demolition of the three domes are registered in the country's mind as its real victory. This victory creates the perception of 'ruler' versus 'the ruled' in our subconscious. For the last hundred years, the country's politics has been revolving around these domes. There have been innumerable arguments on the Ayodhya issue in independent India. Narratives went on for years. But nobody tried to really understand it. Everything happened around these domes. Even now it's all about the domes, even when they don't exist anymore. But its axis is as it is. There hasn't been an intellectual ritual to measure its depth, sharpness and truth, which has the power to connect the present and the future along with history; so that you can analyse the truth against the lies on the basis of evidence and history.

What happened in Ayodhya on 6 December 1992 is not valid or honoured by the Hindu religion. But why did this happen? Our leaders were not willing to even think over this. No one even wants to understand where the roots of this anger originate, except for political parties blaming each other for the demolition. Once you get down to the history of it, this picture starts becoming clear. In 1934, a huge Hindu mob demolished the three domes of the Babri Mosque. Later the English District Magistrate of Faizabad got them restored. At the time, The Vishwa Hindu Parishad (VHP) did not even exist to provoke the Hindus. Before this in 1855 also, there was a huge struggle in Ayodhya. According to one of Nawab Wajid Ali Shah's reports, twelve thousand people surrounded the structure. It was a violent and bloody struggle. Seventy Muslims were killed. One portion of the structure collapsed once again. At that time, the Rashtriya Swayamsevak Sangh (RSS) hadn't even been established. There were no upcoming elections either. This goes to show that there was anger and resentment surrounding these domes at all times. But no one has tried to understand why or tried to resolve it. This is not election politics. This is actually a clash between two different ideologies. One was based on freedom of faith or worship, all-round harmony and religious tolerance whilst the other was based on religious expansion and intolerance.

Ram, Krishna and Shiv are the three embodiments of completeness in India. All three of these divine beings have different ways. I consider Dr Ram Manohar Lohia one of the most secular people of my time. He was also born in Faizabad. He used to say, 'Ram's completeness is in his restricted personality, Krishna's in his free spirit and Shiv's in his incredible persona. I know that Ram, Krishna and Shiv have played a role in crafting the psyche and mindset of India. Though it is pointless to the cultural history of India whether these great people of Indian mythology were even born on earth or not. Ram was the god of India's north-south unity.' But look at the irony. Lohia's followers could not understand this. They went on to fight Ram after taking on Advani. If our leftist friends had seen Ram from Lohia's and Gandhi's perspective, they would have understood what actually lay at the heart of the Ayodhya movement much more easily.

The demolition of the domes in Ayodhya had shaken the entire country deeply. I was witness to this destruction. I have been a witness to everything from the strategies behind the demolition to the hollow efforts at saving it. I have closely observed changing shades of politics in the name of 'secularism' as well. This book is a document of what I saw and heard both inside and outside Ayodhya from the time when the lock to the disputed site was opened to its ultimate demolition. I am giving back the Ayodhya of that time, as I found it and experienced it. I have neither added nor deleted anything. If you wish to experience the Ayodhya of that time, live the tension and crisis of that time, want to feel the pain and panic that it went through at the time, you can read 'Ayodhya Ka Chashmadeed', my compilation of reports printed in *Jansatta*.

Most narratives usually begin with construction. Demolition is considered to be the culmination of construction. I have gone against the nature of set norms and dared to start this book with demolition. The incident of 6 December 1992 carries so many hidden mysterious stories within it that your curiosity will be constantly piqued while reading it. Whatever is out in the open about that day is just a small part. A much bigger part of it all is still a well-kept secret. It wasn't just Ayodhya where things had begun to stir up that day. The most influential and powerful lanes from Lucknow to Delhi were also very busy. Ayodhya wasn't an ordinary city at the time. It was a city that was silently witnessing the country's changing politics and society. Full of anger and vengeance, Kar Sevaks were looking at L.K. Advani and Murli Manohar Joshi also with suspicion. They even pushed these two, their most accepted and popular leaders, aside that day. They were not willing to cancel Kar Seva at any cost. The RSS (Sangh) becoming a part of Ayodhya's plan, officially, also happened for the first time. Three of the Sangh's main leaders, H.V. Sheshadri, K.S. Sudarshan and Moropant Pingle, had been in Ayodhya since 3 December. All sources of the campaign were held by these individuals alone. I was standing at a point from where each and every brick of the disputed site was clearly visible. This was the roof of Sita Rasoi (Sita's kitchen). The police control room was also based here. While plans to demolish the site in Ayodhya were in full swing, Delhi and Lucknow were looking to encash the opportunities from this entire episode. The then Prime Minister P.V. Narasimha Rao, was constantly telephoning Vinay Katiyar in Ayodhya. Uttar Pradesh Chief Minister Kalyan Singh was upset with the fact that he had not been made a part of the secret plan of the demolition. Why had he been kept in the dark? Despite this, he had given clear instructions not to fire at Kar Sevaks. He had given written instructions after a meeting with senior officials, so that later, no officer could be held accountable for the same.

Ayodhya also witnessed how strange and twisted politics could be on that day. The Bharatiya Janata Party (BJP) has always been held responsible for the demolition of the disputed structure. But how different was the role played by the Indian National Congress? That night at 9 o'clock, president's rule was imposed in Uttar Pradesh. Ayodhya was now under the rule of the Central government. And yet, the Congress government at the centre was unable to take any action in the next thirty-six hours to save an Ayodhya that was burning. It was not able to get the Kar Sevaks to vacate Ayodhya. It's also true that Ram Lalla's (Lord Ram) statue was established in Ayodhya for the second time when Ayodhya was under the Central government due to president's rule having been imposed on it. Ram Lalla's temporary temple was also built during the same time. The governor of Uttar Pradesh at the time, B. Satyanarayan Reddy, was sending shocking secret reports to the Central government. He was clearly disageering with the need to either dissolve the state assembly or impose president's rule, citing the peaceful attitude of the Kar Sevaks. Not only this, he was also hinting that violence may spread in the country if any such step was taken. Moreover, Kalyan Singh had resigned three hours before Narasimha Rao called a cabinet meeting and voted for dismissing the Kalyan Singh government. Despite this, the whole drama of dismissing the government took place. Ayodhya was learning about the true colours of its alleged caretakers. This knowledge would shock her at times. At other times it made her aggressive and sometimes made her feel so helpless that she begged for the protection of her god, Ram!

What did happen on 6 December 1992 from 7 a.m. to 7 p.m. on ground zero? The whole incident is reported hour by hour in this book. Everything! Right from what happened when Prime Minister Narasimha Rao called Vinay Katiyar at 7 a.m., to the president's rule being imposed at 7 p.m.; all known and unknown facts are noted here. Even the First Information Report (FIR) filed by the in-charge of Sri Ram Janmabhoomi Police Station is given here as it is. This FIR mentions slogans like *'ek dhakka aur do, Babri masjid tod do'* (push one more time and break the Babri mosque). The FIR also contains eight names of well-known individuals. The condition of the security forces in Ayodhya was also appalling. They were deployed through the whole of Ayodhya but were not functional. The state government was sending outrageous reports about this to the Central government. Some of the reports even claimed that the forces were creating a ruckus in the red-light areas. There was a clash between the state and Central government on this matter. The letters written by Kalyan Singh and the home minister at the time, S.B. Chavan, are available here as evidence to show how well-planned efforts were made to compromise the security forces. These letters pointed towards Ayodhya's future. After the demolition, the image projected of these very security forces was even more shocking. The temporary temple of Ram Lalla, built after the demolition of the disputed structure, was swamped with these security personnel. There were queues of security personnel waiting for their turn to pay a visit and worship. Despite innumerable warnings from senior officials, the process of jawans queuing up at the temple for worship continued. Their faith lay here. All jawans deployed around the temple had taken off their shoes and socks.

On the other hand, conspiracies surrounding Ayodhya were breaking all limits. PM Narasimha Rao was willing to destroy the unity of the saint society. He had given this responsibility to his personal secretary, P.B.R.K. Prasad who was an IAS officer of the Andhra Pradesh cadre. He had previously been secretary of the Tirupati Tirumala Devasthan Trust for a long time. Therefore, he had good relations with saints and religious leaders. The chiefs of Dwait, Adwait, Vishishtadwait peeths; Shankaracharyas of Kanchi, Dwarka, Badri, Puri; Jiyar of Tamil Nadu; chiefs of all maths following Ramanuj tradition in the North; chief of Udupi and Uttaradi math; the saint of Vallabhacharya tradition; Gadiya and Chaitanya sects—were all Rao's targets. The idea was to do something that tore the entire saint community into two.

Amidst all this, there was one decision that, if taken on time, would have changed the face of Ayodhya. This decision came five days after the demolition. The case was regarding the 2.77 acre of land that was the root cause of the dispute in Ayodhya. The Allahabad High Court had yet to give its verdict on its acquisition. If this verdict had come through before 6 December, there was a fair possibility that the disputed structure could have been saved. The Central government was in talks with the RSS and the BJP for a long time regarding this. Politics played a role here as well. People conducting these talks were playing two-way tricks. On 6 December, Kar Seva had to happen on this very land. Before this also, Kar Seva had taken place on this 2.77 acre land. This verdict by the High Court (HC) could have controlled things in Ayodhya. The Supreme Court (SC) had also asked the HC to expedite its verdict. On 3 November 1992 also, this verdict had been reserved. But destiny had something else in store. The domes had been demolished and the verdict came in five days after. Words such as patience, calm and tolerance had drowned in the stormy river Saryu. I have given an account of all the important meetings that took place one month before the demolition, that were about expediting this very decision. All the characters involved in these discussions are very important.

These meetings which took place on various dates in November 1992, included people like Sharad Pawar, P.R. Kumaramangalam, RSS leader Rajendra Singh 'Rajju Bhaiya', Moropant Pingle and BJP's veteran leader Bhairon Singh Shekhawat. After this, PM Narasimha Rao and L.K. Advani had a meeting on the same issue. Home Minister S.B. Chavan and L.K. Advani also met. Everyone from Kalyan Singh to Mahant Ramchandra Das Paramhans, Nanaji Deshmukh and even Atal Bihari Vajpayee spoke to the Prime Minister. In all these meetings, movement leaders only stressed upon one demand, that the state and Central governments together push the SC or HC to speed up the verdict, so that Kar Seva happens peacefully adhering to all the rules. Why was this golden opportunity let gone? Who were the faces behind crushing the situations that were likely to offer solutions to the Ayodhya issue? I have investigated all of this.

Destiny had decided my role too in the Ayodhya case. My editor, the late Prabhash Joshi was also part of the initiative called 'How to resolve Ayodhya?' Prabhash Joshi, Nikhil Chakravarty, Vijay Pratap, Ram Bahadur Rai and I met the chairman of All India Muslim Personal Law Board, at the time, Ali Miyan. After this, we all had a meeting with Mahant Nritya Gopal Das. The chief minister at the time, Kalyan Singh is also witness to this effort. Later the Central government also became part of this talk. But the matter remained stuck at the intent. A solution to this big problem could not be reached at. This crucial effort, to which I wasn't just a witness but also a part of, is available in this book exactly as it happened.

Talks for resolving the Ayodhya issue have been ongoing for years. But then why weren't such discussions ever successful? The reasons and politics behind it are very clear. There is mention of every discussion on this subject and the characters related to it in this book. Efforts made in the name of resolving the issue lacked the intent to resolve. Whatever was done to resolve the issue in fact invited new trouble. This wasn't happening on its own. Behind it lay the political game of loss and gain. At least four ministers of the Narasimha Rao government were holding talks at different levels. These were Sharad Pawar, P.R. Kumaramangalam and Kamal Nath. Later Dr Balram Jakhad also became part of these talks. To come up with the right formula, a group of journalists and a senior intelligence officer were also included. Personalities like Udupi's Pejawar Swami and former President R. Venkatraman also got into reconciliatory talks. It reached a point when the temple could have been constructed twenty feet away from the disputed structure. On the other hand, Nanaji Deshmukh was also talking to PM Narasimha Rao and Kamal Nath was meeting L.K. Advani. What was interesting was that the proposal brought forward by one of Rao's ministers was dismissed fully by the other! For example, Kamal Nath's proposal was rejected by P.R. Kumaramangalam. Kumaramangalam himself was involved in talks. Rajasthan Chief Minister, Bhairon Singh Shekhawat was also trying his best to bring matters to a constructive ending. On the outside, Rao was confronting the RSS but he was also secretly talking to them. He was in direct contact with the Sangh's head office in Keshav Kunj through some journalists.

Rao also tried to intervene through Chandraswami. This was his blatant attempt to create cracks in the Ayodhya movement. Deceptions prevailed in the name of Ayodhya. How a confidential conversation between Prime Minister Rao and Faizabad MP Vinay Katiyar about Kar Seva became part of the court proceeding was a mystery. Rao's moves were sharp and shrewd, but the problem was that his numerous attempts were failing to break the Ayodhya movement. To understand the situation on 6 December 1992, it's important to go through some other previous important dates of this year. These dates were a mirror that reflected the true image of the forthcoming destruction in Ayodhya. I have kept a log of all these dates. From Ayodhya to Delhi, these dates are a living proof of many political meetings and the conspiracies surrounding them.

History belongs to Ayodhya. Ayodhya belongs to Ram. And Ram belongs to the entire abode. In this book I have also attempted to carve the history of Ayodhya. History which has journeyed from mythical and mythological stories, and has been expressed by foreign invaders and English travellers alike. The writings of many travellers, like the English traveller William Finch to Austrian Padre Joseph Tiefenthaler, are part of this book. An attempt has been made to compile whatever anyone wrote about the temple of Ram Lalla and its destruction. From the granddaughter of Aurangzeb to Nawab Wajid Ali Shah's reports, from gazettes of Walter Hamilton to the confession of Faizabad court officer Hafizullah—how and who all had linked Ayodhya with Ram and what was the evidence given. It turns out that those who linked Ayodhya with Ram had nothing to do with Ram.

The court cases over Ayodhya's disputed premises are quite interesting. Whether it's the report of the station in-charge Sheetal Dubey of 1 December 1858 or the objection of the caretaker of the Babri mosque, Mohammed Asgar, they all seem to bear the seal of the true character of Ayodhya. The correspondence between administrative offices on the night of 22-23 December 1949, when the idols of Ram Lalla were placed in the disputed premises, is documented. The language used between the District Magistrate (DM) of Ayodhya and the chief secretary of UP reflects the mindset of those days. Officers appear to be in conflict between devotion and duty. The pain of historical injustice is visible behind the inspiration of devotion. India was then, a mere two-year-old inexperienced democracy. The fumes of hatred, right after partition, were fuelling communal tensions. In this scenario one would have to understand the pressure put on these officers by the public. Even Pandit Jawaharlal Nehru and Sardar Vallabhbhai Patel had to give in to these pressures. They failed to have the idols removed. The dreadfulness of partition had reminded the nation of its pride. This self-realization remained at the centre of the temple movement. I have inculcated, in totality, all these aspects in my writing.

The people behind the destruction were not only those who were provoking Ram-bhakts on 6 December 1992 or those who called upon the Ram-bhakts. The so-called secular powers played a big role in it, whose politics danced around the two factors of minority appeasement and emotional compensation of the majority. The laying of the foundation of the Ram temple at Ayodhya was a result of this. I was present there, at the time of the foundation laying. Among the people associated with the foundation laying decision were some of my friends. They opened up all the layers in their conversations. The private secretary of Rajiv Gandhi, R.K. Dhawan, told me that Rajiv Gandhi was advised to lay the foundation at the Ayodhya Ram temple and to begin his election campaign from Ayodhya itself. Rajiv Gandhi started his election campaign from Ayodhya. In his speech he expressed his commitment towards 'Ram Rajya' of the Congress Party. Mani Shankar Aiyar was the writer of Rajiv Gandhi's speeches. He later said that there had been no mention of Ram Rajya in the speech that he had written. Under the mood prevalent in the country then, Rajiv Gandhi himself had called upon the idea of 'Ram Rajya', to benefit from the prevailing sentiments and thereby getting him an edge in the elections.

Devraha Baba also had a special role in this foundation laying. He was playing the role of a mediator between the VHP and Rajiv Gandhi. Rajiv Gandhi's mother Indira Gandhi also used to go to Baba Devraha for solutions whenever she faced any problem.

Rajiv Gandhi met Baba at Vrindavan on 6 November 1992. Baba

said, 'temple should be constructed. You have the foundation placed. But the location of the foundation should not be changed.' At this point it was decided that the foundation laying will take place. But political paradoxes within the Congress were clashing. Prime Minister Rajiv Gandhi and the then UP Chief Minister, Narayan Dutt Tiwari were unable to come to an agreement. I was a witness to it. Narayan Dutt Tiwari was especially annoyed with Buta Singh. He told me that Buta Singh was adamant that the administration should prove that the place of foundation laying was not in dispute. But what had to happen, did happen. Narayan Dutt Tiwari had to remain dissatisfied. He was terrified at the possibilities arising out of this decision. History did prove him right.

One more important event took place in Ayodhya just before the laying of the foundation. This was the unlocking of the disputed structure. During this time, I was in Ayodhya. The lock was opened following court's orders. But this decision was extremely surprising. It had happened for the first time in the history of India that a court order was implemented within forty minutes. The Faizabad district judge gave the order to open the lock of the disputed structure on 1 February 1986. The decision came at 4:40 in the evening and at 5:20 p.m. the locks were removed from the disputed structure. At that time Congress was ruling at the centre as well as in the state. It was all preplanned. The *Doordarshan* TV crew was already there at the spot to cover the entire unlocking. There were no other news channels in those days. That evening this was telecast throughout the country. *Doordarshan* did not have a centre at Faizabad. The camera team had come from Lucknow. It takes three hours to reach Faizabad from Lucknow. The script of this entire event was being written in Delhi. Only actors were present at Ayodhya. My sources had confirmed the story behind this event, which said that the UP government had been kept in the dark about this whole incident. Except for chief minister Vir Bahadur Singh, who was instructed to communicate directly with Arun Nehru on the Ayodhya matter, the remaining government had no inkling of what was happening at Ayodhya. After vacating the office as Chief Minister, Vir Bahadur Singh opened up to me on the issue. According to him Arun

Nehru had been managing the whole issue along with advice from Rajiv Gandhi. Vir Bahadur Singh told me that the Faizabad commissioner was getting his orders straight from Delhi. Delhi had ordered that all efforts be made to see that the application for the opening of the lock is accepted. I also had a talk with the district judge of Faizabad, Krishna Mohan Pandey, who had ordered to open the lock. Judge Krishna Mohan Pandey was a religious man. He lived in New Hyderabad colony in Lucknow. I met him often during evening walks by the banks of river Gomti. He frequently spoke about religion and sprituality. He shared a detailed theory of a monkey and the divine inspiration behind his decision. He also said that through this decision he honoured the divine inspiration. He told me that this decision made by him had been deeply gratifying to him. The Honourable Judge mentioned that on the day of writing the decision a black langur was sitting on the roof and was not ready to eat anything. Later he saw the same langur at his residence as well. It was some kind of sign of a divine power. This power was the inspiration behind the decision. You may laugh, but this is what he said.

After the removal of the lock at Ayodhya, the inner and outer politics of the Congress party began to heat up. A tug of war broke out within the Congress party at various levels, starting from Rajiv Gandhi to Arun Nehru, Mani Shankar Aiyar to Vir Bahadur Singh and governor of UP Mohammed Usman Arif. This tug of war was interesting and clear in its intention. What *was* the intention of the characters that were at the centre of the act of the lock opening? A true account of it is also there in the book. I also learned of many other interesting stories of this period. The situation reached a point when the chief minister's office had to look for reasons to refuse to provide an aircraft to the governor's office so that the governor would not be able to reach the spot. This was because the governor at the time was adamant to personally survey the spot and assure the Muslim public.

I had many proofs in front of me to show how resolute Rajiv Gandhi was to construct a grand Ram temple at Ayodhya. Devendra Bahadur Rai, who was the Senior Superintendent of Police, Faizabad, at the time of the structure demolition, told me about an important meeting on the issue. He was the security officer of CM Vir Bahadur Singh. This meeting was held at the behest of Rajiv Gandhi and was between Vir Bahadur Singh and Mahant Avaidyanath. In this meeting Vir Bahadur Singh told about the 'Rajiv model' of a grand Ram temple. However, this did not materialize due to certain reasons. I have tried to draw out a comprehensive picture based on these events at Ayodhya. The Archeological Survey of India (ASI) report and the important points of the order by the Allahabad High Court which was based on this report have been included in this book.

From these events it becomes crystal clear that the assumption, that only BJP and Jan Sangh fought or were resolute for the Ram temple construction, is wrong. My conclusion is that the Congress party was firmly behind this movement and controversy. The policy of the Congress party had been pro-temple right from the time of independence. The dispute began on 23 December 1949, when, in the middle of the night, idols appeared or were placed in the disputed structure. At that time the Congress was ruling both at the centre and in the state. It was the then CM Govind Vallabh Pant who surrendered to the communal situation that prevailed right after the turmoil of partition. The idols started to be worshipped. In 1986 the lock of the disputed structure was opened in accordance with the wishes of Prime Minister Rajiv Gandhi. Ram Lalla was freed for the devotees to see. The foundation laying in 1989 took place with the active participation of Home Minister Buta Singh and CM Narayan Dutt Tiwari during the Rajiv Gandhi government. The laying of the foundation was done at the disputed place, keeping elections in mind. This is apparent from the documents. Later Rajiv Gandhi started his election campaign from Ayodhya itself. For the destruction on 6 December 1992, it is the Congress government at the centre which is more responsible than the BJP. The government under PM Narasimha Rao sat by quietly and did nothing for thirty-six hours after the president's rule was imposed. Security forces were stopped from acting. Where is the presence of the BJP in all this? Why did the Central government not allow any action to be taken after the destruction? Why was the placement of Ram Lalla permitted despite the fact that four hours after the demolition,

Ayodhya was under the Central government?

In the year 1990, Ayodhya's famous Kar Seva happened. Mulayam Singh's government ordered open firing on unarmed Kar Sevaks. Ayodhya's lanes turned red with the bloodshed. The politics behind this is very important. Ego clashes between Mulayam Singh and V.P. Singh along with politics of opportunism brought the situation to this point. In the year 1990, the Janta Dal government was ruling in the state of Uttar Pradesh and at the centre. But the distance between PM V.P. Singh and CM Mulayam Singh Yadav was far more than the distance between VHP and Babri Masjid Action Committee on the Ayodhya issue. Their relations were based on mutual mistrust, fraud and conspiracies. I was close to Mulayam Singh Yadav. He often discussed politics with me. He believed that V.P. Singh was looking for an excuse to dismiss his government. He was provoking the saint community against him. This was the reason why whenever V.P. Singh started a dialogue with the protestors of Ayodhya, Mulayam Singh went against him. V.P. Singh also told me about a lot of things that went on behind the scenes. He told me that once he had almost reached a compromise after talks were held. At that time, Mulayam Singh got only those saints arrested with whom talks were on. Chandra Shekhar was supporting Mulayam Singh then and Chandra Shekhar was very strongly anti-V.P. Singh. There was a big conflict going on between V.P. Singh and Mulayam Singh over L.K. Advani's arrest during the rath yatra. Mulayam wanted to get Advani arrested and champion secularism. But V.P. Singh spoke to Lalu Prasad Yadav and foiled his plan. The Kar Seva in Ayodhya began amidst all these conspiracies. I witnessed the blood-stained demolition with wide-open shocked eyes. Ayodhya's temple bells stopped ringing. Prayers were not offered in the evening. The scene, after the firing took place, was unbelievable. There was sorrow and anxiety all around. Faizabad's general public was on the roads. I saw a shocking picture outside the commissioner's residence on the day after the firing. Wives of government officials and military officers had surrounded the commissioner. They were shooting fiery questions at the commissioner regarding the firing upon unarmed Kar Sevaks. The wives of military officers carried a protest rally in the city. This rally started from the cantonment area and reached the commissioner's office. They were holding banners and placards that said slogans like 'stop killing unarmed Kar Sevaks' and 'don't become General Dyer'. All of Ayodhya had turned rebellious. The route between Faizabad and Lucknow had been closed. Commissioner Madhukar Gupta had left his residence and ran away.

I have also mentioned some characters in this book that played a role backstage but these were trying to control the entire Ayodhya movement. Moropant Pingle was one such character. He was the actual craftsman and strategist of the entire Ayodhya movement. According to his plan, about three lakh Ram statues were worshipped throughout India. About twenty-five thousand shila yatras were taken out for Ayodhya from villages to tehsils and districts and from there to the state headquarters. Rocks from forty different states had reached Ayodhya. This meant that six crore people became directly and emotionally associated with Ayodhya's shilanyas or foundation laying. Before this, no other movement had ever taken place in the country that was so intense and that had reached so many households.

The sources for my information on Ayodhya movement are many personalities associated with this issue, with whom I have interacted from time to time, though not knowing that I will write about it someday. Those whom I held long conversations with, included people like Ashok Singhal (strategist of the movement), Vinay Katiyar, Ramchandra Paramhans, Guru Basant Singh (son of Faizabad city magistrate, Gurudutt Singh, at the time idols were placed), Mohammed Hashim Ansari (party to the suit pending in the court of law for the Babri mosque since the pre-independence era), Arun Nehru (a confidante and minister in the Rajiv Gandhi and V.P. Singh governments), Vir Bahadur Singh (Chief Minister of UP at the time of unlocking), P.R. Kumaramangalam (appointee minister for Ayodhya issue by Prime Minister Narasimha Rao), King of Ayodhya, Vimlendra Mohan Pratap Mishra, Swami Karpatri (founder of Ram Janmabhoomi freedom movement), Mani Shankar Aiyar (Private Secretary of Prime Minister Rajiv Gandhi), Subramanian Swamy (activist for the temple movement from the beginning), Krishna Mohan Pandey (judge who ordered to open the locks of the disputed structure), Mahant Avaidyanath (president of Ram Janmabhoomi Nyas), Narayan Dutt Tiwari (Chief Minister at the time of foundation laying), Devendra Dwivedi (Secretary General of Congress and leading strategist of Prime Minister Narasimha Rao), Mulayam Singh Yadav (Chief Minister of UP at the time of firing upon Kar Sevaks), Kalyan Singh (Chief Minister of UP at the time of Babri demolition), Indu Prakash Pandey (District Magistrate, Faizabad at the time of unlocking), Uma Bharti, Dr Murli Manohar Joshi, Ramashankar Agnihotri (chief of Vishwa Samwad Kendra, who gave authorized and unauthorized information of the movement), Moropant Pingle (who readied the blueprint of the Ayodhya movement), Umesh Chandra Pandey (lawyer with Congress background who requested the opening of the locks), Dr Ved Pratap Vaidik (emissary of Narasimha Rao who held talks with the saints), Ram Bahadur Rai (journalist, part of many conversations), Shrish Chand Dikshit (link between VHP and Devraha Baba, also the Director General of Police of the State of Uttar Pradesh), Jitendra Prasad (political advisor of Narasimha Rao), Yogendra Narayan (Chief Secretary to UP Chief Minister Kalyan Singh at the time of Babri demolition), Nripendra Mishra (Chief Secretary to UP CM Kalyan Singh at the time of Babri movement and Kar Seva), Ashok Kant Saran (Inspector General, Faizabad at the time of demolition of the structure), Ashok Priyadarshi (Lucknow District Magistrate at the time of Movement), Maulana Ali Miyan Nadvi (President, Muslim Personal Law Board), Zafaryab Jilani (convener of Babri Action Committee and party to the suit pending in the court of law for the Babri issue), Mukhtar Anees (Shia leader and a socialist who held talks with V.P. Singh on behalf of Muslims), Surendra Pal Gaur (Commissioner of Faizabad).

Whatever I have written on Ayodhya, it is mostly based on my talks with these people, along with whom I was a witness of the dispute. Sometimes I watched quietly and at other times participated in conversations. I have also played a role in some events.

There are various interpretations of the Babri demolition. Some say it's an attack on democracy, the judiciary, the executive and journalism while some others call it a blast resulting from piled up historical emotions. There are some who also call it the will of Ram or the will of God. Some others term it as a betrayal of the law, constitution and democracy. So this demolition means different things to different people. In our first book of Dharma it's written—'*Ekam Sat Vipra Bahudha Vadanti*' meaning there is only one truth but those who know it define it in many ways. In the midst of all this, there were many questions around Ayodhya. The biggest question of all was—why did the Ayodhya that rejected the idea of war, remain entangled in an endless war? Why was war thrusted upon Ayodhya? Ram accepted only dignity and never dispute. Despite this, why was he always kept amongst disputes?

All this happened even though natural conflict was missing from Ayodhya's character. Every time, it was outsiders who pushed Ayodhya into a conflict for their own selfish reasons. Ayodhya was constantly deceived, cheated and conspired against. Ram was always for Ayodhya but Ayodhya never showed propriety towards him. He never received the pleasures of being born royal. He was never at peace there. He left for battles when he was young and never received a pleasurable family life. He always kept battling and struggling. When he ended his life by submersing himself, he left long-standing disputes behind him. Ayodhya seems to be cursed. It appears to be marred with sorrows. It is also a curse that even after being a centre for nationalistic awareness, Ayodhya remained untouched by the kind of progress that transformed so many other cities.

The temporary temple in Ayodhya, after the demolition, has sixteen steps. On the first step it is written, 'Hindu Vijay Diwas 6 December 1992'. It was an expression of the resentment I have mentioned earlier. This resentment was not extempore. This has existed in the consciousness of Hindu masses for ages. Whenever it found fertile land, it has erupted. That's what happened on that day as well.

A question arises in the mind. In such a big movement what was the role of the biggest leader of the BJP, Atal Bihari Vajpayee? He did not appear in the meetings for talks and to form strategies as he should have been. Neither in the movement nor in this book does he make an appearance. In reality, there was a difference of opinion between Vajpayee and Advani on the temple movement, although he never made it public.

Vajpayee was always in favour of a campaign for Ram Mandir in Ayodhya. But he did not approve of the campaign that was being run to construct the temple. That is why he was never vocal about it. But he never expressed dissent as well. When the party needed him, he would come forward to defend it because he was the party's most trusted leader. People listened to him the most. After the demolition when the whole party was guilt-stricken and quiet, at a time when no one could think of anything, Vajpayee came forward to defend his party. He gave a long speech in the parliament.

Vajpayee was known as the Ayodhya case's liberal face. His belief in the culture of good faith and harmony was as deep as his faith in Ram. He was a big supporter of the construction of a grand temple in Ayodhya but without any bitterness or struggle. He clarified his stand on Ayodhya in a letter he wrote to Communist Party of India (CPI) MP Hiren Mukherjee. Hiren Mukherjee had spoken about constructing a national memorial at the disputed site in Ayodhya. He had written an open letter to Vajpayee asking him about his views on Ayodhya. Vajpayee replied to Mukherjee asking him what the memorial would signify. Besides, one religious group demolishing the worship space of the other community! This communication is part of this book's chapter, 'This is also important'. Vajpayee was a poet along with a political leader. He gave a speech in Lucknow one day before the Ayodhya demolition i.e., on 5 December 1992. He supported the proposed Kar Seva in Ayodhya that was to happen the next day. He also spoke about yagya and construction. This speech conveys a lot even though he has always maintained a distance from the Ayodhya issue. He arrived at Ayodhya on the death of Mahant Ramchandra Das Paramhans to attend his last rites. He had come there for the first time in the last two decades. At that time he was the country's prime minister. Vajpayee announced on this day that the Ram temple will be constructed in Ayodhya and Ramchandra Das Paramhans's last wish will be fulfilled. Not a single case was registered against Vajpayee regarding the Ram Janmabhoomi movement. People who question his stand on Ayodhya must definitely read his speech made in the parliament on the issue. This speech is an answer to all such voices. You can read this speech in the chapter, 'This Too Is Important'. This speech was given at a time when other BJP leaders did not have any answers to the demolition that took place.

It is a fact that polarization became a part of Indian politics with the Ayodhya episode. Some wise men try to spread the misconception even today that the Ayodhya movement is a religious movement. You can change the interpretation of history but you cannot change history itself. Going back in time and looking for a valid justification of the present day issues is not a solution. The analysis of history must be done taking into account the situation and the society at the time of its making. Taking all that into consideration we can say that what happened in Ayodhya was a result of the sensitivities that were hurt and egos that remained unsatiated. It was an eruption of anger that had been suppressed for years. This eruption or this situation did not rear its head up in one day. Political parties did the job of nurturing these sentiments for years and it became a mass movement because it got massive public support.

As an adolescent, I had witnessed the Jayaprakash Narayan (JP) movement also. But the JP movement was not as widespread as this one. The movement did not go beyond the hills of Vindhyachal. Its presence was not felt in South India. Although that movement was a purely political movement, it had nothing to do with religion. The Ayodhya movement was massive in comparison. It had reached everywhere from the north-east to the south of India.

Now you can probably begin to understand the reason behind my writing this book. I have been a witness to the dates that changed Ayodhya's face, character and its entire meaning. I went to Ayodhya for the first time when I was thirteen. At that time it was strange to think that even God needed salvation! Later I went to Ayodhya to report for the first time, in 1986. And thus it went on. I have been to Ayodhya over 150 times in about 32 years. I had become so familiar with the route that I could tell where we had reached just by looking at the tea and paan shops on the way. Ayodhya turned me into a journalist. It gave me fame and a reputation. From the opening of the lock to the demolition, I was present there. So I am returning the work done in these thirty-two years by writing this book. God knows how many people I have spoken to about Ayodhya in these years and in a way, this book is like a book of Ayodhya's history.

I have seen Ayodhya very closely. I have seen its religious culture, its spiritual culture and its criminal tradition. Although most saints in Ayodhya follow the Ramanandi tradition there are some Ramanuj maths as well. The difference between the two is that in Ramanuji tradition, only Brahmins are accepted for the position of a mahant of the math, whereas in the Ramanandi tradition a saint of any caste can become the mahant. There is a criminal 'tradition' also followed by the mahants. Criminals come to Ayodhya from outside and take refuge in these maths. Later they become saints by working for the other saints and offering their services to them. After a few days this criminal-turned saint kills the mahant and becomes the mahant himself. That is why there is a popular saying in Ayodhya, 'you become a saint by pressing one's feet and a mahant by stifling him'.

We were the people who followed the 'Jai Siya Ram' (cheer for Sita and Ram) tradition. In folk culture, Ram is never seen alone. Sita is with him. But in the temple movement, Ram is alone. Sita is not present. 'Siya Ram' is the Ram that the public believes in. 'Jai Shri Ram' is the Ram of the mahants and abbots. In the Ram Janmabhoomi movement, only slogans of 'Jai Shri Ram' were heard. This exclaimation was brought to the public in Ramanand Sagar's show *Ramayana* for the first time. I feel that even that show had an impact on the Janmabhoomi movement. The show's popularity was at its peak in the 1980s. No one would enter a room wearing slippers while the show was on. Incense sticks were lit. The entire nation would be gathered around their TV sets consumed by their devotion for Ram. In such an atmosphere, it was natural to have the same kind of love, devotion and passion for Ram's temple as well.

After having been through all the lanes and bylanes of the society and the country at large, Ayodhya has reached a point where it cannot go back. It has to move forward. Now it is up to the nation and society to see what role they play in the infinite journey of Ayodhya. My role is to present this journey of Ayodhya to the readers in its most real, cleanest objective form. So I am making an effort to fulfil this role by combining my mind, heart and soul as I write this book. Let me just say that if, in this endeavour of mine, I am able to add to the readers' knowledge, enrich them with these stories, add value to their lives or fulfil them in any way, I will consider it a blessing from Ayodhya.

Chapter 1

DEMOLITION

I was standing about three hundred feet away from the building. Shocked and speechless! I was wondering if what I was witnessing was reality or just a bad dream. Negativity, anger, vengeance! People were literally swearing vengeance! Everything happened all of a sudden. Kar Sevaks or volunteers had climbed the disputed structure. Police forces and the entire administration were in a state of shock—bewildered, puzzled and helpless. I was seeing such a Gandhian face of the Indian police for the first time. The entire area of forty acres was in a rage of destruction. The scene was terrifying. About two hundred Kar Sevaks were on top of the conflicted mosque with iron rods and were breaking it with all their might. Down below, about one lakh volunteers had encircled it.

That day everyone took some kind of liberty and crossed their limits in the name of Ram. One by one all three domes broke and what came crashing down were the credibility, commitment and dependability of the Hindu society.

On one side were the frenzied Kar Sevaks and on the other were VHP and BJP leaders in a state of shock. They could not understand how all this was happening all of a sudden. Was it preplanned? Our culture and values were covered in smog filled with anger and rage. 6 December 1992 became associated with hatred and religious violence in history forever. It wasn't just the four hundred and fifty years old structure that was getting destroyed in front of me, but also the trust associated with the legislature, judiciary and the executive. 6 December was the anniversary of the *Bhagavad Gita*. In *Dwaparyug*, *Mahabharat* was fought on this very day. And a new *Mahabharat* was taking place right in front of me.

The VHP had announced a symbolic Kar Seva. It may have been 'shocking' for the government, who itself was constantly changing statements, filing false affidavits and getting into misleading pacts. But Kar Sevaks had come here with this very purpose. They were doing what they had been called for. They had been called here to conquer the structure and to erase the symbol of slavery. These Kar Sevaks were brought here from places as far away as 200-2000 kilometres. All chanting one slogan, *'ek dhakka aur do, Babri Masjid tod do'*. So obviously, they weren't here to sing devotional songs! What did they have to do with politics or agreements and pacts made in closed rooms? 2,50,000 Kar Sevaks had gathered in Ayodhya, obsessed with hatred and madness. How could they be told to retreat after all the aggression they had been fed with?

I could see the violent nature of these Kar Sevaks from 9:30 in the morning, even though it had been decided the previous night that the Kar Seva will only be symbolic. In July's Kar Seva, there was a platform made at the disputed site. At the chosen auspicious time, priests were supposed to clean up the area and begin the creation of a symbolic pillar. Volunteers were supposed to shower flowers and water here. So according to plan, at 10:00 a.m., there were about a hundred and fifty priests sitting there, ready with all that was needed.

Just then the Additional Superintendent of Police (ASP) Anju Gupta reached the spot along with L.K. Advani, Ashok Singhal and Murli Manohar Joshi. Kar Sevaks got aggressive after seeing L.K. Advani. They thought he had come there to suspend the Kar Seva once again, so they got violent, broke barricading and tried to get to the platform where rituals were to be performed. Looking at the aggression of the mob, the police became active and tried to push the mob out. But by then, some Kar Sevaks had crossed the barricading and had reached the platform. They pushed Advani and Joshi. Ashok Singhal tried to control the situation. But nobody was even recognizing them at that point.

Volunteers of the Sangh and workers of Bajrang Dal somehow took the three of them to the stage at Ramkatha Kunj. This was the stage from where all leaders were supposed to address the audience. This stage was about three hundred metres away from the disputed structure. The broken barricading was repaired after moving Advani, Joshi and Singhal from there. Because of increasing numbers, the main entrance to the disputed site was closed before time. Visitors had come since morning to get a glimpse of Ram Lalla. But nobody had any inkling that Ram Lalla's gates were being closed for the last time.

Close to the disputed site and opposite the sanctorum was Manas Bhavan. This was a religious rest house. From its roof, the entire expanse of sixty-five acres was clearly visible. The VHP had been in charge of making journalists sit here. About a dozen cameras were placed on the roof. On the second floor, there were cameras of Intelligence Bureau. The entire scene appeared saffron in colour and all we could see was an outburst of rage. Along with the police, there were RSS's volunteers, the Ganveshdhari, who were trying to control the mob.

This was the first time during this incident that I saw the Sangh taking part in it officially. Three prominent leaders of the Sangh, H.V. Sheshadri, K.S. Sudarshan and Moropant Pingle had been in Ayodhya since 3 December. Every single movement was known to them.

By 11 in the morning, the dormant volcano started erupting. The mob of Kar Sevaks started trying to break down the barricading again. They even captured the roof of Manas Bhavan, where we were standing. We felt that the roof would collapse. Fearing this, we came downstairs and went to the roof of Sita Rasoi, which was about a hundred yards away from the disputed structure. The police control room was also on the same roof. This was the safest place for me and everything was visible from here and all the information was also accessible.

The link between this place and Delhi, Lucknow was also clearly visible from this position. What could be a better place than this for a journalist? I got access to this facility because when I was downstairs, I was noticed by Faizabad's commissioner Surendra Pal Gaur and the zone's Inspector General, Ashok Kant Saran. Both of them called me upstairs. Till then, everything was normal. There was no tension on their faces. Senior Superintendent of Police, Devendra Bahadur Rai was standing downstairs giving instructions to people.

Just then information came through the wireless that the district magistrate R.N. Srivastava was coming here with Tej Shankar, the supervisor deployed by the Supreme Court. Tej Shankar was Muradabad's district judge. The Supreme Court had sent him as an observer to keep a check that no temporary construction or anything against the order of the Supreme Court would happen in the name of Kar Seva.

We were on the roof of Sita Rasoi. From here we could also see Ram Lalla being worshipped inside the disputed structure. Chief Minister Kalyan Singh had called the commissioner on the hotline twice since morning. He was anxious to know if all was well. 'All is well I hope? No fear of anything going wrong?' This was the era before mobile phones.

The situation was so tense that despite no activity happening at that point, everyone feared any kind of sudden development. At 7 in the morning Vinay Katiyar's phone rang at his residence. PM Narasimha Rao was on the other end of the line. Before Vinay Katiyar could say anything, Prime Minister asked, 'All under control I hope?' Prime Minister expressed his concern over the news of some Kar Sevaks getting violent. Vinay Katiyar assured him, 'All is under control. The stage is at a distance of about three hundred metres from the disputed structure. Kar Sevaks will remain there only. We are trying to contain them here. Away from the conflicted building, people will give a symbolic service at the stage we have set up and return home from here only.'

Advani, Joshi and Singhal were discussing the Kar Seva over breakfast at Vinay Katiyar's residence. From here the three reached Ramkatha Kunj only to realize that about one lakh people had congregated as a public gathering. 30,000 people were living in tents put up at Ramkatha Kunj. The leaders of the BJP and the VHP had started their speeches at Kunj. Everyone's speech was about a symbolic Kar Seva. But the reason for the anger and resentment of all those present there, was the structure. All of them were pointing to the structure and calling it a symbol of slavery.

Sometime before noon, when Advani was giving his speech, the crowd from the Sheshavtar temple started pelting stones at the police force. The forces were not equipped to shield themselves. Behind them was the disputed site and on their right and left were open fields. Just then, about two hundred people broke the barricading and marched forward. Within minutes, these people had entered the Ram Janmabhoomi area.

When this happened, there was chaos everywhere. Some people from the Sheshavtar temple started throwing stones at the disputed structure. The same thing happened from behind the structure as well. Mobs went out of control and within no time, about one thousand people were inside the Ram Janmabhoomi area. Despite all efforts to stop them, Kar Sevaks crossed the barbed wire fencing and climbed the walls and domes of the structure. The entire situation had transformed within seconds. By the time security forces could act, all the Kar Sevaks present there changed direction and started moving towards the structure. The entire management failed. About two hundred people were on the dome and almost twenty-five thousand inside the conflicted zone. Lakhs of Kar Sevaks, who were listening to speeches in Ramkatha Kunj, also started mobilising towards the disputed structure.

The Central Reserve Police Force (CRPF) Deputy Inspector General (DIG), O.P.S. Malik rushed there and somehow made it inside the structure. He was wearing casuals. Four of his units were present inside the disputed structure. These forces tried to stop the Kar Sevaks. Ashok Kant Saran, IG, Lucknow zone, was standing next to me in a state of shock. The DIG over the wireless was asking him what they should do. (Later O.P.S. Malik retired as DG, narcotics, in the Indian government and A.K. Saran retired as DGP, Uttarakhand government.) The district magistrate and SSP had left their seats and were running towards the disputed structure. The Supreme Court's supervisor, Tej Shankar was also with them.

On the other hand, requests and appeals by L.K. Advani were being made to the Kar Sevaks. He was asking them to retreat from the structure. These were constantly being aired. Merely fifteen minutes after the Kar Sevaks entered the disputed structure, CRPF and PAC left the structure and came out. By noon, the whole area was under the siege of Kar Sevaks. Upon entering the area, the first thing they did was to disconnect the hotline. Then they took the steel pipes used for barricading and attacked the domes with these. While the domes were facing the wrath of the Kar Sevaks above, journalists and photographers were facing it on the ground.

The Supreme Court's advisor, Tej Shankar was in a state of shock.

He had come to check if there was construction material instead of havan material on the stage where Kar Seva was supposed to take place. But here, the entire scene was different. The offerings for the havan had been destroyed. Things to be used in the prayers were being crushed under the feet of people. Priests had returned to their ashrams and maths. The District Magistrate was still with Mr. Shankar. He had his own limitations. It was Chief Minister Kalyan Singh's order to keep Tej Shankar obliged at any cost. His unhappiness could mean trouble if he sent a report of permanent construction instead of Kar Seva. Tej Shankar was running towards the control room. He was also taking his tie off while running, so that the Kar Sevaks would not recognize him. Tej Shankar's crisis was bigger because he had got his son as well with him. He wanted to give his son a tour of the site and Kar Seva.

I was also nervous. I had not seen such frenzy and hysteria in my decade-long career ever. When I had left the hotel in Faizabad in the morning to cover the symbolic Kar Seva, I had not imagined any of this! I had been reporting about Ayodhya for the last five years regularly and for that, I had visited Ayodhya more than sixty times. But I could not believe my eyes today.

By now, the situation had become so bad that it wasn't possible to control it without using a shield. After being surrounded by thousands of Kar Sevaks, the few state police personnel and PAC present there also moved aside. Now no security forces were inside or even near the structure. All security forces became inactive. The relationship between the Kar Sevaks and police forces had changed. Seeing the non-violent attitude of the police, their relations became friendly. One Kar Sevak whose clothes carried Ganesha's picture was blowing his whistle and constantly giving instructions from the watchtower opposite the disputed structure. This watchtower was created by the security forces for themselves. But this fellow was giving instructions to destroy from that tower. Just then, a mob of Kar Sevaks cut off all the telephone lines in Ayodhya. They uprooted all the tools of communication inside the control room in Ram Janmabhoomi. All this happened within twenty minutes of the attack on the structure.

A storm erupted on the roof of Manas Bhavan. Kar Sevaks had

attacked the journalists there. All cameras on the roof were broken. The DM and the SSP rushed over to Manas Bhavan. When both officers tried to get on to the roof of Manas Bhavan, Kar Sevaks present there opposed them. They feared that the police forces would capture Manas Bhavan and fire at Kar Sevaks on the dome from there.

Both officers somehow got on to the roof. But neither were they successful in getting the Kar Sevaks down nor in saving the journalists from getting a beating from them. The attack on the dome continued. The Kar Sevaks made a hole in the dome, strung a rope with an anchor at the end of it thus more people could climb up. There was no place to find a firm footing on the dome. So every few minutes one or the other Kar Sevaks would fall off. In five hours, more than a hundred and fifty Kar Sevaks fell down and injured themselves. VHP had formed a team to attend to the injured. This team had beds and an ambulance. The team was picking up injured Kar Sevaks and taking them to the hospital in the ambulance.

The situation was out of control in the eyes of the administration. It was in control for Kar Sevaks. But overall, the situation did get out of control. No one was ready to listen to anything. Advani was requesting the Kar Sevaks from the Ramkatha stage to return. He was also scolding them. Seeing all his appeals go in vain, Ashok Singhal took over the mic. He announced that the disputed structure was not a mosque, but a temple and therefore Kar Sevaks should not damage it. For the sake of Ram Lalla they should come down. When this also had zero impact, Ashok Singhal and Mahant Nritya Gopal Das got off the stage and walked towards the structure. Everyone respected Nritya Gopal Das. But the frenzied mob misbehaved with them as well. They tore the clothes of one of them. Both returned feeling hopeless. Just then someone informed that the Kar Sevaks on the dome were from South India. The top leader of the Sangh, H.V. Sheshadri appealed in all four languages of South India one by one. He said that breaking the structure is not part of the Sangh's or VHP's agenda. 'You all please get down'. But no one was ready to listen to him either. After some time, such appeals could not be heard. It came to be known later that someone had cut the wire of the mic.

Gradually everyone turned up at the roof where I was standing; from the DIG to the IG, the zonal IG, PAC and CRPF DIG, Malik. One and a half hours of destruction had gone by. None of the domes had fallen yet. Prime Minister Narasimha Rao's son Prabhakar Rao's family servant had also come for the Kar Seva. He got buried in the debris and died. Regular updates about him were sought directly from Delhi. Then the priest Satyendra Das was seen coming out of the *garbhgrah* with Ram Lalla's idol. Someone stole that idol later. At 1:45 p.m., the control room received a radiogram from Lucknow. It asked local administration to use central forces to control the situation. But it also asked to ensure that there was no firing.

That historic wireless was somewhat like this, 'in your service, IG zone DIG Faizabad SSP Faizabad, transmitter, A to DG, I have been directed to convey that you contact the officers of the central police forces and get full support from them. But ensure that there is no firing'. After getting this message, District Magistrate R.N. Srivastava gave a written request to the CRPF DIG Malik, who was present there, to send a company of fifty CRPF to the spot immediately. Malik said that they were ready. But he suggested that a magistrate and PAC jawans should walk on either side of the company for their safety. SSP D.B. Rai got really angry at this irrational demand. He argued that if they had such a huge force with them, why would they ask for the help of central forces? He said that such a thing must be happening for the first time in history when, to control a violent mob, a police force demanded another police force for their security! 'From where should I get fifty gazetted officers, fifty magistrates and a company of fifty PAC?' he said

After this, eighteen instead of fifty central security forces left for Ayodhya from Faizabad with the city magistrate and the circle officer. But barely two kilometres away from the site, near Saket Degree College, some unruly men stopped them. Kar Sevaks had blocked the way ahead. What the security forces should have been doing to stop these Kar Sevaks, was instead being done by the Kar Sevaks to stop the forces. They did not have barricades. So they blocked the way by lighting up huts and shanties in the middle of the road so that no security forces would be able to cross it and reach the location. I felt though, that if the police had fought a little harder, they could have forced them to retreat. But the local administration did not intend to let the central forces reach the site of conflict. Using this as an excuse, the local administration asked central forces to return. City Magistrate, Sudhakar Adeeb gave instructions in writing to DIG, CRPF to ask central units to return. He wrote that the advancement of the forces has been stalled near Saket Degree College because of a violent mob not letting them move ahead and so they should be called back. At 2:45 p.m., the city magistrate asked the units to return. This was when the first dome of Babri Masjid fell. The central forces returned. The central home ministry asked the Indian army to arrange for a helicopter and plane in Lucknow. Destruction continued to be wrought all this while. Local administration and police watched as mute spectators.

The chapter is not complete without understanding the mentality and devotion. Outside the control room, a gazetted police officer was living every moment of this agitation in the true sense. His eyes were closed and he was chanting the name of lord Ram. At times, when he opened his eyes, he would look at the structure and say, 'A lot still remains.' Then he would close his eyes again and start chanting the name of Ram. He was waiting for the structure to collapse desperately. The only difference between Kar Sevaks and the police was that the volunteers were shouting slogans of Ram loudly whereas police forces were only chanting in their minds. The entire atmosphere resonated with the name of Ram.

In the meantime, the beating of the journalists on the roof of Manas Bhavan turned more violent. Kar Sevaks were grabbing the cameras from the photographers, swinging them by the straps and flinging them away. There was not a single journalist on that roof whose head was not injured. It was even more dangerous for the white-skinned. Kar Sevaks were looking for a BBC photographer and his team. More than thirty cameras had been broken. One cameraman from an American television channel was soaked in blood as he ran towards the police control room. Kar Sevaks were chasing him. Suddenly four or five stones pelted down over our roof as well. We sat on the floor. Police officials had left this place. When we looked up, we saw some women standing above us holding big stones in their hands. They were shouting at us and asking us to leave immediately or else they said that they would throw the stones at us. One of these women was using tongs, used by priests, to encourage Kar Sevaks and keep their spirits high. We wanted to get off that roof. But just then we saw the police running towards Manas Bhavan. The Kar Sevaks were making them run for their lives. It was a strange fix that we were in. The male Kar Sevaks ready to beat us up were downstairs and the female Kar Sevaks all set to break our heads, upstairs. I stood on the staircase praying to Ram.

Downstairs I could see badly beaten up journalists running towards Manas Bhavan. All the journalists were being held inside a room which was guarded by a steel barrier so that they remained out of reach of the Kar Sevaks. What the Kar Sevaks actually wanted was that till the time their Kar Seva was complete, any news or photographs should be prevented from reaching the world outside. I was now standing downstairs. Sahara's photographer, Rajendra Kumar came there, soaked in blood. The Kar Sevaks had taken away his camera. They had broken his jaw. They misbehaved with BBC's Gillian Wright as well. We proceeded towards the cars to take our injured colleagues to the hospital. The screens of the cars were broken. Tyres were flat. We removed the 'press' stickers from the cars, replaced it with 'Jai Shri Ram' stickers and sent our colleagues to the hospital. Shri Ram was a source of strength for Kar Sevaks. The same Shri Ram became a safety cover for the journalists. By now, the outerwall of the structure had collapsed.

In a Kar Seva lasting five hours, first the exterior and interior walls were broken. After that, at 2:45 p.m., the structure's right dome came crashing down. Two volunteers died, buried under the rubble. At 3:45 p.m., the structure's right dome came down. The main and the central dome, which VHP called the 'garbhgrah' came down at 4:40 p.m. By this time, all the important leaders had left. They were in a meeting somewhere else. VHP's devotional leaders, Vinay Katiyar, Uma Bharti, Hritambhara and Acharya Dharmendra were constantly challenging Kar Sevaks from the stage.

Acharya Dharmendra was making appeals to Kar Sevaks sitting at Ramkatha Kunj to come and take 'prasad' if they hadn't. He was referring to the bricks of the structure as 'prasad'. Uma Bharti said, 'the task is not complete yet. Don't leave the area till the area becomes even.' The role of Uma Bharti, Hritambhara and Acharya Dharmendra in this drama was most crucial. Uma Bharti gave two slogans to the crowd – 'Ram Nam Satya Hai, Babri Masjid Dhwast Hai' and 'Ek Dhakka Aur Do, Babri Masjid Tod Do.' These two slogans could be heard echoing in the area for a long time. Uma Bharti showcased Meerut's Shiv Kumari as the first woman to get on the dome. She also presented, to the crowd, parents of two brothers, Ram and Sharad Kothari, who had lost their lives in the Kar Seva, held on 2 November 1990. She said, 'see there are tears of joy in the eyes of the mother of the Kothari brothers. The sacrifices of her sons were not in vain. The revenge for their deaths has been taken.' After this, it was Hritambhara's turn. He appealed to Kar Sevaks to get on with this pious task. In the meanwhile, the rest of the saints were reading Hanuman Chalisa and Hanumanashtak on the mic.

As the first dome fell, L.K. Advani, Ashok Singhal, Dr Joshi and Vinay Katiyar left from there. The meeting regarding the next strategy took place at the stage below Ramkatha Kunj itself. During this meeting, PM Rao called Katiyar many times. Katiyar did not speak to him. On the other hand, an angry Kalyan Singh told Advani over the phone that he was going to resign. Advani advised him not to. He said that if he resigned, there will be centre's rule in the state. The central forces will manage the situation. 'Kill some time', he was advised. Kalyan Singh was angry at being cheated. If all this was preplanned, why hadn't he been kept in the loop of things? But looking at the nervousness of these leaders, it did not appear as though any of this was preplanned.

Seeing the PM calling frequently, Ashok Singhal told Vinay Katiyar to talk to him. Katiyar said that he didn't know what to say to him. In the morning, he had assured the PM that all will be well. Singhal said that he must talk and update him of the current situation. Katiyar finally spoke to PM Narasimha Rao. The PM said, 'Whatever has happened is not good. But now you please help. Get Ayodhya free of Kar Sevaks. I am sending 16 special trains. Send back the volunteers in these trains.'

The PM told Katiyar to send the South Indian volunteers first. The state of the country was deteriorating. In that scenario, he wanted to push the Kar Sevaks out of Ayodhya before there was any more bloodshed.

Once the structure collapsed, the Kar Sevaks aimed their entire strength at levelling the base so that Ram Lalla could be established there once again and that too as soon as possible. Police forces, the Central government and the Kalyan Singh government, all three were eagerly waiting. So Kar Sevaks started clearing the area by throwing the debris in the ditch behind. On a land of fifteen square yards, a five-feet-high wall was built in a hurry. Eighteen steps were made leading to that temporary platform. Just then the news broke out that Ram Lalla's idol was missing. On the one hand the Kar Sevaks were under danger of the Central government taking action against them and on the other hand they were in a hurry to build the temporary temple and place the idol there. From the Central government's side, Central Minister of State, P.R. Kumaramangalam was looking after the Ayodhya matter. He had called many times to inquire if the idols had been placed in the temple.

After demolishing the structures, there was almost a war-like situation to establish the temple. Minister in the Rao government, P.R. Kumaramangalam was in touch with the king of Ayodhya, Vimlendra Mohan Pratap Mishra (a.k.a Raja Ayodhya). Raja Saheb had a Congress background. Curfew had been imposed on Ayodhya. Shops were closed. Raja Ayodhya sent idols of Ram Lalla from his residence. These idols were made for this very purpose and placed in a temporary temple by his grandmother. Raja Ayodhya informed P.R. Kumaramangalam after completing the task of placing these idols at the newly built temporary temple. Immediately after this, PM Narasimha Rao called a cabinet meeting and proposed to dismiss the Kalyan Singh government. This was strange because Kalyan Singh had already resigned three hours ago. Even then, the whole drama of dismissing him was played out. The cabinet's appeal was taken to the President's house by Home Minister S.B. Chavan. President Shankar Dayal Sharma immediately issued the notification of president's rule in Ayodhya. Ayodhya was now in the hands of the Central government.

The story around Ram Lalla's idol in the Ram Janmabhoomi is also very interesting.

The idol that had gone missing during the demolition of the disputed structure wasn't the original idol. During the falling and scaling up of the structures, the idols also kept changing. The idol that was taken by Kar Sevaks was placed inside the *garbhgrah* on the midnight of 22 December 1949.

Five hundred years back when Mir Baqi razed the temple at Ayodhya and built a mosque in its place, Vikramaditya's established idol went to Tikamgarh's Orchha Rajmahal. Orchha's queen had come to Ayodhya and taken that idol. That's the reason why Orchha is still ruled by Ram Raja and the Ram Raja there is not Ram, but Ram Lalla. Even today every morning and evening, the state police of Madhya Pradesh salutes Ram Lalla's temple in Orchha.

The most bitter truth in the Ayodhya case is the fact that all the people, especially Congress leaders, who wanted to take quick action in Ayodhya and wanted to save the structure did not act at the time it was most needed. That night at nine, the president's rule was imposed in Uttar Pradesh. Despite this, the Indian government did not take any action in Ayodhya for the next thirty-six hours? It was unable to get the area rid of Kar Sevaks? All this wasn't without reason. Behind all this lay the cunning plan of riding on the Hindutva agenda. This policy opted for by the Congress did not do much good, it in fact stained its secular image. The Congress had to face the consequences during the elections. Years later, during the 2014 Lok Sabha elections, Rahul Gandhi had to cover up the inaction by saying that Babri Masjid would not have collapsed if the Prime Minister at the time had been from the Nehru or Gandhi family.

After the disputed structure had collapsed, Muslims living behind it were attacked. The Babri Masjid case litigant, Mohammed Hashim's house was set on fire. Indefinite curfew was imposed in Ayodhya. Kar Sevaks were setting houses on fire while coming back from the site of demolition. Although owing to the tense situation in the area, most of the people had fled leaving these houses empty. There was communal tension throughout the country. The army was alerted in seven states: Andhra Pradesh, Assam, Bihar, Gujarat, Rajasthan, Madhya Pradesh and Himachal Pradesh. Curfew was also imposed in the cities—Allahabad, Lucknow, Kanpur, Meerut and Banaras in the state of Uttar Pradesh.

If we take a look at the events that took place that day in order of their occurrence, the picture will get clearer. The true intentions of the state and Central government will be known. We'll also get an idea of who all were intentionally ignoring this disaster and why.

7:00 a.m.: on the morning of 6 December 1992, Prime Minister Narasimha Rao talks to VHP leader Vinay Katiyar and takes an assessment of the situation. The Prime Minister telephones at Vinay Katiyar's residence, Hindu Dham. Vinay Katiyar assures him. All will be fine. Kar Seva will be symbolic, as was decided yesterday. You can rest assured.

8:00 a.m.: BJP leaders Lal Krishna Advani and Murli Manohar Joshi reach Vinay Katiyar's place. Ashok Singhal was already present there. They had breakfast together and the strategy of how to keep the Kar Sevaks under control was made. The constantly increasing numbers of the Kar Sevaks was their biggest worry.

8:30 a.m.: Chief Minister Kalyan Singh spoke to all three leaders at Vinay Katiyar's residence and requested them to keep the situation under control. Even Kalyan Singh was worried about unforeseen dangers.

9:00 a.m.: a meeting between the district magistrate, SSP and the Supreme Court's observer Tej Shankar takes place.

9:30 a.m.: Union Home Secretary, Madhav Godbole told the Director General of Indo-Tibetan Border Police (ITBP) that they should be ready with central forces. The minute state government asks for their help, they must not wait for official orders from the centre but should send help immediately. ITBP's Director General was camping in Faizabad.

9:45 a.m.: all VHP leaders and saints including Advani and Joshi reach the stage at Ramkatha Kunj.

10:00 a.m.: Kar Sevaks get angry seeing Advani and Joshi on the platform where symbolic Kar Seva was supposed to happen in the form of *yagya* and *havan*. Kar Sevaks begin sloganeering. Kar Sevaks break the barriers for the first time.

11:30 a.m.: the news about the presence of one lakh Kar Sevaks in Ramkatha Kunj reaches Delhi. Speeches are being made by leaders there. On the stage were present BJP's, VHP's and Sangh's senior leaders. There is excitement all around but everything is under control.

12:00 noon: home ministry receives news through Intelligence Bureau that about two hundred volunteers have forcefully entered the conflicted building. State police and PAC could not stop them. Local officers also abstained from interfering. Kar Sevaks turned violent. This information was conveyed to the prime minister and home minister immediately. IB had put three cameras in one of the rooms of Manas Bhavan from where they had done video recording of the whole day. Later this very recording became the basis of CBI enquiry.

12:10 p.m.: the Union Home Secretary called UP's chief secretary. But he could not talk to him. Then he told the Director, State Police to use the central forces employed in Faizabad immediately.

12:25 p.m.: Home Minister S.B. Chavan spoke to Chief Minister Kalyan Singh and expressed his concern over the attack on the structure. He appealed to him to take action and get the building area vacated immediately. The Home Minister told the Chief Minister to use the central forces. Kalyan Singh told the Home Minister that he will investigate and give him a report on the matter. But he never called him again.

12:30 p.m.: Chief Minister Kalyan Singh contacted the Ayodhya control room and spoke to the police commissioner. He expressed his anger on the developments. But he also said that the situation should be controlled without use of firing. In the meanwhile, the Supreme Court's supervisor, Tej Shankar told Supreme Court registrar that some

	volunteers have climbed the structure but no temporary construction is taking place. (Actually Tej Shankar was there to supervise if there was any temporary construction taking place. But only destruction was happening there.)
12:40 p.m.:	Director General ITBP informed the home ministry that damage is being done to the structure. But, the UP police are not taking any action. Two battalions of the Rapid Action Force are ready to take action. Both battalions are waiting at Faizabad's Dogra regiment centre for the state magistrates.
1:00 p.m.:	The Central Home Minister spoke with B. Satyanarayan, the governor of UP. He informed him about the attack on the Babri structure and asked him to intervene.
1:15 p.m.:	The District Magistrate, Faizabad demanded a company of fifty central forces from DIG, CRPF. Director General, ITBP demanded magistrates to accompany these forces, because according to the law, security forces cannot march ahead without the presence of a magistrate with them.
1:30 p.m.:	Ayodhya control room receives a written message from Kalyan Singh that there will be no firing. 'Get the disputed site vacated without firing.'
1:50 p.m.:	a magistrate and a circle officer reach Faizabad's Dogra regiment to take the central forces with them to the Babri Masjid/ Ram Janmabhoomi site.
1:50 p.m.:	ITBP Director General again told home ministry that the structure has received a lot of damage. But the UP police are not doing anything about it. Three battalions of the central forces left for Ayodhya with a magistrate.
2:00 p.m.:	Home Minister Chavan again asked Chief Minister Kalyan Singh about what is being done for the security of the structure. Kalyan Singh said that he was doing everything to save it but that they weren't allowed to fire.
2:20 p.m.:	DG, ITBP informed home ministry that the three battalions of paramilitary forces that had started from Faizabad had to face resistance and obstacles. People

	had blocked the way. Stone pelting also took place. Then the magistrate gave them written instructions to return. All three battalions returned. The situation remained unchanged.
2:30 p.m.:	The Union Home Secretary told the Director of UP police that all three battalions of the central forces have been returned by the local administration. 'You please advise them to use the security forces'.
2:40 p.m.:	Union Home Secretary spoke to the Defence Secretary and asked him to keep some helicopters ready, so that if need be, the central forces could be flown to Ayodhya. He also asked him to keep one or two transport planes ready.
2:50 p.m.:	IB informed the home ministry that the structure's first dome has fallen. The situation was getting worse fast. Cases of communal violence are also reported. There is fear of communal riots taking place. Central forces are unable to reach the location. DGP, UP informed that the situation cannot be controlled now without the use of firing. Hence, the permission for this was being taken from the CM. The CM had not given any order till now. Advani, Joshi and Singhal come on to the stage at Ramkatha Kunj again. All three looked very worried. Uma Bharti was jumping with joy. She climbed on to the back of Dr Joshi in her excitement.
3.00 p.m.:	Dr K. Srinath Reddy, PM's personal doctor comes to the PM's residence at Race Course Road to check on PM Rao's health, for a second time. He had made an earlier visit the same morning. Reddy tells that Rao's BP was high and his face was red. The PM appeared quite tense. 'His heartbeat and pulse rate was escalated. He wasn't saying anything. 'Normally, he spoke to me in Telugu or English. But today, he said nothing.' Reddy said.
4:30 p.m.:	The Union Home Secretary asked all the state home secretaries and the Director of police to keep an eye on any rising communal tension. If the situation gets

bad, then they must take help from the centre. Help can also be taken from military officers directly. The Home Secretary said to the Army General and to the Defence Secretary that they must be prepared to help the local administration.

4:40 p.m.: The main dome of the disputed structure, which is also called the *garbhgrah* by VHP, also collapsed. All local officers now left their positions and ran away. Now there were only a few saints and priests at Ramkatha Kunj. Acharya Dharmendra, Hritambhara etc. were challenging the volunteers. The volunteers also started returning and the whole area started looking like a mindless head.

5:00 p.m.: Attacks begin on Muslims living in Ayodhya. Their homes and shops were being set on fire. Volunteers returning from the demolition site were doing this task. Many Muslims were killed in this violence. The violence began after a rumour started about a Kar Sevak going missing post his argument with Babri leader, Haji Mehboob.

5:15 p.m.: Dr Murli Manohar Joshi wrote a letter on his own, where he congratulated Kar Sevaks for the Babri demolition. An appeal was made to the Kar Sevaks to spare the Muslims living in Ayodhya and not attack their homes or shops because they hold nothing against them. Joshi gave this letter to Lallu Singh and asked him to go around in a jeep and appeal to the Kar Sevaks. But looking at the Kar Sevaks' anger, Lallu Singh vanished. The administration could not find him.

5:30 p.m.: Kar Sevaks were returning to the bus stands and railway stations. All were holding bricks, barricading pipes and some rubble from the demolished structure in their hands. These were souvenirs of their victory, for them.

5:30 p.m.: The Union Home Ministry told the UP government, which had already resigned, that the army is ready. The army's transport plane was also on alert. The army can be sent if the district magistrate wishes. The Home Ministry told

	the Defence Ministry to keep three N12 planes ready at the Lucknow airport.
5:40 p.m.:	Faizabad's central camp had not yet received any letter asking for paramilitary forces from the Faizabad district administration.
6:00 p.m.:	an Additional District Magistrate (ADM) reached Faizabad's paramilitary camp without a magistrate and took six companies of security forces out of fifty with him.
6:45 p.m.:	Ram Lalla's idols were placed at the base of the platform of the Babri structure. The construction of a temporary structure started.
7:00 p.m.:	the Central Cabinet proposed to suspend the legislative assembly, oust the UP government and impose President's rule.

From the beginning of the demolition to the making of a temporary temple by day three, I was really excited as a journalist on one side, but also very nervous on the other. The concern for the basic and day to day activities had taken a backseat. We were running frantically from pillar to post. To gather as much of history as we could. At one moment there was a fire in the residential settlements and the other marked the arrival of the central forces. The Kar Sevaks began to gather again at the temporary temple. So we ran to it to see if there was any action being taken to remove the idol from there. We had literally turned into *chakarghinnis* in these forty eight hours. We were in the midst of a major upheaval. We were witnesses to the history's most tragic yet thrilling moments, the kind of bewilderment was unimaginable. The indecisiveness, the lies, the absolute state of shock the administration of the country, the chief minister and prime minister spent these forty-eight hours in, is their truth. That will remain etched in the history of India, forever. These forty-eight hours also gave this country an unparalleled understanding on the conflict between faith and society.

With these incidents being put in such an order, can the role of each one be figured at least? Who was helpless? Who wanted to get the structure demolished? Who was under a false impression? Who was lying? The picture of destruction becomes clear after reading this.

After the structure collapsed, we were in a hurry to send out news. For this, we had to return to Faizabad even though Ayodhya was still in the hands of rioters. Kar Sevaks were now on to the task of levelling the ground. Floodlights had been installed in the entire area. There was festive-like fervour all around. There was no fear of security forces. Although there remained a doubt that during night time, the central forces could take action and get the area vacated. When we were returning to Faizabad, we saw some houses burning up in flames. Adyodha and Faizabad are twin cities. Although the distance between the two cities is about seven kilometres, due to spread out areas, one can hardly tell where one ends and the other starts.

During this time, another major incident was prevented from happening. My friend Wasim Ahmad was a Rajya Sabha member. He was very close to V.P. Singh. He had also come to Ayodhya to give every minute update to V.P. Singh. Kar Sevaks surrounded him outside Manas Bhavan. They were asking for Wasim's identity card. Wasim got very nervous because he knew that if they came to know of his secret, the Kar Sevaks could get violent. No one knew what would have happened.

I understood the matter. I quickly ran towards him and pulled him out of that mob. I explained to the Kar Sevaks that he is my editor and has come from Delhi. I took him to the police control room. He was relieved. Then I got him to Faizabad in my car. Wasim still gets emotional when he thinks about that day. This incident also reveals how deep the hatred was at the time.

I was put up at the only decent hotel in Faizabad, 'Shaan-E-Awadh'. More than a hundred Indian and foreign journalists were staying here. The entire hotel was full of journalists. The unique selling point (USP) of this hotel was that the telegraph office was right opposite and residences of the District Magistrate and the Commissioner were also close by. This meant that it was the centre of all news. Communication tools were not revolutionized at that time. These were times of telegrams, telex and fax. Photographers had turned the hotel staircase into a dark room. Journalists were sitting with their typewriters in the restaurant and reception area. The hotel's owner would come himself and offer STD calls services to all. We were all anxious to be the first to send out our reports to our respective offices.

I had to give all details of the incident to my editor, Prabhash Joshi. Prabhash ji was one of the people who were moderating between the centre and the Sangh for Kar Seva. Looking at the crowd in the hotel, I came out and called him from a phone booth. Rambabu took my call and said that the editor had been looking for me. Rambabu was the editor's secretary. I told Prabhash ji the whole story of the Babri demolition. Prabhash ji started to cry. He was silent for some time. Then he said, 'this is betrayal, deception, lies. This is treachery. This is not our religion. Now we will fight these people.'

Prabhash ji was very disturbed. He could not understand anything, and I was in a hurry to tell him the whole story of the destruction in five minutes. After briefing him, I went to write my report, which you will find in my next book, *Ayodhya Ka Chashmadeed*.

The FIR for Babri demolition was registered in Ram Janmabhoomi Police Station that very night. One FIR was filed by Station Officer Priyabanda Nath Shukla and the other by Ram Janmabhoomi station-in-charge, Deputy Supervisor Ganga Prasad Tiwari. The enquiry of both these were given to Circle Officer, Inayat Nagar, R.P. Tandon. Later it was transferred to the Central Bureau of Investigation (CBI). The report number 197/92 reported at the Ram Janmabhoomi Police Station was filed under Indian Penal Code (IPC) sections 395/397/332/337/338/295/297/153 and the case was booked under 7 criminal law amendment acts. The other FIR, based on the report by Ram Janmabhoomi station-in-charge, Ganga Prasad Tiwari, was filed as FIR number 198/92 under section 153A, 153B/505 of IPC. This was filed against eight people. The FIR said –

Based on this FIR, Lal Krishna Advani, Vishnu Hari Dalmiya, Ashok Singhal, Murli Manohar Joshi, Uma Bharti and Vinay Katiyar were arrested on 8 December. All those arrested were kept at the guest house at Mata Teela Dam, Lalpur. Everybody was released on 10 December after Lalitpur's Chief Judicial Magistrate R.R. Yadav gave a verdict in their favour at 6:30 p.m.

The magistrate said in his six-page-long verdict that the government was unable to provide supportive evidence in support of its initial report.

The twenty-seven injured Kar Sevaks recovering in the district hospital were also arrested. They were arrested under section 153. All these were admitted in the orthopaedic ward of the hospital.

Among the ones arrested were:

Hemraj (Kota, Rajasthan), Hazari Lal (Batlaiya), Girja Shankar (Barabanki), Dinesh Sharma (Misrauli, Rajasthan), Mahendra Kumar (Kareeb Nagar, Rampur, UP), Rajjan Lal (Fatehpur, Barabanki, UP), Vinay Kumar Rai (Roopalpur, Gopalganj, Bihar), Laxmi Narayan Das and Digambar Singh (Pauri, Garhwal), Lokeshchand (Raebareli), Sachidanand (Nalanda, Bihar), Om Prakash Shastri (Azamgarh), Rameshwar Suman (Kota, Rajasthan), Satya Narayan (Kota, Rajasthan), Ramesh Tyagi (Chhapra, Bihar), Devendra Singh Rao and Shiv Mangle (Ayodhya), Arjun Prasad Ojha (Balia), Vineet Kumar (Madhya Pradesh), Anchal Singh (Bhopal, MP), Sukhdev (Maharashtra), Ram Lakhan Das (Ayodhya), Satya Prakash Tripathi (Kanpur Dehat), Kishan Bihari (Itawa), Chhedi Shah (Bihar), Ramesh Pachauri (Aurangabad), Kuber Singli (Bhojpur, Bihar).

After the demolition of the structure and construction of the temporary temple, about one lakh Kar Sevaks spent the whole night of 6 December in that area only. They feared that action would be taken to remove Ram Lalla's idol from the temple. Construction work of the temporary temple continued all night. The next day, Kar Sevaks present there created a ruckus from early in the morning as the police had pushed out the temple's official pujari. The pujari's assistants, Subhash Chandra Tripathi and Sunil Das were also sent away. So no rituals took place at the temple that morning. The news spread fast making all of the Kar Sevaks angry. The administration became alert. A search for the pujari and his assistants began. They were found and taken to the temple. The prayer and other rituals began. The pooja that takes place in the early morning started at noon. The rituals that started then still continue. So on an official level, the temporary temple got a legitimate status after the government organized a pooja.

Twenty-four hours after the centre took over Ayodhya, the central forces could not gather the courage to move towards Ramkot area of

Ayodhya. The district administration and central forces were in a fix.

The Centre's claim that paramilitary forces will get the disputed site vacated in forty-five minutes if need be, was proven baseless. Next day, the task of getting the Kar Sevaks out of the area peacefully, went on. But the Kar Sevaks' madness would not abate. Almost all houses where Muslims lived were burnt down in Ayodhya. Most of the mosques had been damaged. The religious madness had consumed the lives of six Muslims so far. The Babri Masjid and Ram Janmabhoomi cases ligitant, Mohammed Hashim's house was also burnt down. Kar Sevaks took over his place. Faizabad's District Magistrate and Senior Police Superintendent were not bothered about this anarchy because they were waiting for action against themselves. By evening, both the officers were suspended and the Commissioner was transferred. The central forces had surrounded the Janmabhoomi area and Ramkatha Kunj and had tried to create pressure, four times, since the demolition. But each time, they had to retreat.

When the disputed structure had collapsed and the debris had been cleared, many remains of the old temple were found. All these were collected and kept at Ramkatha Kunj. More than a hundred white marble pieces were found from under the structure. A brass urn and pieces of some old statues were also found from the beneath the structure. Kar Sevaks were worshipping these remains with devotion.

After Prime Minister Narasimha Rao announced in Delhi that the mosque will be rebuilt, there was fear that Ram Lalla might lose his abode. VHP President, Ashok Singhal challenged the government saying, 'Ram Lalla cannot be removed from his birthplace. If anyone tries to do it, a far worse situation will be created in the country.' Singhal ordered all Kar Sevaks who were still in UP, to come to Ayodhya and leave only after they had visited the Ram Lalla temple. But he also instructed that those who had not not left their homes yet should not leave as of now. They were told to wait for the next order so that the pressure built by Kar Sevaks in Ayodhya remains and the government is not able to take any steps regarding the idols.

The biggest problem in Ayodhya was regarding the central forces. They were present in the entire city but were not in action anywhere.

Late at night, district administration and security forces got into a tug of war on the deployment of security forces. The security forces said that till the time there is a magistrate and a gazetted officer with each of the companies, they will not move because already the state government had been spreading rumours about them saying that the paramilitary forces had been drinking and creating a ruckus in the red light areas. The Union Home Minister had to deny this. Then magistrates from nearby areas were called in a hurry at night. It was after this that the forces took positions the next day.

The Kalyan Singh government had been ousted the previous night. Kar Sevaks targeted the Muslims, living in Ayodhya, who were against this. Muslims were facing a lot of trouble. Sabid who worked at Kaziani's sawmill, was burnt alive. 40-year-old Shaukat Ullah was a teacher at Faizabad Municipality School was also killed by the rioters. His twelve-year-old son was also murdered. Azmat Ullah (46) was a senior clerk at Hydel. He was also consumed in the riots. Salman (22) owned a tailoring shop. The shop was burnt down and he was also killed. Aslam's ten-year-old son, Guddu, from Kajiana also died. Almost all houses in this locality were burnt down. The curfew imposed on Ayodhya and Faizabad had no impact on the Kar Sevaks. Narasimha Rao ruled at the centre and state level. But Ayodhya was free for all.

Some Kar Sevaks were seen packing their bags and moving towards the railway station. A lot of tents at the Ramkatha Kunj began to get vacated. Police, PAC and security forces were present, but only as mute spectators. At intervals, there would be rumours heard of central security forces reaching the site. Hearing this, Kar Sevaks would gather around the temple under construction and would shout slogans of devotion to make their presence felt.

At about 3:15 in the morning on 8 December, there was some kind of noisy disturbance outside our hotel. When we went out, we saw that cars containing paramilitary forces were rushing towards Ayodhya. The flow of cars was continuous. It did not take us long to understand that the plan was 'Operation Flush Out'. 108 Rapid Action Force (RAF) battalions and eight companies, CRPF were rushing towards Ayodhya for this mission. B.M. Saraswat was leading them. My local correspondent,

Triyug Narayan Tiwari and I followed the caravan.

At exactly 3:30 am., the RAF commandoes enter Ram Janmabhoomi area from behind the structure and from Manas Bhavan and Sita Rasoi side. At that time, only about five thousand Kar Sevaks were present there. All of them were singing devotional songs. Kar Sevikayein were sleeping in the pandals next to the tents. Devotional songs suddenly stop at Ramkatha Kunj and noises begin to be heard. In just a few minutes, a stampede breaks out. After a short struggle, the entire area is easily vacated.

In this easy but scary operation, the RAF managed to get Manas Bhavan and also Ramkatha Kunj vacated.

Dealing with a scared and already apprehensive public, only a mild lathi charge and tear gas were used in this operation. This would be considered a mild use of force. That's all that was needed. The speakers at Ramkatha Kunj stopped playing devotional songs and began making announcements, 'CRPF is here. Please leave.' Late at night, VHP president Ashok Singhal had made an announcement to stop Kar Seva considering the current scenario. This was the reason that the number of Kar Sevaks had decreased. The remaining were guarding the temporary temple.

Now one could see how the governments worked. When there was the pressure of a large number of Kar Sevaks, then for thirty-six hours the central forces did not dare to come around to the area. When the Kar Sevaks had mostly left, then the area was vacated using, merely, five tear gas cannisters. But more than sixty members of the team sent by the centre for getting the area vacated were awarded with medals. Faizabad's then SSP, D.B. Rai said to me, 'it is another story that they cannot show this medal to their children even. How will they explain that many thousands of jawans equipped with all the ammunition went after a mere hundred unarmed Kar Sevaks and got the area vacated. They have won this medal for this bravery only.'

One day before 'Operation Flush Out', Vinay Katiyar got a message from the Prime Minister that they do not wish to use forces against the Kar Sevaks. 'You guys get the area vacated. After that, we will try to postpone the Kar Seva'.

Kar Sevaks were returning from the disputed site. The condition of the central forces in Ayodhya was really pitiful. They had become like a 'football' between the centre and the state and were being regarded as opposing the construction of the temple. The state government was also accusing them of different things and creating a mindset that they were the biggest hurdle in making the temple. But this wasn't true. Now that the work of worship in the temporary temple was their responsibility, their hidden faith was being revealed. Right in the morning, they would line up to visit the temple. The senior officers would get anxious looking at these queues. Jawans who had come from far away places were also hell-bent on visiting the temple. This morning the whole programme of temple visits went on for about an hour. But later, seeing the photographers, it was stopped.

Despite this, the jawans remained on the platform waiting to pay a visit to the temple. D.P. Singh, deputy commandant, RAF had to announce many times that jawans must return to duty and not create chaos by gathering at one place. He said that everyone would be given a chance to visit the temple in the evening. But even then one or two jawans still kept visiting the temple. Ram Lalla's temple was closed to the general public. But the jawans were getting prasad and giving offerings as well. This was an amazing scene. All the jawans around the temple had taken off their shoes and socks. At short intervals, crowds of jawans would gather in front of Ram Lalla's idol.

Of the ones visiting the temple, most were Sikh jawans. One of them said, 'I have come to Ayodhya for the first time. God knows if I'll ever come again. So let me visit the temple for sure. I was sick of being on duty in Punjab. Here I am at peace.' Many jawans were even ringing bells with the priests during aarti. They were overwhelmed with faith and devotion. Despite the curfew they weren't even bothered about the paan shops, tea-stalls and fruit sellers on the way to the Ram Janmabhoomi temple. The day they captured the Janmabhoomi area, they put barbed-wire fencing around the whole area to guard it. The tents in Ramkatha Kunj for the Kar Sevaks were now rest rooms for the paramilitary forces.

Faizabad's new district magistrate, commissioner and senior police superintendent took charge the next morning. Immediately after taking charge, District Magistrate Vijayshankar Pandey said that the prayer service is being continued at the disputed site to create a sense of trust between the public and the security forces. He said that worship and religious rituals are to be carried on at the site and will continue the same way. Central forces were being controlled by S.N. Chaubey, IG, CRPF.

After a short meeting with the BJP leaders in Lucknow, VHP President Ashok Singhal left for Delhi with Lal Krishna Advani, Rajmata Vijaya Raje Scindia and H.V. Sheshadri in a Madhya Pradesh government chartered airplane. They all met with Kalyan Singh in Lucknow. This was their first meeting with Kalyan Singh after the Babri demolition.

The central forces captured the Janmabhoomi area on 8 December and Kar Sevaks had returned to where they came from so we were also preparing to leave Ayodhya. I witnessed a very pitiful scene at that time. A one-year-old boy, son of a Kar Sevak couple who had come from Maharashtra had died due to the cold. Both of them were crying and asking for permission of the security forces to go to the Ram Janmabhoomi. The man was holding the body of his dead son. They wanted to touch their son's body to the soil of Ram's birthplace. The empathetic security forces gave them permission for this.

This was the level of faith and devotion in the people and all logic failed in front of it. This scene, filled with tears of faith and compassion was evidence of a storm that was so powerful that the sovereign powers had no option but to accept it. They could not fight it. This scene was the answer to the question that despite being the ruler, despite being aware of the consequences, why did Prime Minister Narasimha Rao not use forces to stop the Kar Sevaks?

Now let us understand why we arrived at this situation of destruction in the first place. Kar Sevaks were very angry with the check and mate game being played by the VHP and Narasimha Rao. Before the Babri demolition, around half a dozen temples were broken near the Babri site during the July Kar Seva. These were all old and known temples. VHP obtained the ownership rights of all of these and got them razed to the ground, so that the path to the disputed site could be made. BJP acquired 2.77 acres of land around the disputed site on 10 January 1991. The government handed it over to the Ram Janmabhoomi Trust immediately after acquisition. On this land, there were Sankatmochan temple, Sakshigopal temple, Savitri Bhavan owned by Chauburji's mahant, Ram Arsey Das and saint Lomash's ashram, Sitakoop, besides many other small temples. After the acquisition, about a hundred labourers worked day and night to demolish these structures. This task went on for some days. Among these, there was one temple where Sheshnaag was worshipped. Demolishing this particular temple was considered inauspicious. So Kar Sevaks started constructing (Ram's) brother Lakshman's temple. Lakshman is considered to be Sheshnaag's incarnation.

While levelling the disputed site, the steel barricading outside it was removed. All the priests had done the registry in the name of the Trust saying that were giving up their temples for the construction of the grand Ram Mandir. But everyone knew the hermits of Ayodhya. No one was over their greed for money there. Most of the temples were bought by the Ram Janmabhoomi Trust. There was anger all over the country over demolition of these temples. The Home Minister had to give an explanation about this matter in the Lok Sabha.

The Sankatmochan temple was exactly opposite Ram Janmabhoomi. Hanuman's idol was taken to some other place from there. This task was carried out at midnight under the supervision of the temple's priest, Ram Asre Das.

They had already filed an application to the DM and had taken permission to remove Hanuman's idol for the construction of Ram Mandir. There was a misunderstanding throughout the country that temples were being demolished in Ayodhya. But soon this misunderstanding was cleared up and it was known that the reason for the demolition of the temples in Ayodhya was to widen and smoothen the area for the construction of the Ram Mandir. All this was happening with the consent of all parties related to the construction of Ram Mandir. The district magistrate said that temples had been demolished for widening the area. Temples had been demolished by the ones who owned it. No law or court's order were an obstacle. The truth behind the Sankatmochan temple, (over which there was so much anger) was that Chauburji's ashram's mahant, Ram Asre Das himself took Hanuman's idol from the temple.

A meeting held by the priests took place in Ujjain in May 1992. It was decided in this meeting that on 9 July 1992, the next session of Kar Seva will start. Anxious with this announcement, the PM's political advisor, Jitendra Prasad met the priests and requested them to meet the prime minister. Narasimha Rao met the priests in Delhi. Among those who met the PM were Mahant Avaidyanath, Vamdev, Paramhans Ramchandra Das, Mahant Nritya Gopal Das, Swami Parmanand, Swami Chinmayan and Udupi's Pejawar Swami. These priests said to the Prime Minister—'it's been almost a year since you became the PM and till now, you haven't discussed anything on the temple issue. That is why we have ourselves come to you. So that it doesn't feel like we are doing one-sided work. We have decided to start Kar Seva from 9 July. We are giving you this information so that later you don't turn around and say that we conducted it without your knowledge.' The PM mostly remained quiet during the meet. Later he said, 'I also want this issue resolved soon and the temple to be constructed in Ayodhya. But this issue has become political now. Politics should be kept away from this. Matters related to religion should be handled on the basis of religion only. I need your blessings to resolve the matter.'

At this the priests had to say, 'there is no politics in this. This is about political willingness. The dialogue that was started with Muslims by Chandrashekhar Ji, you take it forward.' The meeting ended. But the Prime Minister did not give any hint as to what he going to do although neither did he discourage the priests to start the Kar Seva.

In these circumstances, Kar Seva started again on 9 July 1992. This created a stir in the court and parliament. Kar Seva went on for seventeen days from 9 July to 26 July. Nothing went wrong in Ayodhya or anywhere else. If we disregard the court and the parliament, no impact was seen in any other place.

Actually this was the real danger in Ayodhya—that the court and government became active only when Kar Seva was announced. The moment Kar Seva would be suspended, talks and court proceedings would also stop. This time also the same thing happened. After the announcement of 9 July's Kar Seva, everyone became active. Before that, no one was worried.

From 7 July, preparations for the Kar Seva began. The Central government said that it would be disrespectful to the court if Kar Seva took place. The UP government said that they will hold Kar Seva on the no-conflict zone. The central and state governments were up against each other on the issue of Kar Seva. On 8 July 1992, Home Minister S.B. Chavan told the UP government that the Central government has some constitutional responsibilities which need to be fulfilled. We will not let Kar Seva happen. Despite this, the construction of the platform started on 9 July 1992. Construction started at a place called the Singhdwar. Its length was 138 feet, width was 116 feet and depth of the foundation was 6 feet.

Court orders were ignored and the construction of the temple started in Ayodhya. The temple was being built on the 2.77 acres of land acquired by the state government. With fourteen hundred Vedpathi pandits reading the Ved paths, construction of the platforms at the Singhdwar and Nrityamandap began for the proposed temple at 8:40 a.m. The first scuttles of concrete, cement and sand were emptied by MP Vinay Katiyar and VHP leader Ashok Singhal. Besides the Ram Janmabhoomi Trust, the VHP and the priests related to the central guiding committee being witness to the task that started under the supervision of government officials, there were two ministers from the state government as well.

After Kar Seva began, VHP president Ashok Singhal said, 'Now the construction will go on uninterrupted. The obstacles at the Singhdwar and Nrityamandap have been removed. So the construction of these will happen first.' He said, 'We don't acknowledge stay on the transfer of the land acquired by the state government because we believe that neither government nor the court can stop us from building on the land that belongs to Ram Lalla.'

Close to the foundation stone, the land where the Ram Janmabhoomi Trust had started construction was under the state government. The Allahabad High Court had put a stay on the transfer of 2.77 acres of this land. This area was part of the conflicted plots as well.

The foundation stone was placed here on 9 November 1989. The government had banned any kind of temporary construction but Ashok

Singhal said, 'we had made it clear earlier itself that this matter is out of the jurisdiction of court. The land opposite the temple is Ram Mandir's land. We don't know what the state government has acquired and what it hasn't.' The attitude of the VHP was altering and it appeared that they were in the mood to fight it out. Pillars were also to be built on the hundred feet long and eighty feet wide platform on which work had already begun. The temple's Singhdwar and Nrityamandap would stand on these pillars. After which the sabhamandap and garbhgrah would be built. To ensure that the temple continues to exist for over a thousand years, iron was not to be used in the construction at all. The Bridge corporation of UP government known as Setu Nigam was roped in. The project manager, Vinay Katiyar said that the Janmabhoomi Trust was getting the temple constructed. Setu Nigam's truck and the mixing plant were working day and night. The entire task would take two months. The foundation plan was made under the supervision of Roorkee University's ex-chancellor and five engineers.

At the historic moment, when the construction was about to begin, the excitement of the saints and priests was the same as at the time of the 1990 Kar Seva. But this time there were fewer people. Ashok Singhal said that if the crowd had been too big the situation could have gotten out of control. The scene of this Kar Seva was totally different. The police who were in charge of the security of the structure were seen carrying the luggage of the saints and the priests, and they were waiting for their turn to do Kar Seva. Confusion in the first half an hour led to chaos initially. Acharya Giriraj fainted because of this chaos. Among those transporting raw materials for the construction, were Rajmata Vijaya Raje Scindia, Ashok Singhal, Acharya Giriraj Kishor, Mahant Nritya Gopal Das, Paramhans Ramchandra Das, Mahant Avaidyanath, Uma Bharti, Sadhvi Hritambhara, Swami Vamdev, Acharya Dharmendra, Dau Dayal Khanna, Vishnu Hari Dalmia and there were hundreds of saints and priests as well. The programme was being coordinated by MP Shrish Chandra Dikshit, Faizabad's DM R.N. Srivastava and Police Captain D.B. Rai. Before Kar Seva began, the land was cleansed with the river Saryu's water after which Banaras Hindu University's Ved Department head; Vishwanath Vamdev conducted a Ganesh puja there.

An application had been filed in the Supreme Court as well to stop this Kar Seva. On 10 July1992, Justice M.N. Venkatchalayya, who was the Supreme Court's vacation judge, sat for a proceeding at his place. He asked the Uttar Pradesh government for details pertaining to the construction work. He asked if the construction is temporary or permanent. Whether it was at the disputed site or at the no-conflict zone. On 11 July 1992 Chief Minister Kalyan Singh and Home Minister S.B. Chavan held a meeting. Justice M.N. Venkatchalayya presided again and he said that if there was any permanent construction made then it would be demolished.

On 12 July 1992, Home Minister Chavan went to Ayodhya to see the nature of the construction and observed that the Central government was carrying forward the court's perspective. The Union Home Minister also visited the garbhgrah. He offered prasad, flowers and a cloth with Ram's name on it. He prayed and then announced that his visit to the temple is done and that now he should be taken to the mosque. People laughed at his statement. They explained to him that this structure was called the mosque as well. He could not really understand this. A team had come along with Mr. Home Minister and they duly filed their report.

On 14 July 1992, Chavan proclaimed in the Rajya Sabha that Kar Seva may continue, but the government will not allow anyone to touch Babri Masjid.

On 15 July 1992, Allahabad High Court put a stay on Kar Seva. But VHP refused to stop the construction work. In the meanwhile, the Supreme Court ordered the UP government to file an affidavit explaining if there is any permanent construction happening in Ayodhya's disputed site. The team that had gone to Ayodhya with the Home Minister said in their report that the Babri mosque was safe but that the ongoing construction work did not appear temporary.

On 16 July 1992, the UP government's lawyer expressed his inability to give a detailed report on the construction because the saints on the site did not let the officers reach the location. Hence they could not assess and file the report.

On 18 July 1992, Faizabad's administration refuted the possibility of using forces to enforce the court's order, because it would lead to violence and it would be almost impossible to push Kar Sevaks out. It was a difficult situation. Kar Seva was on despite the High Court's order to stop it and the state government was not able to get the court's order enforced.

On 20 July 1992, Faizabad's district magistrate started a dialogue with VHP leaders to enforce the High Court's order. Faizabad's lawyers went on strike in support of the construction. Chavan told Lok Sabha that the government has a plan to control the situation.

The Supreme Court ordered the UP government to reveal the true nature of the construction. On 22 July 1992, the Supreme Court suggested that if the UP government is willing to stop the construction, the court will combine all matters pertaining to the case and hand it over to a big bench for daily hearings, so that the court would be able to decide whether a temple should be built on the acquired land or not.

On 23 July, the Prime Minister again attempts to break the deadlock by meeting with the saints. He appeals to them to stop the construction work so that the issue can be resolved within a stipulated time.

On 25 July 1992, the Prime Minister gave assurance to Ashok Singhal, through a representative that he will be personally involved in the matter and that he will resolve the matter within three months by talking to both parties. On 26 July 1992, VHP stopped the construction work on the PM's appeal. But Ashok Singhal hinted that Kar Seva will start again in the beginning of October or November.

The VHP's Kar Seva resulted in the entire atmosphere around Ram Janmabhoomi-Babri Masjid having had changed by August. Now there were three ways to get to the disputed structure. One of these was to be called 'Raj Marg' or the main path leading to it. It was newly built. The other two were narrow roads.

The scene here was changed now. If one stood a little away from the disputed structure and looked at it one could see uneven land in front of them. Small temples and structures had been razed to the ground to create this. The Babri Mosque stood at the centre of a big empty ground. This was the new scene. There was a sense of liberation in this. The other picture was of the disputed structure. It stood there alone. Earlier it was surrounded by structures around it. Now it stood alone.

Till about a year ago, the atmosphere around Ram Janmabhoomi-Babri Masjid had been the same since 1949. Only two incidents could be counted as changes. The lock was opened in 1986 and in 1989 a foundation stone was placed at one place. Till last year, this place was easily recognizable. But now, it looked different. Now its identity had been attached to a flag. In 1990, the *chhatri* was removed from the place where the foundation stone was placed by Mulayam Singh, secretly one night. But there were huge protests against this and therefore, he had had put it back. Now, the same *chhatri* had been removed again, this time by the VHP.

It is important to know what the Babri structure, that was demolished, looked like at the time of demolition. What was its vastu like and how evolved was it? It was a beautiful model that was established in the medieval era. There was a well near it and the water from this well had medicinal qualities. The Babri Masjid had a grand architecture with three domes. Out of these, one dome was bigger. The two smaller ones were on either side of it. Next to the well was a big terrace. This well was known for its cool and sweet water. The stone above the main entrance had two inscriptions on it in Farsi.

The inscription said that Mir Baqi had had this building constructed on the orders of Babur. While Babri Masjid's walls were made of white sandstone, the domes were made of small thin baked bricks. Both of these were plastered with a mixture of grainy sand and thick lime powder. The courtyard was surrounded by slanted pillars. This was done to increase the height of the ceiling.

The acoustics and the cooling system of Babri Masjid was also a great example of Mughal architecture. Standing in one corner of the Masjid, one could hear the sound of a piece of paper being torn at the other end of the Masjid. According to Lord William Bentinck's (1828-1835) vastu expert, Graham Pickford, 'Any whispers in the arch of the Masjid could be heard upto twenty feet away.' He mentions this in his book, *Historic Structures Of Awadh*. The book also mentions, 'In comparison to the other structures of the sixteenth century, the audibility of sound was much better here. This really astonishes the visitors.'

There were many stories about the well too, that was located at the centre of the structure. Ayodhya is a pilgrim city for Hindus. More than five lakh Hindus and Muslims celebrated Ram Mahotsav here every year. Many devotees came to this well to drink its water. There was a belief that many diseases could be cured by drinking the water of this well. Hindus believed that the well actually belonged to Ram Mandir, whereas Ayodhya's Muslims believed that this was a blessing given by Allah or their god. Local women came to the well regularly with their infants to feed them this magical water. There was a neem tree growing next to the well whose roots reached deep inside the well and added medicinal value to its water. The well was made of bricks from the ground level to about thirty feet. There was almost no sodium in the water which made it popular as it was sweet in taste. One had to climb a three feet tall platform to get to the well. The well was covered with a thick wooden plank on top and had stairs at the back of it. Since it was claimed that the water had 'spiritual qualities', it was used only for drinking. But now, the existence of the mosque and its well is a subject of history.

In the Ram temple movement, Kar Seva took place about half a dozen times. But every time it would get associated with a symbol and become symbolic. 6 December's Kar Seva was being done to make a decision once and for all. This last Kar Seva once again turned symbolic.

But this time Kar Sevaks decided to listen to 'Ram's orders' and not their leaders. The leaders did not even realize when exactly they had lost control over them. By 6 December, all Kar Sevaks had decided not to listen to their leaders. Now they had their eyes open and their minds were aiming at the 'bird's eye'. A structure was demolished on one hand and on the other, the building of politics got a new roof. In response to the politics of appeasement, the politics of Hindu fundamentals also gathered strength. This 'structure' became so big and strong that it could be seen clearly from anywhere in the country.

Amongst the many layers of my memory, I was trying to hold on to one picture of destruction in my mind. The ends of the threads to all the conspiracies were in front of me. Where did these threads begin, where they turned and where they joined, I had been a witness to their movement and nature from Ayodhya to Lucknow and Delhi. Having covered news about Ayodhya for such a long time, my relations with politicians and other involved parties were both professional and personal. Many things that they wanted to keep from me as a journalist, they would tell me openly on a personal level. This was the reason that I was able to understand the obvious and the unobvious. The old bricks of the disputed structure turned out to be very useful. Kar Sevaks demolished the structure and moved on. But the political parties held on to these bricks. They painted these bricks the colour of their choice and adorned their offices with these new showpieces.

It is ironical but it's a fact that even today, the country's political system stands on the rubble of the Babri Masjid. Whenever there is communal violence in the country, the dust of this very rubble fills the atmosphere. It is also a fact that some lessons learnt the hard way are also buried in this very rubble. There is a need to recognize these lessons and accept their relevance in time. Traditionally, a religious revenge has never been considered worthy. Our traditional roots go very deep. Emotions don't erupt because of treachery. Did this eruption not damage the entire Hindu society's trustworthiness, their promises and their ability to be answerable? This is food for thought.

Chapter 2

POWER POLITICS BEHIND THE GAME OF DEMOLITION

The Kar Sevaks who demolished the structure were merely pawns in the entire movement. The central force was elsewhere. The ones controlling the whole movement belonged to a different world. Although it's a different story that Kar Sevaks left their side at the time of demolition and wrote the story's climax according to what they deemed right. On the other hand, there was an equally active world of politics that wanted to kill the movement. The important thing was that both parties had the same goal. Their destination was the same. Only the route was different. The fight was only for credit and ownership, and the benefits one got from it.

In the world of Ayodhya politics, there was Congress and the so-called secular people who wanted to break this BJP and RSS led movement and follow their plan to get the temple built. They wanted to take credit for building the temple and then reap the political benefits of the same.

The entire political arena from Delhi to Lucknow was hyperactive and overflowing with enthusiasm at the time when the Babri structure was attacked by the Kar Sevaks. While the Prime Minister was sitting in front of his television at 7 Race Course, his residence in Delhi, Chief Minister Kalyan Singh was basking in the sun on the roof of his government residence at Kalidas Marg in Lucknow.

The news of vandalism and destruction was conveyed from Ayodhya's control room to the CM's house in Lucknow. He was shocked. Kalyan Singh demanded the area to be vacated without the use of firing, at the same time he was angry because he felt that if the VHP had had any such plans, he should have been kept in the loop about it. In the meantime, violence had erupted in Ayodhya. The PM's personal secretary P.V.R.K. Prasad called Faizabad's commissioner and asked him to control the situation and use the central forces.

There is no doubt that during the first five hours of demolition, Chief Minister Kalyan Singh decided to believe that he had been cheated just the way Prime Minister Narasimha Rao had also agreed to believe. Kalyan Singh seemed as hurt and disturbed as Narasimha Rao. He felt that he had been given the wrong impression although he had received some kind of a hint about it. On Saturday night, the report sent by the district administration to the Home Secretary said that there was a segment of Kar Sevaks who were unhappy with the changed face of Kar Seva. It meant that the idea of a symbolic Kar Seva was not acceptable to them. Having understood the sensitivity of the situation, Kalyan Singh had sent BJP Chairman Murli Manohar Joshi and Lal Krishna Advani to Ayodhya on Saturday night itself. According to the programme planned earlier, they were actually supposed to go to Ayodhya on Sunday.

After the demolition, Kalyan Singh stayed away due to shock. He called a meeting with the Chief Secretary, Home Secretary, Director General of Police and other senior officials at his residence in Lucknow.

He had given orders in writing for 'no firing' so that no officer could be held responsible later on. Kalyan Singh created goodwill for himself within the bureaucracy through this meeting. After consulting with his officers and top ministers, he decided to resign.

Kalyan Singh wanted to meet the governor, B. Satyanarayan Reddy and resign. But the governor wasn't giving him time because he wanted to talk to Prime Minister Narasimha Rao before meeting Kalyan Singh. He probably wanted to ask the Prime Minister whether Kalyan Singh's resignation was to be accepted or whether he was to be terminated. But Narasimha Rao refused to speak to the governor. Narasimha Rao was upset with Governor B. Satyanarayan Reddy because when the entire nation was demanding the dismissal of the UP government, the governor was constantly sending reports in favour of the UP government to the centre.

Narasimha Rao felt that even the governor had had a role to play in misleading him in the matter. The last report that the governor had sent two days before the demolition, even stated that if the Kalyan Singh government was dismissed, the Babri structure could be in danger. The structure could become victim to anger against this decision.

Kalyan Singh reached Raj Bhavan and submitted his resignation to the governor at five thirty in the evening. In his one line resignation he wrote, 'I am resigning. Kindly accept.' He had not suggested that the legislative assembly be dismissed with his resignation.

It wasn't just the Opposition that was trying to corner Prime Minister Narasimha Rao, but members of his own party were turning against him as well. He addressed the nation that very night under pressure from his colleagues. In his speech, Narasimha Rao referred to the demolished structure as 'Babri Masjid' many times. It was understood nationwide and globally that the demolished structure was a mosque. At no point in his speech did the PM mention that there had been idols kept in the structure for the last 44 years and that namaz was not being read there. The PM's address aggravated the tension in the country. You can read the whole speech by the Prime Minister in this book's 'This Too is Important' chapter.

As time went by, Kalyan Singh was gaining courage. At first, he was shocked and claimed that he had been cheated. But now, he had accepted the responsibility for the demolition. After his resignation, he announced that it was an outburst of Hindu feelings and emotions because all three—the administration, legislation and judiciary—were responsible for delaying action in the matter. He said that although it was true that he had taken the responsibility for the security of the structure, but he had also said that his government would not fire at saints and Kar Sevaks. He said that no officer was responsible for firing at the Kar Sevaks to get them off the structure. 'The files have my signature on them. When I had found a way out, no one listened to me. I wanted to separate Kar Seva and the disputed site. My plan was to create a 2.77 acre zone between the disputed structure and the area where Kar Seva would be held. This was the "safety valve". This could have avoided the 6 December 1992 violence. But no one listened to me. Non BJP parties created hurdles. They used judiciary to have their way.'

He said, 'there is still time. The non BJP parties must understand the public emotion. There have been 76 fights over Ram Janmabhoomi now. More than three lakh people have been killed. We should not ignore this. What was the reason behind the Centre not acting forty hours after taking over. By not using any force against Kar Sevaks for forty hours after taking over, the Central government gave approval to my decision of not firing.'

I also met Kalyan Singh that day. He said to me, 'people who are going mad at the demolition of Babri, where were they when 45 temples were razed in Anantnag (Kashmir)? If this is not hypocrisy, then what is it?'

The demolition of Babri had shaken up my editor, Prabhash Joshi. He wrote on the day after the demolition—'Deceitful devils who praised Lord Ram blackened Maryada Purshottam Ram's Raghukul's tradition. That religious place was Babri Masjid as well as the temple of Ram Lalla. People who think they can demolish such a structure deceitfully and build a temple there don't believe in Ram. They don't know Ram. They don't understand him. This is an offence. The deceitfulness in this is an attack to our democracy and our secular constitution'

The Babri structure would not have crumbled on 6 December 1992 if the provoked Kar Sevaks had not turned violent. What happened was an eruption of a sleeping volcano of history. A lot of people were aware that a tragedy was imminent and they wanted to do something about it immediately. *Jansatta*'s editor Prabhash Joshi was also one of these and one such attempt was made by him as well. In this attempt, he and many other politicians hoped that nothing much would happen with a symbolic Kar Seva. So when the structure was demolished, it was also an attack on all the efforts made through talks.

If you look at the sequence of events that happened just before and after 6 December, you will realize that everyone including the Centre and the Prime Minister took the whole thing very lightly. Politicians only thought about political gains at every level.

Very few people were aware of the fact that Prabhash Joshi was involved in the mediation of Ayodhya between the government and the Sangh. They were trying to find a way out and reach a consensus. He was trying to get this done with utmost honesty. He was also part of the meeting between Prime Minister P. V. Narasimha Rao and Sangh's Prof. Rajendra Singh (Rajju Bhaiya) on 3 December. It was decided, at this very meeting that the structure will not be demolished and permission will be given for Kar Seva outside the disputed area. Prabhash Joshi was shattered when this trust was broken.

He was also disappointed after the July 1992 Kar Seva. He wasn't hopeful that talks would work as both sides were rigid about the matter. Prabhash Joshi went to Lucknow for a programme during this time. I took him to Ali Miyan in Nadwa in Lucknow. He had a long chat with Ali Miyan. After talking to Ali Miyan, he became a little hopeful.

That day, Gandhian leader Achyut Patvardhan had also come to attend a programme on Acharya Narendradev. Achyut Patvardhan was staying at the Raj Bhavan. He had lunch with Prabhash Joshi. He told Prabhash ji to get into mediaton again. He said that Ayodhya was a national issue after all. This had an impact on Prabhash Joshi. That very night, Prabhash Joshi and I met the chief minister, Kalyan Singh. The talk with Kalyan Singh was positive. He clearly said, 'We will separate Kar Seva from the disputed site for the time being. The structure will remain and the Kar Seva can happen elsewhere. We are ready for this. Talks regarding the structure can continue with related people alongside.'

Prabhash Joshi conveyed Kalyan Singh's positive attitude to Achyut Patvardhan the next day. Achyut Patvardhan had to go to Banaras that very day. Unfortunately Achyut Patvardhan suddenly died in Banaras on the third day i.e. 5 August 1992. Prabhash Joshi wrote, 'Achyut Patvardhan's last wish and Kalyan Singh's faith had given us a mission. That is when *dada* (Nikhil Chakravarty) asked us to get on the job, we said, "Yes dada".'

After Lucknow's exciting conversation, Prabhash Joshi spoke to Rajasthan's chief minister Bhairon Singh Shekhawat. He knew Shekhawat at a personal level. Shekhawat met the Prime Minister with this very input that Kar Seva should take place and the structure should also be secure. The meeting was more or less on these lines. On 3 December when final talks on avoiding a bloody crossfire were happening, this was what was agreed upon. On 3 December, Bhairon Singh met the Prime Minister along with Prabhash Joshi, Nikhil Chakravarty and R.K. Mishra. Immediately after this, Prof. Rajendra Singh (Rajju Bhaiya) came to meet the PM. Rajju Bhaiya was the Sangh's commanding officer at the time. Delhi was his centre. Commanding officer Madan Das was also with him.

According to Prabhash Joshi, talks were happening in the right direction. The formula was clear. First, the court is to give its verdict on the 2.77 acres before 6 December. The government and VHP request the Supreme Court to tell the High Court to bring forward its decision. Second, the government is to send a one point context according to article 143 that before the Babri structure, there was a temple there. Third, the State Government is to take care of the security of the disputed site by taking help from the Centre if need be. They had reached an agreement that day on these three points.

Prior to the demolition, Atal Bihari Vajpayee had said in the Lok Sabha that attempts were still on to find a way out. Later he even said to some of the print journalists that the editors' guild was active. 'I want them to be successful in their efforts. If they fail, they should accept with honesty that they failed due to the government's dogmatism.' He said. After the demolition, Prabhash Joshi was writing with this 'honesty' that they had all been cheated. The promises made for the structure's safety were broken. Prabhash Joshi was really upset with the whole incident. He felt cheated. But he continued to write freely and gave everyone the freedom to write freely. He said to his editorial colleagues that he had taken a stand. But this was not to be misunderstood with the news. While reporting news stories, I was taking a stand opposite to that of Prabhash Joshi, because the excitement on the ground and the public anger had had an impact on me. Also the campaign that the VHP ran against Muslim appeasement had such a widespread basis that even I was affected by it.

Of the whole event, the maximum impact had been on Narasimha Rao. He was duped. Actually, in his heart, the Prime Minister was in favour of the temple. He wanted to find a way out. Despite pressure from his entire cabinet, he did not sack the Kalyan Singh government before 6 December. That is why he was attacked from all sides. Narasimha Rao felt that all would go according to what the VHP had promised. But his trust had been broken. On 6 December, the Prime Minister remained silent at the central cabinet meeting that was called to sack the Uttar Pradesh government. Arjun Singh writes in his biography *A grain of sand in the hour glass of time*—'Narasimha Rao was so languid during the meeting that not a single word came out of his mouth. All eyes had turned to C.K. Jaffer. Jaffer Sharief said that the country, government and Congress party will have to pay a heavy price for this incident. Rao was silent like a post. Makhanlal Fotedar had started crying during this meet.'

Makhanlal Fotedar was a Congress family loyalist. His loyalty lay more towards the Gandhi family. He has explained the whole incident in his biography, *Chinar Leaves*—'I requested the Prime Minister over a call that he should tell the security forces to ask Air Force helicopters employed at Faizabad to release tear gas and push Kar Sevaks out. Narasimha Rao said, "How can I do this? This is the job of the state government." I said to him again, "Save one dome at least so that we can keep it in glass box and show people that we tried our best to save Babri Masjid." The prime minister kept quiet for some time. Then he said, "Fotedar ji! Let me call you back."'

Due to another meeting that he had with President Shankar Dayal Sharma, Fotedar reached that cabinet meet fifteen minutes late. Everyone was silent there. Fotedar says, 'Looking at the silence I asked, "Why is everyone so quiet?" Madhav Rao Scindia said, "Don't you know? Babri Masjid has been demolished." I said in front of all ministers, "Rao Sahab, only you are responsible for this." The Prime Minister did not utter a word.'

Cabinet's senior member Arjun Singh strongly criticized Narasimha Rao in the matter. Just like the VHP wanted to uproot the structure, Arjun Singh was using this opportunity to weaken Narasimha Rao. He was waiting for Narasimha Rao to fail completely in the matter. Makhanlal Fotedar confirmed this. He wrote in *Chinar Leaves*—'Arjun

Singh very well knew what's going to happen on December 6. But even then, he left Delhi and went to Punjab. I believe that his absence in the cabinet meet on December 6 and then his move to resign from the cabinet put him through a great political loss. He remained close to me. But I knew that he does not have the courage to accept challenges.'

Former president, Pranab Mukherjee remained Narasimha Rao's associate for a long time. In his biography, *The Turbulent Years*, he has written, 'Not being able to stop the Babri demolition was P.V.'s biggest failure. He should have given the responsibility of talking to other parties to a senior leader like Narayan Dutt Tiwari. S.B. Chavan was a good negotiator, but he could not understand the emotional angle of the rising circumstances. P.R. Kumaramangalam was also young and comparatively less experienced. He had become the state minister for the first time'. Pranab Mukherjee further wrote –'I have worked with Narasimha Rao for decades. I did not need to read his face. I could clearly feel his misery and despair'.

P.V. Narasimha Rao answers these questions. He writes in his book *Ayodhya 6 December 1992* –'I am bombarded with questions on this issue the most that why didn't I impose president's rule in Uttar Pradesh to save Babri Masjid on 6 December1992?' Narasimha Rao explains his helplessness –'According to Article 356, a government can be dismissed only when law and order is broken and not when there is a possibility that law and order may be broken.'

He says, 'In such cases, governor's report is the basis. Who would impose president's rule after seeing the report that governor, B. Satyanarayan Reddy sent three days back.' Satyanarayan Reddy wasn't from the Sangh. He was a socialist and came from the Telugu Desam party.

Let's look at parts of the report sent by Governor B. Satyanarayan Reddy three days prior to the demolition.

'Reports say that Kar Sevaks are reaching Ayodhya in large numbers. But they are peaceful. The state government has given assurance that it will protect the disputed site and that proper arrangements will be made to protect the site. The court has accepted it.'

'In my opinion, the time hasn't come when a step like dismissing the Uttar Pradesh government or the assembly or imposing president's rule needs to be taken. If such a step is taken, it can have far reaching consequences. This can lead to violence not just in the state but in different parts of the country. The danger of damaging the disputed structure also cannot be denied. So my suggestion is that we must be very careful in the matter and only after considering the pros and cons of different options should we come to a conclusion. We should avoid any decision taken in haste.'

This was the secret report sent to the Central government by the governor. Narasimha Rao did not have an option in such a situation other than to trust the promise made by the state government. Although this faith was nothing more than a political miscalculation and which made him sorrowful until the end. He was also upset with Satyanarayan Reddy. That is why he did not take his call on 6 December.

Narasimha Rao writes in his book, '*Ayodhya 6 December 1992*'— 'An appeal was also made to the Supreme Court that the Centre be made receiver of the land property in Ayodhya (Babri structure and some of the nearby areas). This would have been a useful step. The structure would have got security and the Centre would have got more time to look for better and more impactful options. Because giving the entire state to the Centre in one go according to section 356 would have created many dangers. The Indian government had already agreed to give any kind of support that was asked for. The state government opposed this move and said that it is well aware of how to give security to the disputed site. So it is irrelevant to appoint a receiver.

On the basis of these assurances, the Supreme Court dismissed the appeal of appointing a receiver on November 28. Instead the court appointed one of its judiciary officers as the supervisor whose job was to oversee the Kar Seva and update the court with all details.'

Narasimha Rao said, 'The Central government had only two options in such a scenario. One, to go and act against the clear advice of the governor putting at stake the security of the structure, or inspiring the state government to utilize the 30,000 central forces in order to keep the structure secure. It is important to note here that the state government never denied using the central paramilitary forces. But the fact was that they were not allowed to work.'

This helplessness of Narasimha Rao sounds like a story. But it is not. It is beyond understanding how at noon on 6 December, the situation of law and order ended. Everyone including the police, administration, Chief Minister and Prime Minister were in a state of shock. Kalyan Singh was announcing again and again that there will be no firing. The central forces were not able to enter Ayodhya. In such a situation, what was stopping Narasimha Rao from dismissing the Kalyan Singh government? Why did Narasimha Rao wait for nine hours before dismissing the government when the demolition had been ongoing?

It's simple. Narasimha Rao did not want to take the blame for any bloodshed that may happen due to him taking action. He was avoiding his primary responsibility.

P.V.R.K. Prasad was the Prime Minister's additional secretary and also his most trusted officer. He was an IPS officer of the Andhra Pradesh cadre. He had been the secretary for the Tirupati Tirumala Devasthan Trust for a long time and that is why he had good relations with saints and priests. When Narasimha Rao was trying to create a divide in that section of people, he had used Prasad. Prasad has made an apt description of Rao's state of mind on 6 December in his book, *Wheels Behind The Veil*. This description gives a clear understanding of the mind of the Prime minister and his faith in the temple. According to Prasad, 'When the structure was falling, Narasimha Rao was walking in his room and anxiously talking to himself loudly. He was angry. He wasn't even aware of someone else's presence in his room.'

His book is also a description of his long relationship with Narasimha Rao. He writes –

The PM would habitually call me on Sundays. 6 December was also a Sunday. When I went, he was alone in his room. He asked me to sit down. I saw that he was talking to himself loudly. I was listening very carefully to him. He was saying, "We can fight BJP. But how will we fight Lord Ram? BJP's attitude is such as if only they have a right over Ram. When we say that Congress is a secular party, it does not mean we don't believe in God, that we are atheist! Lord Ram is our God as well. Like them, we also worship him. For how long will they fool the public in the name of God and building a temple in Ayodhya?" Probably Narasimha Rao was unaware of the fact that there was an officer sitting in front of him. He was going on talking, "If they were in power, they would have realized their lines. If VHP is committed to safeguarding the Hindu values and traditions, there is no issue. But if VHP becomes a puppet in the hands of a political party, then how can the government allocate Ram Mandir land to it? Just by adding some saints and priests to their group, how can they claim to be representing all Hindus?" After this, P.V. was quiet for sometime. Looking at his passion to find a solution for the issue, I did not interrupt him. Little later, I heard him talk about the strategy for the solution.'

"The Ayodhya issue has become very sensitive. Court case has been on for decades on the ownership of land and structure. Even if court clears pending cases, the dispute will still go on. It is true. Courts cannot resolve such religious cases. I can see only one resolution for them and that is through talks, discussions and mutual agreements. Our party is committed to the constructing of the Ram temple in Ayodhya. Rajiv Gandhi had only kept the foundation stone. After demolition, I had announced as the PM that a mosque will be built there. The aim was to have both. But not through courts or politicians. This will happen by holding talks with people of both religions".

Talking to himself, the Prime Minister then said, "Now there is only one way. The issue of Ram Mandir is handed over to a committee comprising people representing maths, peeths, priests, people representing our traditional values along with politicians. May be only then we will find a solution."

Narasimha Rao's secretary P.V.R.K. Prasad writes–'It seems prime minister was so engrossed in talking to himself that he did not even realize my presence there. To test this, I coughed a little and asked, "'Ideally who all should be members of this committee?'

Narasimha Rao instantly answered, 'Dwait, Adwait and Vishishtadwait peeth's head, Shrangeri, Kanchi, Dwarka, Badri and Puri's Shankaracharya, Tamil Nadu and Andhra's Jiyangars, head of all peeths in the North that follow the Ramanuj tradition, head of Udupi and Uttaradimath that follow *Dwait* tradition, saints of the *Vallabhacharya* tradition, representatives from the *Gaudiya* and *Chaitanya* communities, Mahants from Ayodhya and other Hindu groups.

If you can bring all these people together and hand them the task of building the temple, no one will be able to say that this trust is political. This is how we will be able to curb political parties taking advantage of the issue. All my efforts of a peaceful solution between Hindus and Muslims in the matter failed. Previously, even Vishwanath Pratap Singh's government had also failed in getting all interested parties to sit and talk. Actually those people don't trust each other. If the government gives a verdict, it will not be accepted peacefully. It will also be difficult to implement it. This is an emotional and sensitive issue. The only way is that representatives of both sides sit and talk it out.' Prasad says, 'VHP and BJP will oppose making such a trust and create a pressure on the chief of *maths* to not become part of it.'

P.V. said, 'They will definitely put pressure. So it should not seem like an initiative by the Congress party or government. Instead it should seem like an initiative by the chiefs of *maths*. All this should happen so secretly that no one should come to know about it. First of all, we will have to talk to all of them individually. We will have to get their consent. They will have to be made clear that the government will fully support the trust and will not side with any group.'

Prasad said, 'If this is can be made possible, your suggestion is great. But who will do all this?'

'You will only have to do all this', said Narasimha Rao. I was shocked. The Prime Minister was thoughtful for a while. Then he started speaking—'Yes, you will have to do all this alone. You have good relations with chiefs of all *peeths* and *maths*. After all, being the executive officer you had given all of them land!'

'Sir, that's true. But most of them were South Indians. Very few come from North India. I don't know the ones from North India', said P.V.R.K. Prasad.

'You don't worry. I will make all necessary arrangements. Dwarka's Shankaracharya is still the Shankaracharya for Badri. He and VHP are not on the same track. Although an effort was made to get all five Shankaracharyas together. But that effort did not get any direction.

Dwarka's Shankaracharya was considered close to Congress by all. There is no problem in getting him to become part of the trust. But he would like to become the chairman of the trust which will not be possible. If he becomes the chairman, the trust will be called a Congress body. In that case, our motive will remain unfulfilled.'

'Although we have friendly relations with Kanchi's Shankaracharya. He has good relations with both VHP and BJP. Udupi's Pejawar Swami Vishveshwar is associated with cause of building a temple. He has once been to the jail also. He is one of the main members of the Ram Mandir trust and the vice president of VHP. I believe that he is quite close to you as well.'

'Yes, I have known him for years. I will definitely try. Who should be the president of this trust according to you?'

'It is very difficult to decide that. If Shrangeri Swami, who has never been involved in the matter, is made the president there will be no controversy. The various *peeths* may or may not agree to this decision. But Shrangeri *peeth* is the most important. It is one thing to convince Shrangeri's chief. But convincing Kanchi and Dwarka *peeth's* chiefs to work under them is way more difficult. In the entire North India, Shrangeri *peeth's* followers are in big numbers.'

The Prime Minister then says, 'Whatever you do or whoever you meet must not be promoted. For North India, one of Bihar's DIG rank officer will help you (He was hinting at Kishor Kunal). He had good relations with Uttar Pradesh's and Bihar's religious gurus. Naresh Chandra, Ayodhya cell's incharge at the PM office, who had been the cabinet secretary earlier, will make all these arrangements. Madhya Pradesh's chief minister Digvijay Singh had good relations with Dwarka's Shankaracharya and with chiefs of some of Uttar Pradesh and Madhya Pradesh's Vaishnav *maths*. I will ask them to help you.' Chandraswami had a lot of influence on Prime Minister Narasimha Rao. He often used him in many matters. But Chandraswami's own image wasn't all very good. Senior saints and priests did not consider him anything. Only people who were impacted by his money respected him. Probably that is why P.V.R.K. Prasad told Narasimha Rao to avoid taking help from Chandraswami. Narasimha Rao said, 'Chandraswami can help you with

Ayodhya's saints and priests.' Narasimha Rao said, 'Along with this, we will also have to do something for Muslims. Our own people have done a lot of damage. In trying to put me at a disadvantage, they provoked them and did a lot of damage to themselves and the Congress. You don't have to worry about that. Now this task is your first responsibility.' But efforts of the making of this Trust by Narasimha Rao were never successful. P.V.R.K. Prasad met Shrangeri Shankaracharya three to four times for this. Later Shankaracharya said, 'You are knocking on the wrong door.' The team of these four went to all places including Kanchi, Bangalore, Udupi and Puri in an official jet, but found no success. In fact they were criticized by most. Union Minister Kalhucharan Lenka went to meet Puri's Shankaracharya Niranjandev Teerth. He asked Lenka to leave and warned him not to play with emotions of Hindus. In Vrindavan, Swami Vamdev asked Union Minister P.R. Kumaramangalam to return. Digvijay Singh was M.P.'s chief minister. The Prime Minister told him to help Prasad. Digvijay Singh convinced Swaroopnand Saraswati. He even got Banaras's Ramanandacharya, Ramaneshacharya to agree but at the same time Digvijay Singh told PM's messengers, 'It is not possible for me to visit the Mahatmas. Let me contact them. Then you three can go alone. I will arrange for the jet. Whenever I leave with you all, media raises all kinds of questions.'

P.V.R.K. Prasad, Gauri Shankar and Kishor Kunal visited Ayodhya about seven to eight times for this mission. But no senior priest agreed to their plan. Shrangeri Shankaracharya Bharti Teerth later agreed. He stayed in Delhi during Chaturmas. He met the prime minister also. This mission wasn't getting much success in Ayodhya. So Chandraswami was used in Ayodhya. Chandraswami called Hanumangardi's and two other chief priests to Delhi. After all the violence, Ramalay Trust was registered in 1995. The deed said that the trust will get a temple built on Ram Janmabhoomi. After registration, the Trust's meeting kept getting postponed for two months. By then, the 1996 elections came up. When Prasad spoke to the PM about the matter one day, he said that this was election time. 'It will become political. Now we talk about it only after elections.'

Narasimha Rao was playing at dual strategies. After demolition, he had not talked about reviving the structure while addressing the nation. But in the Congress parliamentary meet, he spoke about the need for reviving it. This was part of his political helplessness. On the eve of 7 December, the Prime Minister made two big announcements. One was that communal organizations like RSS, Bajrang Dal, VHP, Jamaat-e-Islami and Islamic Sevak will be banned. And two, that the mosque will be reconstructed. Both these announcements by the PM were going to enhance the problem. Arjun Singh was going to corner Narasimha Rao at the Congress parliamentary meet. Rao had taken these decisions under that pressure even though these decisions increased the aggression of the Ram Mandir movement. After demolition, a defensive BJP became aggressive. BJP's base and popularity spread. Ideological polarization spread fast.

This was the time when politics around the Ayodhya issue was at its peak and no one was spared. Not even the security forces. Their plight was pitiful. Being tossed around like a football between the centre and state, their image had now become of them opposing the temple. The Central government was sending the central forces without the consent of the state government. So the state government was putting all kinds of accusations against these forces, creating a perception in the public as if the only obstacle on the path to building the temple were these forces.

Chief Minister Kalyan Singh wrote a letter to the Prime Minister telling him that the forces he was sending without inquiring with the state government was an attack at the Sangh's structure. Kalyan Singh even objected to the paramilitary forces collecting near Ayodhya without prior permission of the Kalyan Singh government. He demanded that they be called back immediately, (in his letter to the prime minister) because they were spreading terror and anxiety, showcasing bad behaviour when drunk and hence creating a ruckus in Ayodhya. This letter written by Kalyan Singh to the Prime Minister reveals the deteriorating relations between both governments and the falling political ideologies. The letter written by Kalyan Singh on 30 November to the PM says:

Respected Prime Minister,

For the last few days, the Central government has been sending central forces in large numbers to Uttar Pradesh especially to Ayodhya and Faizabad. In this regard, neither the state government asked for central forces from the centre for the Ayodhya case nor was the state government consulted or taken permission from. Even now, central forces are constantly coming to Uttar Pradesh. This one-sided step by the Central government is against the basic sentiment of the constitution and is an attack at the Sangh's structure. This is totally against the democratic traditions and is an attack at the freedom and liberties of the people of Uttar Pradesh.

The Indian constitution has defined the jurisdiction of central and state governments in detail. According to the seventh article of the constitution, maintaining law and order is the duty of the state government and falls under their purview. If the state government wishes and feels the need, it can request for support from the Central government. But the situation in Uttar Pradesh is not such. The law and order is in place and communal harmony is maintained.

To let the constitution friendly Sangh structure keep functioning properly, it is necessary that the Central and State governments work in their boundaries and do not attack each others' jurisdiction. Encroaching on the lines defined in the constitution by the Central and State governments can prove to be dangerous for the democracy. Constitution says it is necessary that the Central government protects the autonomy of the state governments. Being more powerful, the centre must not misuse its powers by putting pressure and imposing its ideology on the states. If such nature of events is not controlled in time, it will cause a lot of damage to our Sangh's structure.

The Union Home Ministry sent a message and only said that these forces were being sent to various parts of Uttar Pradesh in case the UP government needed them; then they will be available for deployment at a short notice. But these forces were not kept under the state government. Although from the message it seems that the Central government itself accepts that deployment of the central forces can be done on a request from the state government, to work under them.

Should we understand from this that the central forces were only sent to various places, but they were not supposed to be deployed? It is unfortunate that it doesn't seem so from the behaviour of officers in the central forces and the others under them. Few days back the 'Rapid Action Force' commandos showed objectionable behavior on their motorcycles and created terror in Ayodhya. These jawans misbehave with public. Two central forces sub-inspectors went to the police control room situated in Ayodhya and said to the staff there that they had only come to see, but two days later they would come and capture it. Besides this, officials from the central forces said to the press that they will not work under the district magistrate. This is only one technical thing. But actually, by not working under the state government, they would work freely. This undesirable behaviour by central forces is leading to terror and misconceptions in the public of Ayodhya. There is tension and anxiety in the people of Ayodhya towards them. The possibility of a clash between public and central forces because of such behavior in the near future cannot be denied. If this happens, full responsibility for this will be of the Central government.

Respected sir, I will again request you not to attack the Sangh's structure by doing this. Please do not destroy democratic traditions.

I am hopeful that you will think about the points made by me and give orders to call back unnecessarily deployed central forces immediately.

Warm regards

Yours
Kalyan Singh

The limit was crossed when the state government sent information based on Faizabad's DM that paramilitary forces were creating ruckus in the red light area of Faizabad after getting drunk. Faizabad's wine shops and sex workers were facing a great challenge. The three-page report said that these jawans get drunk and also fight with the shopkeepers and the women. Complaints of misconduct with women was becoming routine. Faizabad's electricity department sent a similar report. This report complained of power theft by paramilitary forces which was creating more pressure on the transformers, leading to the danger of them burning or blasting. This was still alright. But there was one more report. In this report, the state administration had called the deployment of CRPF inside the disputed site 'dangerous'. These facts say a lot. Whatever was going on between the central forces deployed to save the structure and the state government is made clear through these letters.

In return, Union Home Minister S.B. Chavan also warned Kalyan Singh that the security that was organized to protect the structure by the state government was not enough. Instead of blaming the paramilitary forces and making baseless accusations against them they were to be used in a better way. Chavan said that if violence in the name of religion led to any damage to the structure, then law and order would get disturbed not just in Uttar Pradesh but in the entire country. Home Minister said that he was not satisfied with the security arrangements for the disputed site by the state government.

Home Minister S.B. Chavan responded to Kalyan Singh's allegations and wrote:

5 December, 1992
Home Minister, India
New Delhi-110001

Dear Kalyan Singh,

I have written to you with regards to the Ram Janmabhoomi-Babri Masjid structure's security many times earlier also.

In your letter dated 2 December 1992, you have reiterated the state government's commitment towards security of the structure.

But we are still worried and Kar Sevaks gathering in big numbers in Ayodhya is only increasing our worries.

We have received reports that Kar Sevaks are agitated and

anxious and many of them are buying *trishool* or trident, which can be used for attacking. We have also found out that some of them are against the central forces. This is also reported that due to Kar Sevaks gathering in big numbers, the crowd of devotees visiting religious places has increased.

Like I had mentioned in my earlier letter, in case of violence the security arrangements by the state government will not be sufficient. We have received a report that there is a lapse in the security at the entrance between outer and inner circle and that is why visitors are putting pressure on entering the disputed zone. Besides this, we have also received a report that people are gathering endlessly at the area where devotional songs are sung. It is being said that because of this huge crowd, there is danger of people entering the place and also damaging wooden circle on 4 December, 1992. This can be stopped only by police interference. Tightening the security around the circle is important. Some more lapses in the security arrangements were brought to notice in the fax (81011/1/92) sent on December 4, 1992.

Keeping this background in mind, there is need for paying attention to security. We don't believe that the steps being taken by the state government will be enough for this. Mainly this is not clear that if Kar Sevaks go against the court order and start construction, and then get violent on being stopped, then in that situation should there be a back-up plan?

You have constantly assured us of the state government's commitment for the structure, but on the other hand already existing security solutions have been removed despite our request. You have said that PAC's fifteen more companies have been deployed at Ayodhya. According to us, if violence erupts in Ayodhya, these arrangements will not be enough. On the other hand, if the forces are not able to face the situation, then security forces can get into unnecessary danger. We have offered to make central forces available at many points earlier as well and have deployed them in the nearby areas now so that they can be sent to the state government at a short notice when needed. I request you to consider my request seriously.

The Ram Janmabhoomi-Babri Masjid security case came up in the High Court also today. The lapses pointed by the centre were noted by the honorary court as well and it was suggested that these lapses be brought to the notice of the state government. The honorary court told the lawyer of the state government to think positively on these suggestions.

This is the reason why Central government has made the state government aware of its worries from time to time and given suggestions that should be considered relevant. I am hopeful that the state government will think positively on the worries and suggestions expressed by the Central government. For maintaining law and order, and seeing that the court's orders are complied with, Central government is willing to give the kind of support needed by the state government.

With compliments,

Yours sincerely
S.B. Chavan

These letters were a way of the political class to treat Ayodhya in line with their own tune. But in the middle of all this, Ayodhya's basic question was still unanswered. The basic question was how did so many Kar Sevaks gather in Ayodhya? That too at a time when Congress was the ruling party in the centre as well as in more than half the states. There was Lalu Yadav's government in Bihar, Biju Patnaik's in Odisha, leftists in Bengal. But why did no one try to stop the Kar Sevaks?

The Supreme Court directed the Uttar Pradesh government to propagate that there is no ban on the symbolic Kar Seva. This promotion was also a reason for the large turn out of Kar Sevaks, because the message that went to the public was that anyone can serve Ram by becoming a part of this Kar Seva. After losing the structure, Narasimha Rao went against his nature and took speedy action although he did this under pressure from the secular leaders. The Central government banned RSS, VHP, Bajrang Dal, Jamaat-E-Islami and Islamic Sevak Sangh on 10 December. BJP governments in Rajasthan, Madhya Pradesh and Himachal Pradesh were dismissed. They were dismissed on the basis that they are associated with banned groups. On the other hand, the Muslim groups that were banned were only for show. Just a day before this the Islamic Sevak Sangh's leader Madni had announced that if RSS was banned, they would automatically dissolve their group. The group ended as RSS was banned. The case of Jamaat-E-Islami is even more interesting. This group was almost non-existent. The kind of allegations used against them to ban them, were related to speeches made by the Jamaat-E-Islami party leaders two years back.

After losing the structure, the High Court also became active. The decision, which all were waiting for, was given by the High Court on 11 December 1992. If this decision had come five days earlier, the structure could have been saved. After the verdict, 6 December's Kar Seva would have been legitimate. The High Court dismissed the acquisition of the 2.77 acre land that the state government had acquired around the disputed structure. This decision was reserved since 3 November. The whole drill before the Kar Seva on 6 December by the state government, VHP and BJP leaders was that the High Court would give its verdict before 6 December. If the court maintained that the 2.77 acres land is legitimately acquired, the land would have gone to Ram Janmabhoomi Trust. The state government had acquired the land and given it to the Trust. So Kar Seva on this would have been legitimate. Even if the court were to dismiss it, ownership of 2.07 acres of land out of 2.77 would have gone back to Ram Janmabhoomi Trust because this land was owned by the Trust even before the acquisition. The Trust had bought this land from different people. This part was with the Trust before the process of acquisition started. 2.77 acres of land was separate from the disputed structure, which means that the Kar Seva on this land would be away from the disputed site. Kar Seva in both circumstances would be legally legitimate. Later Kalyan Singh told me that he had reserved the 2.77 acre land away from the disputed area as the 'safety valve'. The High court said in its decision that this acquisition had been done in a cowardly manner. This acquisition abused the fundamental rights in the constitution.

Kar Seva had happened on this land earlier as well. The founding stone was also kept on this piece of land. Kar Seva had happened on this very land in July 1992. The platform was constructed here at that time. Sumitra Bhavan, Falhari Baba's ashram, Sankatmochan Mandir and Ram Gopal Tiwari's hut was also on this very land, which was registered with the Trust. Later these structures were razed and the land was levelled. The trust had bought this land from different people.

The state government issued the first notification of this acquisition on 7 October 1991. By means of which as per the 1937 administration some parts of *Khasra* plot no. 159, 160, 170 and 172 were acquired to promote tourism.

Later, the state's tourism secretary Alok Sinha gave an affidavit in court saying that the temple construction on the acquired land would also be an important part of promoting tourism. This falls in the definition of public interest. The state government had changed their intent on acquisition to hand over the land of conflict to the Trust.

Mohammed Hashim challenged the 10 October 1991 acquisition's notification in the High Court on 17 October. During court proceedings on 10 November 1991 the High Court passed an order announcing this acquisition legal and gave permission to take charge of it. But the High Court put forth a condition that neither can any permanent construction happen on this nor can this land be transferred.

Later this order was upheld by the Supreme Court as well. There was a controversy over Kar Seva being held in July 1992 on the 2.77 acres of land acquired. The High Court passed an order to cancel Kar Seva on this land on 14 July, because there was a permanent platform being built on this land against the order of the court and the state government had transferred the land to the Ram Janmabhoomi Trust. Since then the matter had been stuck. The state government and VHP both wanted an early ruling from the court. In the talks that were on between the Central government, RSS and BJP, the biggest issue was that the Central government requested the court to gives its verdict before 6 December. The High Court gave its verdict on 11 December, five days after the structure was demolished.

After the Babri structure was demolished, the Indian government had two issues. One was to maintain the status as it was till they had found a solution and two, to conclude if there was a temple there before the mosque. On 7 Janurary 1993 the Indian government gave orders to acquire all the 67.7 acres of land around the disputed site in Ayodhya. This acquisition included Ramkatha Kunj, the disputed structure and the foundation areas.

Even today, Ayodhya's 67.7 acres of land remains centrally governed. This includes the area of the disputed site. Along with this, the government also did presidential reference according to article 143 of the Constitution, through which the Supreme Court asked if there was a Hindu temple or another religious structure at the place where the mosque was built in 1528. According to the presidential reference, the president consults the chief magistrate of the Supreme Court. But this advice by the SC is not binding on the president. This is merely advice.

The Muslim leadership and Babri committee attacked the government's proceedings. Both acquisition and the presidential reference were challenged in the Supreme Court. A special bench of five judges started proceedings of the case in September 1993. In its decision given in December 1994, the Supreme Court declared acquisition of the land to be legal but refused to give an opinion on presidential reference. Under the leadership of Chief Magistrate M.N. Venkatchalayya the five judges' bench said that according to article 143 of the Constitution, the special context given by the president is not necessary. So there was no need to answer this and therefore they were returning this. Also, the Supreme Court had transferred the rest of the cases to the Lucknow bench of the Allahabad High Court.

Under pressure from the public and looking at the communal situation in the country, Narasimha Rao was now beginning to back out from his announcement of rebuilding the mosque. The saints and religious gurus had announced that a mosque won't be built inside Ayodhya. So the government decided to build the mosque outside a pentatonic circuit. According to this plan, acquisition of 40 acres of land was being planned in Faizabad's Sehnawa village. A team of central officers also went and conducted a recce of Sehnawa along with I.B. Faizabad district administration marked 40 acres of land in Sehnawa. This land was registered under Mir Baqi's family in the revenue records. The documentation of this plan was secretly completed.

Four kilometres away from Faizabad, on the road that went to Sultanpur was Sehnawa, the village with a Muslim majority. Most people depended on agriculture or related income sources in this village. This village also had Mir Baqi's *Mazaar*.

Mir Baqi was Babur's army commander. He was the one who had demolished the temple and built the disputed structure in Ayodhya, the same structure that was demolished on 6 December 1992. There was a mosque already present beside Mir Baqi's epitaph. A proposal that said that Babri mosque should be built in this village had come from the Shia Muslims of Faizabad earlier, as a solution to the problem. After acquiring 67 acres of land in Ayodhya on 7 January 1993, the government said that there was some more land that would be acquired. The Prime Minister was in trouble after his announcement that Babri Masjid will be rebuilt. People of his own party, the Congress Party were against his announcement. Taking all of this into consideration, Congress had looked for a place in Sehnawa village for the reconstruction although the Babri Masjid Action Committee openly opposed any such plan. Mir Baqi's descendants live in the same village even today. Narasimha Rao stepped back from this proposal also. He would change his decision instantly under pressure. Nothing stayed with him.

We need to go back a little, to understand Ayodhya's political struggle, before the date of demolition. The truth is that if the lock had been opened, the structure would not have been demolished. Even if the founding stone hadn't been laid, the structure could have been saved. If the Chandra Shekhar government hadn't been dismissed, even then the structure could have been saved. As prime minister, Chandra Shekhar was looking for a way out of the Ayodhya matter with full commitment. It was unfortunate that his government stayed only for four months. He had brought both parties face-to-face on only one question – was there a Hindu place of worship before the mosque was built? There were six rounds of talks between the two parties. Sharad Pawar, Bhairon Singh Shekhawat and Mulayam Singh Yadav supervised these meetings. In the sixth round when the Muslim side had to give proof against any temple being there before the mosque, they did not turn up. After this, Prime Minister Chandra Shekhar decided to bring in an ordinance. On the basis of some points of agreement with Sharad Pawar, Rajiv Gandhi got the Chandra Shekhar government dismissed. Experts from both sides met a total of six times in the Chandra Shekhar government. Documents of about seven thousand pages were exchanged. At the fifth meeting on 6 February 1991, the government decided to compare documents with existing records given by both parties. Before Chandra Shekhar could reach an agreement, Congress took back their support. The Chandra Shekhar government was dismissed untimely and an agreement was not reached at.

At that time, there were two more people who were seriously involved in the talks—Sharad Pawar and Bhairon Singh Shekhawat. Lok Sabha elections took place in May, which the BJP fought on the issue of Ram Mandir and all issues related to Hinduism and nationalism. In the middle of these elections, when half the country had already voted, the country faced a big tragedy. Rajiv Gandhi was assassinated on 21 May 1991 when he had gone for an election rally in Sriperumbudur. The LTTE had conspired to kill him with a human bomb. This incident changed the direction of elections. The Congress party emerged as the biggest party in the Lok Sabha with 246 Members of Parliament (MP). BJP came second with 119 seats. In June 1991 Congress party's minority government took over under the leadership of Narasimha Rao and BJP took up charge of Uttar Pradesh under Kalyan Singh's leadership. BJP had managed to get a majority in Uttar Pradesh for building the temple. Public sentiment was for the temple and the pressure of clearing obstacles in the way of building it was on the BJP. Hence pulling through the struggle at Ayodhya became a part of the democratic responsibility for the then government of Uttar Pradesh.

Prime Minister Narasimha Rao is an indisputable part of the truth of 6th December 1992. The picture of Babri Masjid demolition cannot be erased from his tenure as India's prime minister and this will always be. Most people treat Narasimha Rao as their punching bag in this case. As the prime minister of India, owing to his nature and the nature of his work, he always maintained silence over this. Yes, the stage had been reached at the time of Narasimha Rao, that while there was a Kar Seva campaign going on on one side, talks were on on the other.

The campaign for Kar Seva did not affect the talks and neither did the campaign stop while talks were on. Both went on simultaneously. There were a lot of contradictions in Narasimha Rao's personality. He said something and did something else altogether. The background story of Ayodhya's demolition is full of such examples. Let me give one interesting example. Prabhash Joshi was our editor. He played a role in the talks on the Ayodhya matter. Prabhash Joshi met Narasimha Rao a few days after the incident of 6 December along with Nikhil Chakravarty and R.K. Mishra. Narasimha Rao's behaviour on 6 December was a reason for Prabhash Joshi's anxiety. Prabhash Joshi told Narasimha Rao that it was his attitude on the 6th of December that could not save the Babri structure. 'What were you thinking?' Joshi asked, and was shocked at Rao's answer. Narasimha Rao said, 'You people think I don't understand politics. Whatever I did was done thoughtfully. I had to end BJP's temple politics. I did that.'

In every phase of Ayodhya's dispute, the effort of finding solutions through talks went on. But it never succeeded. Rashtriya Ekta Parishad has been one such platform where harmony has been discussed for decades. In Ayodhya's context, its meeting took place on 2 November 1991 for the first time. Some leaders suggested talking to Maulana Bukhari in this meeting. Former prime minister, Chandra Shekhar raised an objection to this. He said that Ali Miyan was a useful person. If they spoke with him, they could get help in resolving the Ayodhya case. The same way he also spoke about Kanchi Kamakoti's Shankaracharya (head) Jayendra Saraswati. He wanted Jayendra Saraswati and Ali Miyan to try at their personal level for which he felt they needed to talk to them.

For this, the Rashtriya Ekta Parishad's three journalist members, Nikhil Chakravarty, R.K. Mishra and Prabhash Joshi, continuously met with leaders from RSS, BJP and VHP from July 1992 to the end of November. They decided to meet Ali Miyan also in this sequence. Nikhil Chakravarty, Prabhash Joshi, Vijay Pratap and Rambahadur Rai reached Takiya village of Raebareli in the first week of November. They met Ali Miyan. He had a long conversation with Nikhil Chakravarty and Prabhash Joshi. But Ali Miyan did not take interest in initiating any change in the Ayodhya matter, despite his soft image. I was also with that group.

He kept using the same logic that the Muslim Personal Law Board was giving. Ali Miyan was also the chairman of the Muslim Personal Law Board. He said that the Masjid could not be touched. It could not be relocated for building a temple. This was the crux of what he said, which resulted in nothing but hopelessness and disappointment for Prabhash Joshi and Nikhil Chakravarty. While leaving, Ali Miyan also gave them some Hindi and Urdu magazines printed in Nadwa, which he had got published for better understanding of Islam.

The next day I took all of them to meet Chief Minister Kalyan Singh. While leaving, Kalyan Singh asked me what our plan was. When he learned that we had just had a meeting with Ali Miyan, he suggested we visit Ayodhya as well. Kalyan Singh informed the commissioner at the time, Surendra Pal Gaur, about our visit. He received us at the Faizabad border. Everyone took a look at the Babri Masjid. Since the commissioner was accompanying us, we could even go to areas that were restricted for the general public such as the rear side of the mosque where there were loose bricks and an unfinished wall. Upon seeing this, Prabhash Joshi joked. He said, 'Dada (Nikhil Chakravarty), I have found the solution to the Ayodhya case. Either Saryu (river) will take it away some day or someone will take away these loose bricks one by one!'

We also met Mahant Nritya Gopal Das in Ayodhya. We had a similar talk with him as well on how to find a solution to the Ayodhya issue. But no solution was to be seen. Both parties were stuck. Narasimha Rao wanted to be seen as someone holding talks with everybody, rather than looking for a real solution. These meetings were of no use. The Prime Minister only wanted to send out the message that he was constantly doing something about the issue. In the next few pages, you will only read about such efforts, the real intention behind which was to just keep the issue hanging.

When Narasimha Rao started talks in the government, he included Bhairon Singh Shekhawat because Shekhawat was part of the previous talk during the Chandra Shekhar government. The previous government's line of communication was clear. Shekhawat asked Prime Minister Rao as to what was the direction of this conversation, what was its purpose? Rao replied, 'We will figure out the purpose and direction later. You keep the talks going for now. Everyone should know that the talks are on.'

A report was published on 2 October 1992 in the *Indian Express* whose prime source was Shekhawat. The report was never officially refuted. The report said that the PM is only whiling away time through talks. A dialogue has started in the Chandra Shekhar government in a very straightforward manner. This government was on a track exactly opposite to that. In the meantime Bhairon Singh Shekhawat made a shocking revelation about how he came to be included by Narasimha Rao in the 1992 peace talk. Shekhawat said, 'The thought was to begin talks from where they had ended. I was requested to join it, but not to become a part of it. How was this possible? I was told that Sharad Pawar and I had to sit outside the room where the talks were on. As and when required, someone would come and discuss with both of us. I refused to participate in this manner. Subodh Kant Sahay strongly opposed Rao's decision of making me part of the talks in this way. He said that Bhairon Singh Shekhawat and Sharad Pawar should be part of the talk. Later both of us were made part of the talk.'

Narasimha Rao had included so many people in the talk that it became a nuisance. Some indivisuals and groups who were not related to each other at all, were talking separately. At least four ministers of Narasimha Rao were speaking at different levels. Sharad Pawar, P.R. Kumaramangalam, Kamal Nath and even Balram Jakhad were included in the talk. To reach a formula, a group of journalists and a senior intelligence officer were also included.

Many such people, who were only expected to argue and not really reach a solution, were also contacted. Senior personalities like Udupi's Pejawar Swami and former president R. Venkataraman also participated in it. Pejawar Swami said, 'After Chaturmas, I had a meeting with the Prime Minister in September. In that meeting he had made me aware of all situations and suggested that the temple can be built 20 feet away from the disputed structure.'

Later Pejawar Swami said that this proposal will not be accepted by anyone. He also met former president R. Venkataraman in Madras later. Venkataraman's suggestion was that two out of the three domes can be given to VHP for temple construction. And the third one can be left as it is, as a national memorial. Pejawar Swami gave information of this proposal by R. Venkataraman to the Prime Minister's personal secretary, P.V.R.K. Prasad. If permission for Kar Seva was given, this proposal could be considered.

In the meantime, Union Minister Kamal Nath met Lal Krishna Advani and Bhairon Singh Shekhawat. Kamal Nath had first met Advani in July 1992. After this they met many times to discuss the issue of Ayodhya. Such a meeting took place, last, in the second week of October 1992. Lal Krishna Advani informed the Prime Minister about his conversation with Kamal Nath. Advani told him that Kamal Nath has been meeting him regularly on the Ayodhya issue, to which the PM's response was 'OK'. After this Kamal Nath met Advani many times.

In these meetings Advani said to Kamal Nath that the Central government should speed up the land acquisition case going on in Allahabad High Court. Advani also said that if the decision were to come in their favour, VHP will begin construction work. The same would happen even if the verdict was not in their favour because eighty percent of the acquired land was owned by VHP. Kamal Nath told Advani that it was not good to be hopeful regarding such decisions from the court. 'We must talk about our formula.' He said.

After two or three days, on 8 or 9 October 1992 Kamal Nath came back to see Advaniji. He suggested that if the Central government can acquire the land, the High Court could be bypassed. He said, 'if we assume that Central government acquires the land, it hands it over to the Ram Janbhoomi Trust for construction of the temple on the condition that the disputed structure will not be touched till the time there is no instruction. Will this be agreed upon?' Kamal Nath suggested that the issue could either be resolved by holding talks or by hearing the court's order. To this Advani replied that they could think about this.

The next day Nanaji Deshmukh met the Prime Minister. When Nanaji mentioned about Kamal Nath's proposal to the Prime Minister, he said, 'There is no such proposal, nor have I told Kamal Nath to hold a talk.' Then Kamal Nath met Advani and Advani told him about

Nanaji Deshmukh's conversation with the PM. In response Kamal Nath said, 'It is possible that the PM is thinking of it as his last move and is unhappy because of it being revealed early.' The other minister involved in the talk, P.R. Kumaramangalam also disapproved of Kamal Nath's plan. He also said that the PM had not authorized Kamal Nath for any effort on the issue of Ayodhya. An upset Advani distanced himself from the talks after this.

What is surprising is that when Kamal Nath was talking to Advani, he also discussed his plan with Bhairon Singh Shekhawat. Bhairon Singh Shekhawat also approved of it. On 11 November 1992 Bhairon Singh Shekhawat said to the *Indian Express* that involving too many people during the talks was spoiling it. Advani had approved Kamal Nath's 'package' after speaking with the VHP. But the PM said that he did not have knowledge of any such 'package'. Shekhawat said this in an interview. Narasimha Rao kept misleading the public. He sent another proposal to the Sangh through three senior editors and an intelligence officer. All three editors went straight to the Sangh head office in Keshkunj from Rashtriya Ekta Parishad's meeting on 23 November 1992. All four of them met Professor Rajendra Singh (Rajju Bhaiya). These people had taken a settlement draft with them which said that the first phase of building the temple will start from Singhdwar on the 2.77 acre land. In the first phase of construction, except for the 2.77 acre land, the disputed structure and area would not be touched. The responsibility to ensure the disputed structure's safety would be of the Ram Janmabhoomi Trust, the Uttar Pradesh government and the Central government. One supervisor appointed by the Supreme Court would be responsible to keep an eye on the security of the disputed structure.

This proposal also failed because the PM backed away from things he had agreed upon initially even though this formula was based on the PM's initiative. Most of the formulas that came up during this time, to come to a settlement, met with the same fate. All formulas were about separating Kar Seva from the disputed site, which meant that Kar Seva would happen in a neighbouring place and an agreement would be reached at through talks by court regarding the structure. This was basically BJP's proposal. But the PM backtracked from this as well.

On the other hand, the PM was trying to break the leadership of the Ayodhya movement. He tried to do this through a controversial tantrik Chandraswami. Chandraswami was close to the PM. But the saints' community had no respect for him because at that time, Chandraswami was busy increasing his say in the political community. The PM's efforts to demolish the unity of the leadership were confirmed by Swami Vamdev. According to Swami Vamdev, when the PM, along with Viyoganand and Ramta Yogi called him on 5 October, Chandraswami was present there. The Prime Minister openly said in this meeting that the temple would be built but it would be outside the current structure. Swami Vamdev concluded that talking to the PM now, was meaningless.

Swami Vamdev openly announced in the conference of saints on 17 October that he would not meet the PM on a personal level now, because the PM wanted to break the campaign for the temple. His intentions were not clean. After this, on 19 October 1992 a messenger of the PM reached Ayodhya. He asked Swami Vamdev to meet the PM. Swami Vamdev clearly said that after 5 October's meeting there was no reason for him to meet the PM. The Prime Minister went on with his efforts tirelessly. On 12 November 1992 the home ministry's special emissary Mahesh Pathak reached Mathura. He again requested Swami Vamdev to meet the prime minister. Swami Vamdev again refused to meet him. On 25 November 1992 senior journalist Ved Prakash Vaidik reached Vrindawan at 1:00 a.m. as the prime minister's messenger. Ved Prakash Vaidik tells us that the prime minister told him not to take an office car. Balram Jakhad arranged a private car for him. Ved Prakash Vaidik was quite close to the PM. He also invited Swami Vamdev to meet the PM. The conversation went on till 2:30 at night. But Swami Vamdev did not agree and refused him too. But the PM did not give up. On the night of 26 November 1992 at eight o'clock, three people—Rajeev Tyagi (MP), P.R. Kumaramangalam (Union Minister) and Pradeep Mathur (former MLA from Mathura) along with Gokul Chand Sarpanch went to Swami Vamdev and requested him to meet the Prime Minister. The Prime Minister had a proposal.

Swami Vamdev refused these people also saying that now Kar Seva's programme would not change. Swami Vamdev said that if permission for Kar Seva on the 2.77 acre land was to be given, then he would be willing to talk. On 30 November 1992, a mahant, Sevadas, met Swami Vamdev in Faridkot and requested him to change the 6 December date for the Kar Seva. Swami Vamdev said bluntly that that was impossible. This mahant had also come to break the campaign. The mahant also suggested to Vamdev that the saint community should take up the task in their hands and keep VHP out of the construction work. At this time VHP's Acharya Giriraj Kishor also came there. He said, 'If Congress declares that place as Ram Janbhoomi (birthplace of Lord Ram) in the parliament, VHP will back off. After that saints can build the temple according to the plan. VHP will have no role to play in that.' To this mahant Sevadas replied, 'I have come here after meeting the Prime Minister. The government won't allow any construction there nor will it declare it to be Ram Janmabhoomi.' Swami Vamdev then said, 'Then why are you wasting your time?'

Prime Minister Narasimha Rao made one more serious attempt to break the campaign. This attempt was done at a personal level, which was later revealed by Paramhans Ramchandra Das. According to him, during the last days of November 1992, he got an invitation from many messengers sent by the PM that the Prime Minister wanted to meet him alone. Being the chief of Ram Janbhoomi Trust, he could not accept the offer of meeting the Prime Minister alone. So he ignored the invitation.

Paramhans says, 'After this a letter came from the Shankaracharya of Jyotir math, Shantanand Maharaj. In the letter it was written that the Prime Minister wants that Ram Mandir is to be built only by saints. Political leaders are to be pushed out of it.' After reading Shankaracharya's letter, Paramhans Ramchandra Das felt that the PM was seriously thinking of building the temple only by the saints. So he changed his opinion and informed Vamdev Maharaj in Ayodhya that he was going to meet the PM.

Paramhans refused to take the official jet. He asked the Delhi office of VHP to pick him up from the airport. He went to the Prime Minister straight from the airport. The PM told Paramhans that respecting the court's decision, VHP can hold Kar Seva in the no-conflict zone. He also said that if political elements were out, any effort towards building the temple would have his complete support. Paramhans said, 'the saint community had given you time to make a decision on the entire area and not just the 2.77 acres of land. But you declared that campus a mosque in your speech on 15 August.' To this the Prime Minister said that he never used the word 'mosque'.

Paramhans was a straightforward person. He told Narasimha Rao, 'I am not saying that you are dividing saints. But everyone believes that you are using means that will divide. Now, even I am doubtful. Dear Prime Minister, please tell me only what I can go out and tell the press as well as the public.' Gradually Paramhans Ramchandra Das came to his natural avatar. He said to the Prime Minister, 'I have never lied. We never gave you time to think over the 2.77 acres of land. That bit has been under us for the last 43 years. We have laid the foundation stone there. We are going to hold the Kar Seva there only and no one can stop us. You can get me killed, but we will conduct the Kar Seva.' The Prime Minister did not say anything.

News of the meeting between Mahant Paramhans and the Prime Minister got published in the *Indian Express* on 26 November1992. The article said that the prime minister had made the offer to Paramhans that he was willing to lend support to any initiative towards temple building, if political elements were kept out of it. Religious gurus who had gone in a special plane from Ayodhya (though it's not true) told the PM in a half an hour meeting that it was impossible to keep the VHP away from the efforts of building the temple.

All the efforts made to break the Ayodhya campaign by Narasimha Rao were showing no results. So he held evidence collected by the Naresh Chandra committee to create pressure on the saints and also because if this evidence was to come out, the issue could be resolved.

A special cell was formed under the leadership of Naresh Chandra at the Prime Minister's office. This cell had collected some evidence that this disputed structure was built by razing a temple. In Islamic Shariyat, it was permissible to vacate, break or demolish mosques. In other Islamic countries where incidents of vacating, breaking or demolishing a mosque happen, the country knows the reason behind it. The government felt that revealing such evidence was not right.

Looking at his plan fail, the Prime Minister was now despairing. His stand started to change. He started calling the disputed structure a mosque. On 27 July 1992 he once again referred to the disputed structure as a mosque in his speech at the Rajya Sabha. He repeated his appeal that the temple would be built without touching the mosque. On 29 July 1992 in his speech at the Lok Sabha, Narasimha Rao used the word 'mosque'. In his address on Independence Day, 15 August 1992 he said, 'We want a temple in Ayodhya. But the mosque must not be demolished.' The pressure under which he was calling it a mosque again and again led to increased bitterness between him and the BJP. Till now, the BJP had been working with Narasimha Rao. There was a special understanding between Narasimha Rao and BJP. The BJP gave Narasimha Rao and his party a lot of support especially on the economic front. In fact to lend significant support, BJP did not care about its own interest. But now, relations between the Prime Minister and the BJP were fast deteriorating. In the Kar Seva during 1992, he spoke to BJP and RSS leaders. This included Lal Krishna Advani, Atal Bihari Vajpayee and Professor Rajendra Singh. But since November he was maintaining a distance from Bhartiya Janta Party and Rashtriya Swayamsevak Sangh's leadership. There could have been political reasons behind this.

The biggest reason behind his increasing distance with BJP was Arjun Singh. Arjun Singh was constantly attacking the PM without taking his name. He accused Narasimha Rao for being soft towards the BJP. He had formed a group with Congress members who were angry with Narasimha Rao for different reasons. Much against tradition, Bhartiya Janta Party was supporting the government despite being in the chief opposition party.

But they also began attacking the Prime Minister now. BJP had started becoming aggressive towards Narasimha Rao from October. Even Lal Krishna Advani, who had called Narasimha Rao the most capable prime minister after Lal Bahadur Shastri, demanded his resignation after the stock and Solanki Bofors scams. Then on 6 November 1992 BJP came out with its official statement that Narasimha Rao is a national calamity for the country and should be removed.

After this, the environment did not remain the same. This relationship turned so sour that Narasimha Rao met Lal Krishna Advani for the last time on 18 November 1992. At the most decisive and crucial time of the Kar Seva, the Prime Minister had no communication with Advani. He used to talk to Vinay Katiyar. According to Advani, there may have been another reason for this. Perhaps the Prime Minister had been advised that since the decisive protest on the Ayodhya issue could not be averted, maybe it would be best to maintain distance now onwards instead of doing so at the time of election.

Advani was of the view that even if the Prime Minister had distanced himself because of some personal reason, it should not let work get affected. So he advised Atal Bihari Vajpayee to meet the Prime Minister. Vajpayee met the Prime Minister, but as Advani had suspected, the meeting was inconclusive.

These events made it clear that the Prime Minister had decided to act against the Ayodhya movement. The Prime Minister wanted to give an impression through his sharp politics that he was interested in establishing peace. But he was not getting support from the BJP. Here it was important to mention those conditions that led to the announcement of Kar Seva on 30-31 October 1992. Actually the announcement of Kar Seva on 30 and 31 October was not an impromptu announcement. When Kar Seva was cancelled in July 1992, Vishva Hindu Parishad had told workers that the Kar Seva will start again in November.

There were some reasons behind this announcement to the Kar Sevaks, which gave the impression that the Prime Minister did not want to find a way out of the situation. For example, after the talks held with the saints in July 1992, the Prime Minister's stance changed all of a sudden and he walked away from the promises he had made. There was a deliberate delay in holding talks between the VHP and Babri Masjid Action Committee. The evasive attitude of the Prime Minister was obvious because after holding talks on the different proposals with many fractions, he walked away from it all. Also obvious, was the Prime Minister's attempt to break away from the leaders of the movement openly and otherwise getting documents of proof collected by a special team appointed by the Prime Minister and keeping quiet instead of using those papers to resolve the ongoing issues. These facts and the situation created, compelled saints and the VHP to announce the last date for Kar Seva. A 'dharmsansad' was held on 30-31 October. About five thousand saints participated in it and Kar Seva was announced for 6 December 1992. Saints and the VHP were waiting for the decision of the High Court on the disputed 2.77 acres of land.

Since the hearing was already done with in the High Court on 3 November 1992, the decision was kept reserved. Everyone hoped that the decision would come before 6 December 1992.

This was where the complication arose. The Supreme Court had directed the High Court in 1992 to speed up the verdict. The leaders associated with the movement appealed to the court to at least pronounce the 'operative part' of the decision if not the complete decision. BJP leaders had requested the Central government that the government should ask the Supreme Court to direct High Court to pronounce its verdict before 6 December 1992 so that Kar Seva could be started. Meetings were held throughout November. These meetings were attended by various leaders associated with the movement and by ministers of the Rao government. Not a day passed by when a meeting didn't take place at the top level. But the result was nil. If we look at the details of these meetings we will see the evasive attitude of Narasimha Rao.

- On 2 November 1992 Central Minister Sharad Pawar and P. R. Kumaramangalam had talks with RSS leaders Rajendra Singh (Rajju Bhaiya) and Moropant Pingle in Mumbai. Bhairon Singh Shekhawat was also present at this meeting.
- On 6 November 1992 Prime Minister Narasimha Rao and BJP leader Swami Chinmayanand held talks. This meeting was inconclusive.
- On 12 November 1992 Narasimha Rao and Lal Krishna Advani again met. The discussion was on how the reserved decision of the High Court could be pronounced speedily.
- On 17 November 1992 Home Minister S.B. Chavan and Lal Krishna Advani met again. But this meeting did not yield any result.

- On 18 November 1992 Narasimha Rao and Lal Krishna Advani met again on the same issue. Advani was unhappy with Narasimha Rao for repeatedly turning back on his word. This was the last meeting between the two before the demolition.
- On 19 November 1992 Narasimha Rao and Kalyan Singh held a meeting in Delhi. But nothing moved forward in the meeting.
- On 20 November 1992 Narasimha Rao and Professor Rajendra Singh (Rajju Bhaiya) met.
- On 25 November 1992 Narasimha Rao invited and met Mahant Paramhans Ramchandra Das. Mahant flatly refused to leave VHP.
- On 30 November 1992 Narasimha Rao met Nanaji Deshmukh and Atal Bihari Vajpayee. In that meeting an agreement was reached to hold symbolic Kar Seva. It was decided that Kar Seva would be held, but it would be done without any court issue. It was sought that if the court decision were to come, the Kar Seva will become legislatively acceptable.
- On 3 December 1992 Narasimha Rao and Professor Rajendra Singh met again. A three point formula was agreed upon in this meeting.
- On 5 December 1992 Narasimha Rao and Nanaji Deshmukh again met. Purpose of this meeting was to establish mutual trust.

The purpose of mentioning all these meetings is only to establish that the leaders of the movement had expressed only one desire which was that the UP government and Central government should ask the Supreme Court or High Court to speed up the matter. In fact Advani on 18 November 1992, Kalyan Singh on 19 November 1992, Professor Rajendra Singh on 20 November 1992 and 3 December 1992—met to appeal to Prime Minister Narasimha Rao that even if the whole verdict was not pronounced at least its operative part should be delivered by the court.

This appeal was being made on the basis that Kar Seva could be held in Surat peacefully and according to the rules, even if the operative part of the decision was to be against expectations.

On 5 December 1992 Naresh Chandra who was the head of the Ayodhya cell in the PMO, said that he was going to arrange that a request be made by the UP government to the Allahabad High court to pronounce the operative part of the decision. Lawyers of the Central government were to support this move. But when the UP government submitted its plea, the Central government's lawyer did not appear in the court. As a result of this the application in the court was rejected. This increased suspicion against the Central government. Mutual distrust also increased.

The only sensitive suggestion on the Ayodhya issue was that disputed structure should be separated from Kar Seva. The permission for construction should be given sparing the disputed structure. But this proposal was not accepted by the centre. This also raised questions on the intention of the government. The Prime Minister wanted that the Uttar Pradesh Government should give permission under article 138(2) of the constitution to go to the Supreme Court. BJP had made it clear that it was not ready to go to the Supreme Court under article 138(2), but if government desired it could seek legal advice under article 143. Under article 138(2) the advice of the Supreme Court is binding and under article 143 Supreme Court's advice is merely an advice.

While talks were on, the Prime Minister took a stand after 10 November that he would not let Kar Seva happen. On 23 November 1992 on the question of tackling the situation, the National Unity Council asked Prime Minister Narasimha Rao to take an independent decision. On 24 November 1992 the Prime Minister announced that Kar Seva was illegal and Central government would follow the court order.

On this very day the Attorney General requested the Supreme Court to act, because the next two days were going to be critical. But the court refused. Newspapers began to carry reports of central security forces in Ayodhya. On 25 November 1992 the Supreme Court denied the Central government permission to appoint a receiver for the disputed area. On 27 November, 135 battalions of central security forces had reached Ayodhya without the knowledge of the state government. Among attempts of dismissing the state government, the Governor of Uttar Pradesh was summoned to Delhi. He was briefed that if the Supreme Court pronounces an adverse decision then he should recommend dismissal of the state government. The Governor was against dismissal of the state government before something happened. Governor B. Satyanarayan

Reddy was an old socialist although he had joined Telugu Desam Party. But he was not ready to be a puppet of the centre.

In the meantime the Prime Minister asked Bajrang Dal leader and MP from Faizabad, Vinay Katiyar, if there was an option of Kar Seva without breaking the law, so that the PM could get some more time. Katiyar said, 'Yes, there is a part of the platform which is outside the 2.77 acre land area, at the point where earlier there was a police post. The construction can begin from there.' On 28 November the Attorney General requested the Court that Kar Seva should not be permitted in this area as well. But the Supreme Court did not accept this argument. But how could the Attorney General have known about the plan which was shared in confidence only with the Prime Minister by Vinay Katiyar. VHP was of the view that the Prime Minister took this information only to shut all options of Kar Seva and discredit the Ayodhya Movement. Alongside the talks the strategy of confrontation with the government was also being prepared. Also, a strategy was evident behind the conduct of the government as well.

When it was clear that the Central government was prepared for a confrontation, BJP decided to send Lal Krishna Advani and Murli Manohar Joshi for a 'rath yatra'.

Both the leaders would put forth the party's resolve on the issue and the deception of the Central government in front of Kar Sevaks and the general public. Advani started his rath yatra from Varanasi and Joshi from Mathura. This yatra got tremendous support. This yatra was more about exposing the Central government's intentions than it was about consolidating the Kar Seva. The atmosphere was electric. This yatra was garnering so much support that both the leaders had to now appeal to the supporters to cancel their travel to Ayodhya, because Ayodhya was already reeling under the mass of Kar Sevaks already present there.

Kar Seva was planned for 18 days, starting from 6 December 1992. The organizers had planned the arrival of the Kar Sevaks in such a way that it should be spread over 18 days. But after reports of a possible emergency dismissal of the Kalyan Singh government, those Kar Sevaks who were to come later reached Ayodhya early. By 4 December 1992, about 75,000 Kar Sevaks had reached Ayodhya. The VHP had to appeal to the Kar Sevaks that they should stop wherever they were and not go towards Ayodhya. But the Kar Sevaks kept pouring in.

The demolition of the disputed structure was a result of out of control and sudden emotions, which could not have been stopped. The main reason for it was that the government failed to understand the sensitivity of the issue and merely thought it to be a political dispute between Bharatiya Janata Party and the Congress. The Narasimha Rao government, which should have shown tremendous mutual understanding and responsibility, remained full of deceit and arrogance. It's pointless to now argue about who knew and who was unaware of the demolition. But this is for sure that even the investigative agencies had no clue of this.

The disputed structure became a victim of the suspicion of the central and the state government while a game of hide and seek between the government and the courts went on. After understanding the minds of the VHP and the Sangh, I was of the view that the demolition was not preplanned. Home Minister S.B. Chavan also said so later, in the Lok Sabha, that the demolition was not preplanned.

What happened in Ayodhya on 6 December 1992 was the result of an eruption of the historic age old supressed anger. But this eruption had not grown to be this massive in one day so that it could belittle the ideals of the Hindu religion. Its roots were strengthened by opportunistic politics. Those who were openly supporting it by donning religious colors were responsible for fueling the resentment, along with those who were wearing a veil of neutrality over their opportunistic politics yet were active from behind the scenes. The BJP was like an army that could win the siege because the gatekeepers of the fort had opened the gates for them. These gatekeepers were the powerful Congress leaders in the Central government. You can change the analysis of history, but not history itself. Congress is also part of the same history which is responsible for the conditions that led to the demolition of the Babri structure and construction of the Ram temple. But it wants to hide its identity in the oblivion. This is the reason it is as critical to understand the cunning politics behind the demolition as it is to understand the events of the demolition. This chapter is a journey to help the readers understand this. This may be about a journey in the past, but its lessons are a writing on the walls of the present and future. Whatever took place in Ayodhya is not just a description of the past events but it is also an understanding of the political turn-around in the passing time. What took place in Ayodhya is neither an end to this kind of politics and nor is it a conclusion. You can see that after thirty years Congress is still on the same path. Rahul Gandhi has to go from temple-to-temple for votes. Ayodhya is a journey of deceit and opportunistic politics—an endless journey.

Chapter 3

KAR SEVA

The world was changing. African leader Nelson Mandela had been released after twenty-seven years of imprisonment. Both West and East Germany that had become a painful sore on the European map, united again this year. Germany was one after twenty-five years of separation. Both these events had begun to fill the world with hope. It seemed that 1990 would deliver a pleasant end to the Ayodhya dispute. Janata Dal had formed governments in the state and at the centre. Vishwanath Pratap Singh's government at the centre had the support of the BJP. It seemed that now there was a possibility of a solution. But the opposite transpired. Views on the Ayodhya matter were more in contrast between Prime Minister Vishwanath Pratap Singh and Uttar Pradesh chief minister, Mulayam Singh Yadav than the views between the VHP and Babri Action Committee. The relationship between the governments was full of distrust, deception and conspiracy.

At that time, I was quite close to Mulayam Singh Yadav. He often discussed personal and confidential matters with me. He believed that V.P. Singh was using the temple issue to dislodge his government and was constantly conspiring against him. He suspected that the Prime Minister was meeting Hindu saints to discuss and provoke them against him. Ajit Singh had a role in creating distance between Mulayam Singh and V.P. Singh. But this story, I will tell you another time. V.P. Singh was under tremendous pressure from the BJP on the Ayodhya issue, because this dispute had catapulted BJP from 2 to 85 seats. This injected great enthusiasm in the BJP and its associate organizations. When V.P. Singh began his talks with warring communal factions, Mulayam Singh decided to oppose the talks. V.P. Singh once told me that when he was close to an agreement on the Ayodhya matter, Mulayam Singh got the sadhus he was in talks with, jailed. Later V.P. Singh got the sadhus released.

Trenches were dug between V.P. Singh and Mulayam Singh. The Prime Minister initiated talks with the sadhus and saints because conflict with the BJP over the issue was not favourable for his government. After all, the government needed support from BJP. The Central government understood that collision on the matter will not solve the issue and if the situation remained the same, it will become difficult to run the government. But to get even with V.P. Singh, Mulayam Singh chose the other extreme. He switched over to the Babri supporters.

He appointed Azam Khan, one of the three members of the Babri Action Committee, as his minister in the state government. Second was Shafiq-ur-Rahman Barq, who was made an MP from his party and third was Zafaryab Jilani who was made the legal adviser. In this cold war between the two, Chandra Shekhar, who was lagging behind in the race to the Prime Minister's office, was supporting Mulayam Singh Yadav. Chandra Shekhar was a blunt speaking socialist, but he and V.P. Singh never got along well. This 'Babri supportive stand' of Mulayam Singh turned the communal division of Uttar Pradesh murkier. Now the division between Hindus and Muslims in the society was even starker. The situation had worsened. To resolve the issue, the Central government, in agreement with the BJP, implemented ordinance of acquiring the disputed land, but as Chief Minister of the state, Mulayam Singh announced that he will not allow it to happen. This was the extent of mistrust and lack of communication between the two.

Vishwanath Pratap Singh was not as straight and simple as he appeared to be. He was a clever leader. On one hand he was talking to the saints and ascetics of the VHP and on the other hand, he was in touch with those saints who were against the VHP. And he was doing this without the knowledge of the UP Chief Minister. He was talking to these saints through Santosh Bharti who was a journalist turned member of parliament. Santosh Bharti was busy finding non-BJP ways for the Prime Minister. There were a big number of saints who were not with the VHP. Santosh Bharti was trying to find possibilities with them.

In the meantime, the saints who supported the VHP held a conference on 27 and 28 January 1991 by the Sangam in Allahabad.

Kar Seva for the temple construction in Ayodhya was announced for 14 February. This worried the Central government. Ex-judge Deoki Nandan Agarwal, who lead the temple movement went to Delhi to talk to the Prime Minister. The Prime Minister also invited other leaders of the VHP to Delhi. On 7 February, Mahant Avaidyanath, Mahant Nritya Gopal Das, Ashok Singhal, Deoki Nandan Agarwal, Vishnu Hari Dalmia, S.C. Dikshit and Guman Mal Lodha met Prime Minister V.P. Singh. The VHP leaders remained adamant on performing the Kar Seva. Ramchandra Paramhans persuaded VHP leaders to give more time to the Prime Minister. V.P. Singh requested these leaders to postpone Kar Seva for the time being. He proposed that following postponement a committee should be made, to have a continued dialogue on the issue.

VHP gave four months to Vishwanath Pratap Singh. It was announced to postpone Kar Seva. V.P. Singh told in one of his interviews, 'While I was talking to the sadhus and saints at 28 Lodhi Estate residence, I went inside and I wrote a handwritten appeal to them to postpone Kar Seva. It gave me four months time.' V.P. Singh continued, 'But Mulayam Singh got the saints I was talking to arrested. This worsened the situation. I had to work really hard to get those saints released.'

'The question I faced was how to find a solution to the problem? The court could have been an option. But the Sadhu-saints were adamant that they will not listen to the court. That it's a matter of faith that cannot be decided on logic.' V.P. Singh told them, 'But I will have to work within the purview of the constitution. So I formed a committee of three people to take the matter forward. The people in the committee were Madhu Dandwate, George Fernandes and Mukhtar Anees.' Madhu and George were ministers in the V.P. Singh government, whereas Lahiya-ite leader Mukhtar Anees from Sitapur was the health minister in the Mulayam Singh government. Anees was a Shia leader so the Babri committee did not count him. V.P. Singh said, 'I have deliberately not kept Mulayam Singh Yadav in this committee. I had kept Home Minister Mufti Mohammad Sayeed also out of it, because they both had to take the final decision. If both had got entangled in a war of words, then who would make the final decision? But Mulayam Singh took it the other way and opened a battle front. My opponents convinced

Mulayam Singh Yadav that the Prime Minister is taking decisions after side-lining you so that it is easier to dismiss your government.' V.P. Singh was troubled that Mulayam Singh mentioned this lie as a complaint to many of his colleagues.

The Prime Minister was making sincere efforts for reconciliation. He also sought help from Lal Krishna Advani and requested him to contribute to the talks. Advani refused saying temple construction was not on his party's agenda. He advised V.P. Singh to hold talks with the VHP directly. Three years after being the Prime Minister V.P. Singh was keeping unwell. He was on dialysis every second day. But he had very strong willpower. On the days that he didn't have to undergo dialysis, he travelled. I met him many times at his residence at 1, Rajaji road. Now his wife Sita Singh lives there. V.P. Singh used to recall and recount the many meetings that were held by the committee he had constituted. In those meetings Babri Committee leaders had eventually agreed to the daily hearing by the court and that they will not present too many witnesses. They gave in writing that no matter what the decision of the court was, they would agree to it. But the VHP refused to agree to it at the last minute. Their point was that they would not agree to the court's decision.

This was a dramatic change in the VHP's attitude. Just a few months ago, the VHP had given assurance that, if they were allowed to lay the foundation stone, they would accept the verdict of the court.

This promise was given by the VHP in the meeting held on 7 November 1989. Chief Minister of UP, Narayan Dutt Tiwari and Central Home Minister Buta Singh were also present at the meeting. All were in agreement. V.P. Singh said, 'That document was with the government. I showed it to the delegation of saints. Our plan was that the saints who are not in VHP and the Muslim leaders who are not in the Babri Action Committee should find a solution through talks, so that discussions can be held without any prejudice. Some saints had come from Haridwar for this meeting. I told them that I will agree to everything as the Prime Minister after they see the agreement. Those saints expressed their surprise at the agreement and said they had no knowledge of it. They said they had no clue that such a commitment was given by VHP.'

During this period Andhra Pradesh Governor Krishnakant and Bihar Governor Yunus Salim also turned up to sort out the issue. They told the Prime Minister that if he permitted, they would begin to resolve the issue. According to V.P. Singh, after getting his approval they met the Shankaracharya of Kanchipuram, Jayendra Saraswati and Muslim scholar Ali Miyan. A hope for a solution emerged. They made good progress. Shankaracharya of Kanchipuram and Ali Miyan had concluded that a committee of Hindu and Muslim community representatives should be constituted. That status quo should be maintained till recommendations of the committee were made and later, the government should implement the recommendations of the committee.

'Ali Miyan' or Maulana Abul Hasan Ali Nadvi was an international scholar of Islamic traditions. He was also the president of Muslim Personal Law Board. Ali Miyan was from Taquia village of Raebareli and a teacher at Darul Uloom Nadwatul Ulama, a university in Lucknow. He was an amazing scholar and had a humble saint-like personality. I met Ali Miyan many times at his residence. Maulana's father, Maulana Abdul Hakim Hai, had also been an administrator at Nadwatul Ulama. He had written a book in arabic, *Hindustan Islami Ahmade*. Ali Miyan had translated the book in Urdu. In this book Maulana had mentioned seven Mosques which were built after destroying temples. Babri Mosque was among them. In this book, in the chapter 'Hindustan's Mosques', it was mentioned, 'This was constructed in Ayodhya, which Hindu's call the birth place of Ramchandra. Babur constructed this mosque exactly at the same place.'

Someone gave reference of this book to Arun Shourie, editor of *The Indian Express* at that time. This was the time when a debate was on whether Babri Mosque was built after demolishing a temple or whether there was any preexisting religious structure at all. Arun Shourie brought the reference of Ali Miyan's father's book as proof but could not get the book itself. The book was there at the Aligarh Muslim University, but it was not shown to him. At that time I was stationed at the Lucknow bureau of *Jansatta*. Arun Shourie asked me to somehow get the book. I met Ali Miyan and sent a photocopy of the book to Arun Shourie. Arun Shourie wrote a series in *The Indian Express* asking what more evidence was needed on the issue. He said that this was written by the father of the person who is the president of Muslim Personal Law Board. What's worth mentioning is that right after the articles by Arun Shourie were published, copies of the book disappeared from all Islamic institutions including, Darul Uloom Nadwatul Ulama and Aligarh Muslim University. Arun Shourie also wrote news pieces about the disappearance of the books. By that time this controversy had reached another level and the context of the controversy itself had changed. Now nobody was interested in what existed before the Mosque. Not even the Supreme Court. The court also refused to give its opinion on the matter. Now the sole issue was Kar Seva.

Ashtchaap written in the 16th century by poet Kumbhandas said, 'What business do saints have in Sikri. The sandals break in the rounds of the capital and God is forgotten in the whole turmoil'. It was the same story. Both sides of saints and theologians were using unfair means in the company of politicians. Ali Miyan had made his father's book disappear. The saints had hidden facts and got the 'Shilanyas' or foundation laid at the disputed site. V.P. Singh revealed this fact.

To outline the political line of thought that existed in the country, I am quoting two letters here. MCP leader Hiren Mukherjee wrote an important letter to Atal Bihari Vajpayee. Vajpayee replied to the letter and this is even more important.

Now the rest of the story through V.P. Singh–

'When I looked at the documents, I found that the 'Shilanyas' or the foundation laying has been done in an illegal manner. I sent a team of officers. After inspection, they found that the foundation which was laid at the time of Rajiv Gandhi was in the area of the disputed site. At first, I didn't believe that the Rajiv Gandhi government would have facilitated foundation laying within the disputed area. But the documents were the witness to it. My government kept trying to find a solution.'

The VHP had given four months to the government, but they didn't miss any chance of keeping the atmosphere charged up. To take the Ayodhya matter to the people in every corner, four month-long programmess were announced. Parishad announced a thirteen-day

'Dharm-jagaran' or religious awakening from 9 April and Babri Action Committee organized Muslim Conferences in District Headquarters.

Both sides were determined to not let the government breathe easy. And now, the Shankaracharya of Dwarka peeth, Swaroopanand Saraswati also jumped into the controversy. Swaroopanand Saraswati's Congress background is well known. He was always against the events organized by the VHP. He surprised everyone by saying that the foundation laying by the VHP was done during an inauspicious time. So he will lay the foundation again in accordance with the scriptures. An arrangement was made for a second foundation laying. Mulayam Singh arrested Swaroopanand while he was on his way to Faizabad on 30 April. After the arrest, the Shankaracharya was placed in detention at the fort of Chunar. This was the first arrest of any Shankaracharya in the temple movement. This was precarious but Mulayam Singh had well thought of the consequences. This arrest overnight turned Mulayam Singh into a new 'champion of secularism'.

Mulayam Singh was not playing a small game. His secular image needed the arrest of Swaroopanand to be made. On the other hand, the same Mulayam Singh also gave permission to the followers of the Shankaracharya to lay the foundation on 7 May. This action was weakening the hold of the VHP on the temple movement, because Swaroopanand was opposing the VHP. Forty-four followers of the Shankaracharya were arrested at 'bara sthan', which was close to the *Janmabhoomi* premises. They had with them the four bricks, Jaya, Nanda, Bhadra and Poorna, meant to be used for the foundation. The Shankaracharya had given them names based on the 'Purans' or scriptures.

The priest of the Ram Janmabhoomi temple, Lal Das was also among those who were arrested. He was a government appointed priest. Lal Das was against the VHP from the very beginning. He was of the view that the movement was 'fake' and an attempt to occupy the 'birthplace'. Lal Das was a rebel, always ready to pick a fight. He was born in a 'Kshatriya family' (the traditional warrior family), in a village named Shringish near Ayodhya. Before becoming a priest, Lal Das was a secretary for some time with the Marxist Communist Party at Ayodhya. He once said, 'Ayodhya has become like the Chambal valley. If you know of what is happening in the temples, you will become an atheist.' Lal Das was often used by the 'secular brigade'. Lal Das was removed from the position of priest when the new government was formed under the leadership of Kalyan Singh. On 20 November 1993 unknown assailants shot at and killed Lal Das. The Police said that Lal Das lost his life due to a land dispute he was involved in.

The four-month time period that V.P. Singh had got for finding a solution after meeting saints and religious leaders was about to end. No useful proposal had been found yet. The relations between the BJP and V.P. Singh were no less than a miracle. He wanted to remain with the BJP and yet was not seen with them. He supported the BJP on many issues behind closed doors but criticized the party on public platforms. Before the elections, there was duality in his attitude towards the BJP. There was an open conflict on this issue between V.P. Singh and the Bharatiya Janata Party. But he also wanted an electoral understanding with the BJP against Rajiv Gandhi. Lok Sabha elections were forthcoming. Vishwanath Pratap Singh was a leader of mean and dual character. He was willing to sacrifice any ideal to maintain his image. His secularism was a hindrance in creating an understanding with the BJP over seat-sharing. But his hunger for power desired 'seat adjustment' with the BJP in a secret manner. Between May 1989 and November 1989, many talks were held to reach an understanding for seat sharing at various levels between Bharatiya Janata Party and Janata Dal. This was a time when the country was being divided on whether, 'the foundation at Ayodhya should be laid or not'. V.P. Singh was against the laying of the foundation. In the beginning, he was not in favour of having an adjustment with the BJP in Uttar Pradesh and Bihar. He felt that if an adjustment was made with the BJP, Muslims will leave Janata Dal and align with the Congress. Personally, on the ideological level V.P. Singh didn't have any issue with BJP. Nor did he consider BJP as untouchable. He desired BJP's support. But along with that he also desired Muslim votes. Understanding his plan, the BJP made it clear that either adjustment will happen in all matters or will not happen at all.

To break the deadlock between the BJP and Janata Dal, an important meeting was held at the Express Tower in Mumbai. People who were present in this meeting were, *Indian Express* Chairman Ramnath Goenka, Bhaurao Devras of RSS, Rajendra Singh (Rajju Bhaiya) and Nanaji Deshmukh. Charted accountant Swaminathan Gurumurthi was also present at the meeting. He was close to the Sangh and advisor to the powerful publisher, *The Indian Express*'s Ramnath Goenka. He was also in the role of an interlocutor between Hindus and Muslims. Which is why he was always present at all meetings. Along with him was present, Prabhash Joshi, a trusted editor of Goenka. In this very meeting an agreement was reached that BJP and Janata Dal will contest elections together.

This was the famous meeting in which V.P. Singh had asked, 'Arre Bhai! Where is the mosque? There is a temple there now. Prayer is being held. The structure is so weak that it will fall with one push. What is the need to demolish it?' Later Arun Shourie made an issue of this very comment and he gave a reference of it in an article of his, in 1990. Shourie was not in this meeting. But he made headlines of this meeting for months and V.P. Singh kept explaining it all his life.

V.P. Singh wanted assurance on only two things in this meeting. First was that the foundation laying should be symbolic and second that there should be an adjustment of seats, but no combined campaigning of BJP and Janata Party. It meant openly declaring adjustment of seats but for secularism sake, it was not open to a public alliance.

On the other hand, to find a breakthrough on the temple issue, Governor Krishnakant went to Udupi and made three suggestions to Pejawar Swami and V.P. Singh. First – a trust should be formed under Kanchi Shankaracharya Jayendra Saraswati and the disputed site should be handed over to him. Second, temple construction should be done leaving the disputed site 'as it is'. Third, a wall should be constructed between the temple and the disputed site.

In response, Swamiji said that he will have to consult other people from VHP and only then a decision can be taken. Krishnakant immediately flew Swamiji to Delhi in a special flight. Before going to Delhi Swamiji held a meeting with Ashok Singhal and other people from VHP. It was decided in this meeting that the land acquired by the government should be given to Ram Janmabhoomi Nyas. Swamiji gave four suggestions after holding talks with the VHP: First, the disputed site should be handed over to the Ram Janmabhoomi Nyas and no new trust should be formed. Second, minor changes should be made in the reconstruction plan. Third, disputed structure should be kept as it is. And fourth, the temple should be constructed over the pillars around the structure.

Vishwanath Pratap Singh agreed to these suggestions and said that Swamiji should make VHP also agree to these suggestions. Later, Krishnakant, Central minister Subodh Kant Sahai and Bihar governor Yunus Salim called a meeting of Hindu and Muslim saints and held a discussion on these points. The Hindu saints said that for the sake of mutual harmony, Muslims should willingly leave their claim. Temple can be built without demolishing the existing structure. In this situation no one would be defeated and no one would appear as a winner. In response to this the Muslim side said that they should get a place of worship to which Hindu saints agreed. Muslims asked for some time to think over the proposal, but they asked that first the proposed Kar Seva be stopped. One more proposal came which was from the local Shia community. There is a village called Sahnava on Sultanpur road, a few miles from Faizabad. They suggested that the Babri mosque should be transferred to this place. In 1528, the person who constructed this mosque, Mir Baqi, was buried at this place. Descendants of Mir Baqi still live in this village. Nritya Gopal Das, the president of Ram Janmabhoomi Mukti Yajna Samiti supported this proposal. He also made Paramahans Ramchandra Das agree to this proposal.

Nritya Gopal Das was a saint with a heavy build but had a childlike nature. Religiously he was not a hardliner. But he was vocal. Polite and quiet in nature, Nritya Gopal Das was mahant or the head priest of Vaishnav Akhada of Maniram Das Chhawani. These akhadas and chhawanis were constituted in the 8th to 9th century for the protection of religion. We will discuss this in detail in the sixth chapter of this book. The word chhawani is usually not used for temples. In northern India, this word was used for places where there were army garrisons in the British era. Weaponry, ration and means of commuting were stored there. Ayodhya has many garrisons of sadhus where they stay for the protection of religion. Ayodhya has two big garrisons, one is Maniram Das garrison at Vasudeva Ghat and Raghunath Das garrison near Ravidas Temple. Nritya Gopal Das does not let any visitor leave without having food. In Ayodhya, the control room of the Kar Sevaks was at Char Dham temple in this garrison. All decisions were taken here. Directives for the next strategy of the Kar Sevaks were given from this garrison. It should have been seen as bad luck that both parties opposed the proposal of shifting the structure. Both, VHP and Babri Action Committee questioned how the local people could decide on something that belonged to both the communities? Hindu saints said that Kar Seva could be stopped but it could be done somewhere else, leaving the disputed structure as it was. The Muslim side did not agree to it, but they asked for some more time to think over it. In the meanwhile, the Kanchi Shankaracharya appointed a prominent leader of the Ayodhya movement, Mahant Avaidhyanath, as his representative to talk to the government. This again got murkier. Including a saint from VHP shook this effort because the primary purpose of it was to keep VHP and Babri Committee at a distance. On the other hand, as V.P. Singh would inch towards a solution, Mulayam Singh increased his rallies against the Ram Janmabhoomi Temple movement. At this time his rallies were quite provocative, even though they were named 'Sampradayik Sadbhav Rally' meaning 'Communal Harmony Rally'. Mulyam Singh had adopted a provocative posture. He had faith in the repressive power of the government machinery.

Talks for finding a universally acceptable agreement were on when BJP president Lal Krishna Advani left Somnath in Gujarat for Ayodhya on a rath yatra on 25 September. This rath yatra was to end on 30 October at Ayodhya, where Kar Seva had been announced to begin from that very day. This 'Chevrolet rath yatra' was to pass through eight states and cover ten thousand kilometres. While starting the rath yatra in a rath decorated with marigold flowers, Advani said that all BJP MPs and MLAs will participate in the Kar Seva. He said that if they did not get permission for Kar Seva, they will start Satyagraha. Advani also said that on the personal appeal of Prime Minister V.P. Singh, saints had given him a time period of four months, but now seven months had gone by. The Prime Minister had not made any tangible efforts. In the meantime, the Chief Minister of Uttar Pradesh had vitiated the entire atmosphere with his constant ranting against the temple.

Before starting the rath yatra at Somnath, Advani said, 'When VHP decided on 30 October to begin the construction of Ram temple, I wanted to start a campaign like this so that people come to know of BJP's view on the issue, the view that was passed in 1989 through the Palampur working committee's proposal.' He said, 'Movement for the temple has resulted in bringing people together. No other movement has reached the villages like the Shilapujan (foundation prayer) has. In honour of Ram, this is not only bringing the Hindu community together but the entire country.' The government report says that the rath yatra left communal tension behind. Communal violence took place in all the areas it crossed. But Advani claimed in his autobiography that from wherever the rath passed by, peace prevailed. It is true that violence did happen, but it happened after the rath was stopped, i.e. between 23 October and 30 October. But when BJP formed the government in UP under the leadership of Kalyan Singh, the Inspector General of Police of the state was of the view that Advani's rath yatra was responsible for dividing UP communally. The report was withdrawn when BJP created an uproar over it.

Before sitting in his air-conditioned rath, Advani had said, 'I want that Muslims should also participate in the Kar Seva at Ayodhya. They should accept that the structure they call Babri Masjid has not held namaz for the last fifty-four years, while idols have been placed there since 1949 and are being worshipped. Hindu sentiments in the country are strong over Ram Janmabhoomi. It is because there is a majority of Hindus that the nation is secular. Muslims should not ignore this situation. If they will respect emotions of Hindus for Ayodhya, I feel that the temple will be a monument of communal harmony.' This was the announcement with which Advani started his rath yatra.

Advani was the party president of BJP then. He toed a hard-line which was the opposite of Atal Bihari Vajpayee and considered the temple issue to be beyond the constitution and court. The victory of the party in 1989 brought this Sindh-born leader in the first line of leaders. Advani was a courteous and civil leader. He was slim, had a round bald head and a neatly trimmed moustache. He wore black round-frame spectacles. Advani was an impressive leader but not that good an orator. He was from an affluent family. His initial schooling was done at Saint Patrick's School at Karachi. They also had a Victoria horse-carriage at their house at Jamshed Quarter, which was a symbol of prosperity and wealth at that time. When he came to India after partition and did not shine in politics, he used to be a film critic. He met Vajpayee in 1951 and became his assistant in 1957. When Vijay Kumar Malhotra became the Chief Executive Councillor of Delhi in 1967, Advani was appointed as a councillor in the house. So Advani was an average Sangh leader who managed to reach the top.

Although Pramod Mahajan was the convener of Lal Krishna Advani's rath yatra, it was Narendra Modi who was the strategist and architect of this yatra. Current Prime Minister Narendra Modi was the General Secretary (Organization) in Gujarat state BJP then. Convening this yatra brought Narendra Modi to the forefront of the party leadership. From this perspective Ayodhya remained an important chapter in Narendra Modi's political career. Credit of Narendra Modi's rise in the national politics goes to Ayodhya.

The rath yatra from Somnath to Ayodhya, under the leadership of Lal Krishna Advani changed the direction of the Ram Mandir movement. This yatra created fervour of Ram in the entire country. It was 13 September 1990. Narendra Modi presented the outline for the yatra in front of the country. On this day, Modi informed media about programmes and route of the rath yatra. The rath yatra was to begin on 25 September from Somnath and end at Ayodhya on 30 October. At that time, he described the struggle for the yatra to be part of the cultural consciousness and determination of the entire nation. Narendra Modi was behind the stage management of this far reaching mission of politics. The unprecedented success of the rath yatra immediately increased his stature in the organization. He was also announced the 'sarthi' or the driver for Murli Manohar Joshi's Ekta-Yatra (Unity-march), from Kanyakumari to Kashmir. This rath yatra, under the strategy of

Narendra Modi, not only deposed the V.P. Singh government at the centre but also uprooted Congress from UP forever.

By initiating the rath yatra from Somnath, the party used the holy Shiva temple as a symbol, which was destroyed many times by Muslim invaders. The temple foundation was laid by President Rajendra Prasad after India's independence. This was the reason that this place was chosen as the starting point of the rath yatra, to evoke emotions from across the country. 25 September is the birthday of party founder Deendayal Upadhyay. Advani writes in his autobiography, 'We rode the Ram-Rath (Ram's-chariot) into the battle'. Perhaps that's why he chose a rath to plunge into the election battle. His charioteer was the firebrand leader Pramod Mahajan. More than twenty public meetings were being held from the rath. The atmosphere was so charged that people were not only worshipping Advani but the rath as well. Wherever the rath went, people picked up the dust and touched it to their foreheads in reverence. There is a poem by Guru Ravindranath Tagore–

'Rath bhaveaami dev path bhaveaami, Moorti bhaveaami dev hanse antaryaami'

'Chariot thinks, I am the God. Path thinks, I am God. So many people are coming to see me. The idol thinks I am God. Seeing this the almighty laughs.' He had written these lines at the Bhagwan Jagannath rath yatra procession, where Gods, chariot, horses, path fall prey to the illusion that the mob is there for them. Anyway, even if an illusion, the atmosphere of the nation was changing. Now, the party's movement was turning into a mass-movement.

Seeing the rath closing in, V.P. Singh tried to avoid confrontation and started talks with the Muslim leaders and VHP again on 18 October. It was decided that the government can acquire all the land around the disputed structure, except 30 feet of land around it. Later it can hand over the land to the Trust which will construct the temple. S. Gurumurthi tells that he was called upon by Prime Minister V.P. Singh on 15 October 1990. They discussed late into the night in four sessions and for more than four hours.

Gurumurthi suggested that the government should acquire all the land and give it to the VHP Trust. Government should keep with it only the disputed structure and 30 feet of land around it. And whether there was a temple earlier on this spot should be left to the Supreme Court to decide as per Section 143 of the constitution. Gurumurthi tells that Vishwanath Pratap Singh immediately agreed to it. Gurumurthi asked V.P. Singh that if he agrees then should he inform Rashtriya Swamsevak Sangh and VHP. V.P. Singh replied, 'Sure you can tell them. I am talking to you as a Prime Minister.' Gurumurthi immediately informed the Sangh and the VHP about the decision and informed the Prime Minister of their affirmation for it.

On 18 October two sessions of discussions were held. The railway minister at the time George Fernandes and Information Minister P. Upendra went to meet Ashok Singhal at the Keshav Kunj headquarters of the Sangh. These ministers told Singhal about the ordinance by the government. According to the ordinance, except the sanctum-sanctorum of the disputed structure, government would hand over the rest of the land to Ram Janmabhoomi Trust. Ashok Singhal was adamant that until the government hands over the entire land to Hindus, there could be no settlement.

To discuss the issue V.P. Singh called upon BJP leader Govindacharya that very day, then he called upon Additional Solicitor General Arun Jaitley and journalist Prabhash Joshi. He told them that the disputed structure and 30 feet around it will remain under the government's control. To decide whether there was a temple at this spot, the advice of the Supreme Court will be sought under Section 143 of the constitution. After the meeting an additional secretary from the PMO was called upon and told to initiate the procedure for an ordinance.

The format of the ordinance was drawn up that night itself. At five in the morning, a committee of five officers went to the residence of the PM and the draft was finalized. A cabinet meeting was held at 10 in the morning, in which a three-point programme and the ordinance was approved. Since that ordinance was also to be assessed on other aspects, it was not released immediately.

Gurumurthi was called by Vishwanath Pratap Singh once more that day. He was in Chennai. The next day, 19 October, was a Friday. Gurumurthi reached Delhi in the morning. A meeting was held on Friday morning at Sundar Nagar guesthouse of *The Indian Express*. Lal Krishna Advani also attended the meeting. He had left the rath yatra at Dhanbad. There were Goenka, Gurumurthi, Joshi and some other friends at the meeting. Advani clearly said in the meeting that they also wanted to find a way out. 'We don't intend to depose the government. If, through the ordinance, the land around the disputed structure is given to VHP, we will support the ordinance.' The Prime Minister spoke to Gurumurthi again in the afternoon. By then V.P. Singh had completely turned around. The ordinance had been changed. He was under immense pressure from the Muslim organizations. Some ministers were also not of this view. Mulayam Singh Yadav also announced a revolt against it. Prime Minister said that not only the disputed structure, but the disputed land should also remain under government control. That it couldn't be handed over to the organizers of the Ayodhya movement. Gurumurthi expressed surprise at this because this was not the compromise agreed upon. The Prime Minister asked him to come over once again to his residence in the evening. He told Gurumurthi that Advani should postpone his rath yatra for a day so that a solution for the problem could be found. He told Gurumurthi that if this were to happen then he himself would go with Lal Krishna Advani to Ayodhya for Kar Seva. When Advani was told about this he said that V.P. Singh should be given reprieve. He does not need to go. He said that he would agree to the ordinance only if it was based on its original form.

To break the deadlock, the meeting went on post 9:00 p.m. at the Prime Minister's residence. V.P. Singh told Gurumurthi that he will have to consult his subordinates on this issue. The ministers present in that meeting were Arun Nehru, George Fernandes, Ajit Singh and Dinesh Goswami. Gurumurthi, Jaitley and a senior journalist were also part of this meeting.

The Prime Minister was in and out during this meeting. At the same time, he was talking to many other people. Law minister Goswami said that it won't be possible to bring an ordinance as there were many ongoing court cases on the matter. The reality was that it was not possible to make any law because of the pending court cases. Arun Jaitley and Gurumurthi explained in detail that around the many aspects of this issue, they seemed to be revolving around only three questions: first, was Bhagwan Ram born at this place? Second, who owns these different land pieces? Third, was there an already existing Hindu structure at the site? The law minister was told that there cannot be a legal decision possible on the first issue. On the second issue, legal decision of a mandatory acquisition can be taken under undisputed authority. On the third aspect only advice of the court can be sought.

Late at night, the ordinance and plan were released to the press. This had three points. First, the government would take over the disputed site and nearby land. Second, except for the disputed structure and 30 feet land around the structure, rest will be handed over to the Ram Janmabhoomi Trust. Third, the mystery of whether there was ever a temple there would be solved under Section 143 (A) of the constitution so this was to be handed over to the Supreme Court.

There were mixed reactions to this formula. N.T. Ramarao, CM of Tamil Nadu, M. Karunanidhi, Left parties and some other parties welcomed it. But the Chief Minister of Uttar Pradesh threatened that he would not let this ordinance be implemented. The Babri Committee opposed it saying that it undermined the judicial system. However the ordinance was implemented on the night of 20 October when the Commissioner of Faizabad took control of the acquired land. But suddenly on 22 October, the ordinance was taken back under pressure from Mulayam Singh and other Muslim organizations. This complicated the matter further. The question raised was why had the government acquired the structure and later stepped back from the compromise it had reached.

The reality was that V.P. Singh had decided to have a confrontation with the BJP on the temple issue and that was why he had withdrawn the ordinance. On the other hand on 23 October, BJP leader Lal Krishna Advani's rath yatra was stopped at Samastipur in Bihar. He was arrested from the Samastipur Circuit house. Advani was first taken to Dumka by a government flight and then by road he was taken to Mansanjhor, where under national security law he was detained at the rest house. Bihar police confiscated his Rath. Now a conflict was imminent. What was strange was that even while talks were on, the preparation for a conflict was also going on from both sides. Mulayam Singh's UP government had sealed Ayodhya. All the district collectors were directed to stop Kar Sevaks in their respective districts. Adequate measures were in place to stop Kar Sevaks at the state borders, especially the borders of Madhya Pradesh and Rajasthan, because these two states had BJP governments. The UP government had even gone to the extent of digging a 40 feet wide moat because this was the planned entrance route into Uttar Pradesh for Advani's rath yatra. V.P. Singh aimed at two birds with one arrow. He got Advani arrested and also deflated Mulayam Singh Yadav. Mulayam Singh had become the sole flag bearer of secularism by opposing V.P. Singh's ordinance on Ayodhya land acquisition. Mulayam Singh Yadav was the leader who had stopped the rath. V.P. Singh could not accept this. Arun Nehru said that the Prime Minister had sent a message to Lalu Yadav directing him to stop Advani in Bihar itself so that Mulayam Singh does not remain the only secular leader.

As Advani was arrested in Bihar, BJP announced withdrawal of its support from V.P. Singh's government in Delhi. BJP leader Atal Bihari Vajpayee immediately met with the president, R. Venkataraman and informed him that they were withdrawing support from the government because their leader Lal Krishna Advani has been arrested. Withdrawal of support brought the government to a position of minority. V.P. Singh told the President that under the changed circumstances he will prove majority on 7 November. V.P. Singh knew that his government would collapse because he didn't have the numbers to save his government but he had decided to sacrifice his government in the name of secularism. On *Doordarshan* and *All India Radio* he addressed the nation and said that he was ready to sacrifice not one but many governments for the sake of secularism. It was the same V.P. Singh who had held more than a dozen meetings with the BJP and Sangh to save his government. V.P. Singh said in his address to the nation on 23 October, 'Friends, today I want to talk to about the dispute of Ram Janmabhoomi and Babri Mosque. This is an old dispute but there is a new twist to it. Nation is in crisis. The challenges before us are not only of political and constitutional machinery, but about our humanity and emotional values. Never before have we faced such a test. In the days to come we will know if we will remain true to our values or we will move away from them. Future of India will be written in such times.

'Many times we have not reported this matter in our newspapers, because doing this would have further complicated the process of reaching a solution to the complex situation. Our government constantly held meetings with religious leaders from different faiths. We constantly met different political parties. They include VHP, Rashtriya Swayamsevak Sangh, Left front and Bharatiya Janata Party. We also achieved some success, but parties didn't come close on the core issues of the dispute.'

V.P. Singh told the nation, 'My only request was that until the court decides, no work on such a map should be done that includes the disputed structure. I asked them to have patience and wait for the verdict of the court. But I want to say this with utter grief that this simple and right step was not agreed upon. They remained adamant that they will begin construction only on the decided disputed place. They will not wait for the court's verdict and will not accept it either. Now the country has to decide. If people of all faith were to start saying that they will not accept the decision of the court, how will this country run and how will its unity remain intact?

'With these thoughts, I again asked in the meeting held with the ministers if the country can be given eight months or one more year so that court can hold regular hearings and reach a verdict. Should the people of this country and our future generations not be given this short period? What is the hurry to destabilize the country within 6 days and not give it a chance for a peaceful life?'

'Sardar Patel had said that Ram Janmabhoomi-Babri mosque issue cannot be solved with force. I want to say this without any dilemma that I have tried every possible option for a compromise. I will implement law in every condition, whatever the cost may be. When I took the oath I swore on the constitution to not step back from disposing my responsibilities.'

'If we accept supremacy of any religion, we will be accepting that religion on the basis of political affiliation. In such a situation how will I answer those who were demanding Khalistan on the basis of religion? What will I answer to those who were asking to take people of their religion and merge with Pakistan? In the Northeast, where mostly there is a Christian majority, is it not possible that one day they start demanding for a separate country? How will we encourage them to remain a part of mother India? If we permitted such a thought once, then such aligning on the basis of religion will become routine.'

'This is a country made by Mahatma Gandhi. He has shed blood to make this country the way it is and today, I am being asked if I will be able to save my government? Friends, I want to make it clear that it a very petty thing to save the government now. This is the time to save the nation. To save the temple of mother India, I am ready to sacrifice many such governments. We should not avoid this test. If the question is to save the government or the country, country will come first. Governments come and go but the country should remain. To accomplish this, my dear fellow countrymen, I need your support.'

From 24 October it was all about reaching a finale. Both sides were preparing decisively. Since 1 September 1990, Mulayam Singh's helicopter was landing at three districts daily. Although these rallies were called sadbhavna-rallies or goodwill-rallies, they were promoting animosity. He announced on a regular basis. 'There will be no "14 Kosi parikrama". Even a bird can't enter Ayodhya.' Through his rallies, he was busy finding support of the people who were in a disturbed state, so that public support was seen behind his possible action. But these rallies were fuelling sectarianism. The state government had imposed curfew from 24 October. No one was permitted to enter the Ramkot area, meaning there was a ban on darshan or seeing the God's idol. As the Mulayam Singh government tightened security, VHP got more and more determined to send its Kar Sevaks there.

Retired military and civil officers were managing to send Kar Sevaks to Ayodhya. Ashok Singhal and Vinay Katiyar were given the responsibility to send five lakh Kar Sevaks to Ayodhya. Stopping them from reaching Ayodhya was the job of Home Secretary of the state, A.K. Rastogi and Intelligence Chief, Ram Asre. The barricading was so high that the roads and bridges leading to Ayodhya now had permanent walls. A moat was dug on the UP-Bihar border near Sevrehi. Advani's rath yatra was to take this path. The SSP at the time, D.B. Rai tells that even during the Mughal reign, a moat had never been dug on the state border. On one side of the moat there were armed state police and PAC men. BJP leaders and workers were being arrested on a large scale. At the time of Diwali, people were in jails. Temporary jails had been notified as there was not enough space in the regular jails. Common people were arranging for the food of the Kar Sevaks. People brought food for them from their own homes as the shameless district officers stole all the money that came for the food of the inmates. This definitely will be called Ramrajya in the history of the state's jails. The irony. The temporary jails had unrestricted access to people and the food meant for the inmates was being consumed by the officers.

The responsibility of this movement by the VHP was on three people: Ashok Singhal, Shrish Chandra Dikshit and Vinay Katiyar. All three had gone underground.

Fear, suspicion and uncertainty gripped Ayodhya on the morning of 30th October. The situation was out of control. All the small and big roads that connected Ayodhya were buzzing with the movement of paramilitary forces. Borders were sealed. Chief Minister Mulayam Singh Yadav had announced that not even a sparrow should be able to cross the border. Every officer from the IG to the station in-charge was out on the roads to implement his plan. Ayodhya was under curfew for the last four days. There was no ban on darshan at the Ram Janmabhoomi but no one was allowed to go there. We had reached upto Maniram Das Chhawani. Kar Sevaks were ready to do anything. On one side of the road were the Kar Sevaks and on the other side police force had its cordon circle. We felt this would be the battleground. We sat there at a tea stall. I was with my colleague Triyug Narayan Tiwari, correspondent of *The Hindu*, J.P. Shukla and the representative of *Navbharat Times*, Gyan Prakash Pandey.

Suddenly like a swarm of locusts, lakhs of Kar Sevaks appeared on the Ayodhya roads. The roads got packed with Kar Sevaks. Police forces and paramilitary forces became tense on seeing so many Kar Sevaks on the roads. Unarmed Kar Sevaks were determined that they must perform Kar Seva upon the symbol of shame, the Babri structure. There were two kinds of people in the mob—those who had travelled thousands of kilometres for the purpose of Kar Seva and those who came to Ayodhya every year on the occasion of Kartik Purnima or the full moon of the Kartik month for 14 kosi parikrama. But even this section was equally excited for Kar Seva. On the bridge that linked Ayodhya to Gonda on the Saryu river, thousands of Kar Sevaks had been waiting since the night before. One could only see heads on the bridge. It could not be crossed even on foot.

Ayodhya was divided into two parts. The entire part from the National Highway to Hanuman Garhi was under police control. In this part there were Ram Janmabhoomi, Kanak Bhavan and Hanuman Garhi. The other part was the eastern part that was in control of the Kar Sevaks. This area had Digambar Akhada, Maniram Das Chhawani, Devraha Baba Chhawani, Kaushalendra Sadan, Janki Mahal Trust and Kar Sevakpuram. There were no police present in this area. From Hanuman Garhi to Ram Janmabhoomi there were six steel barricades. These were also under the police. Despite the restrictions imposed, even government officials were involved in helping Kar Sevaks get to Ayodhya. State police had a friendly attitude towards Kar Sevaks. You can understand the attitude of security force personnel with this one instance. The National Highway was closed near Sohawal. Some Kar Sevaks were coming from that side. The police stopped them. Kar Sevaks pleaded with them in the name of religion and Gods. But the daroga or the in-charge didn't budge. He said, 'Not even a bird can go from this road. It's the government's order. I'm strictly following it.' And then Daroga ji changed his stance, 'But I'm not stopping you from going through the farms.' The Kar Sevaks understood. All the Kar Sevaks were given an identity card and a map of small roads and lanes.

This is how Kar Sevaks were reaching Ayodhya even though none of the big leaders had been able to reach Ayodhya. While going towards Ayodhya, RSS leader Rajendra Singh (Rajju Bhaiya) was arrested in Lucknow. President of VHP, Vishnu Hari Dalmia, Mahant Avaidyanath, Swami Chinmayananda, Shankaracharya Vasudeva Nand, Guman Mal Lodha were arrested on the way. Atal Bihari Vajpayee was arrested at the Lucknow airport. Lal Krishna Advani had already been arrested in Bihar. Rajmata Vijaya Raje Scindia was arrested in Sitapur when she was attempting to enter Ayodhya with the Kar Sevaks. But the main protagonists of the Ayodhya movement, Ashok Singhal and Shrish Chandra Dikshit were not found by the police.

The government had been looking for Ashok Singhal for the last ten days. More than one and half a dozen places had been raided in Varanasi, Allahabad and Lucknow. But evading all the security arrangements, he reached Ayodhya on 29th. His entry and appearance in Ayodhya was quite dramatic. Singhal had gone underground in Allahabad. He went upto Kadipur in Aultanpur via Jaunpur by car. Kadipur is a tehseel adjacent to Faizabad boarder. Shrish Chandra Dikshit was also with Singhal. From here both of them changed to shirt and pants as opposed to their traditional get-up of dhoti & kurta and took a scooter to Akbarpur in order to avoid being recognized. From there both reached Ayodhya separately on the 29th October.

After reaching Faizabad, Singhal released a proper press statement of his being there. This made the Kar Sevaks enthusiastic. When Shrish Chandra Dikshit was asked how he reached, he replied, 'If I told this some people will lose their jobs.' Dikshit had been Deputy IG in the state police. Vinay Katiyar was already in Ayodhya along with Moropant Pingle. Now the strategy was to perform Kar Seva at Char Dham temple on the night of 29 October. It was decided that three groups of Kar Sevaks would be formed; one to be led by Ashok Singhal, second by Shrish Chandra Dikshit and the third by Vinay Katiyar. 'Line of command' was also decided. Ashok Singhal's directive would be the 'Supreme Court'. If he was arrested or if something were to happen to him, then Moropant Pingle's words would be final. If he too was arrested, then whatever Vinay Katiyar decided on the spot would be agreed upon by all.

Security forces were fighting on two fronts. On one side Kar Sevaks were creating pressure to enter the city. On the other side those who had entered were trying to reach the Janmsthan or the birth place of Lord Ram. Police were thwarting such attempts again and again. When the first lot moved towards Ram Janmabhoomi, police chased them off. They came and sat at the Hanuman Garhi. They were being led by Andhra Pradesh MLA, K. Narendra. The police announced that they were all under arrest but there were not enough vehicles to take the prisoners away.

While the police was engaged in this, the second lot of people came led by Ashok Singhal. This lot was stopped by the police with lathi charge. Ashok Singhal received a blow on his head. Even with a bleeding wound he tried to move forward. But the police caught hold of him and he was separated from the mob. He was taken away for treatment but the mob that had been with him sat down and began shouting slogans. Other mobs had started to appear at ten in the morning from Hanuman Garhi and its nearby allies. The numbers were increasing and police started arresting people. To take the arrested persons away, a bus was brought. Some sadhus were taken away in this bus with the numberplate UMR 9720. As the bus was about to move, a monk who knew how to drive, pushed the driver of the bus out and took control of the bus. This monk had hijacked the bus. Driving through narrow lanes, this monk broke the police barricading. After breaking three steel gates with the bus, the monk brought the bus to within 50 metres from the Ram Janmabhoomi area.

This bus had about 100 sadhus inside and on top of it. This attempt to reach the Janmabhoomi after breaking the police barricade renewed the enthusiasm of the others. The monk's name was Ramprasad. He was from an akhada of Ayodhya. Security forces were shocked at this incident. Breaking of steel barriers emboldened the Kar Sevaks. The second section of the mob ran on to the road as the bus left. Police kept banging canes on the road but the mob grew bigger. By now the first lot of sadhus had entered the enclosure. Women were throwing stones and bricks on the policemen from rooftops. There was chaos everywhere.

At places Kar Sevaks were touching the feet of the police personnel to let them pass through and at other places they struggled with the forces. Seeing one of their members getting thrashed by the mob, CRPF asked for permission to open fire. The DM announced of a possible firing on the loudspeaker. But that didn't deter the mass. Then lathi-charge began. There were Kar Sevaks on the road and common people raising slogans on the rooftops. Kar Sevaks began inching forward. Tear gas, lathi-charge, barricading, all failed. BSF, CRPF, CISF, PAC and state police all seemed helpless in spite of their automatic guns.

At that very moment, near the Janmsthan, Shrish Chandra Dikshit appeared from nowhere. He was surrounded by three to four hundred Kar Sevaks. It was a tense moment. The mob tried to enter the premises. Some crawled, some jumped the fence and others pushed their way inside. Those standing outside went mad seeing some other Kar Sevaks waving a flag over the dome. The loud chants turned frightening. 'Ram-Lala hum aaye hain, mandir yaheen banayenge' meaning 'young Ram we are here, we will build the temple at this very spot'. All the Kar Sevaks had 'Jai Siya-Ram' and 'Har-har Mahadev' on their tongues. Vandalism on the dome sent the rest of them into frenzy. Shrish Chandra Dikshit and Mahant Nritya Gopal Das thought of making an appeal to somehow make the mob calm down and leave. Dikshit asked for permission for himself and Mahant ji to stand on the mound inside the Ram Janmabhoomi and appeal to the Kar Sevaks to calm them down. When the police opened the gate for Dikshit, a big number of Kar Sevaks rushed inside the gate along with him. This worsened the situation. Dikshit had tricked the police and signaled the Kar Sevaks to barge in with him. Kar Sevaks started vandalizing the interiors of the premises. By now a helicopter was also circling in the sky to scare the mob. After the Kar Seva started in the premises, Shrish Chandra Dikshit said 'lokshakti won today' meaning power of the people had won.

The pressure was building up on the Hanuman Garhi side because of the increasing number of Kar Sevaks and the report of Ashok Singhal being wounded. In spite of lathi-charge and a strict vigil, by noon around 40,000 Kar Sevaks had broken steel gates and entered the Janmabhoomi area. We also followed them up to the birthplace. But the cameramen had not been able to follow us. Police were not allowing them inside. By this time three Kar Sevaks again climbed the domes. The domes were about 30 feet high. The skill they employed to climb the domes and the swiftness with which they placed the flag surprised us. A hole was made in each of the three domes. Then Kar Sevaks quickly climbed down after putting up a flag on each of the domes. One group of Kar Sevaks removed the steel windows and gates from the outer wall. All this was done with ease. Gates were taken down. Para-forces were helpless in front of the huge crowd of Kar Sevaks. Kar Sevaks were being led by leaders of VHP like Shrish Chandra Dikshit, Nritya Gopal Das, Saint Vamdev and Mahant Paramhans Ramchandra Das. They were the ones being chased by the administration for many days now. Police dispersed them immediately.

Around two o'clock the Kar Sevaks were again out of control. Attacking from outside, Kar Sevaks demolished a wall of the building. Police fired rounds in the air. Some Kar Sevaks made their way inside the building. Two of them climbed up on the domes and adjusted the flags. At that moment CRPF fired. Kar Sevaks fell to the ground and died. The police had to struggle for twenty minutes to have the premises vacated and under its control. But outside, the pressure from the Kar Sevaks remained as it is. Police kept chasing Kar Sevaks away and fresh mobs kept coming. After one and half hours, a new wave of Kar Sevaks came. They started digging the foundation. To disperse them, Border Security Force fired 20 rounds. Eleven Kar Sevaks died there. There was much violence after that. Kar Sevaks torched seven jeeps and two buses. The violence at 'Bada-sthan' was worse.

But the paramilitary forces refused the order to fire near 'Bada-sthan'. Kar Sevaks began touching the feet of the soldiers. When soldiers stepped back to avoid it, Kar Sevaks moved forward. This gave them a way forward.

The incidents made it apparent that the government had completely failed. Kar Seva at Ram temple was done. Flags had been placed over the domes. Domes, walls and windows were broken. About one lakh Kar Sevaks were able to move towards Janmabhoomi. Paramilitary forces tried to stop them by firing three times. Two Kar Sevaks died while putting up the flags on the domes. Three died as they were digging the foundation. Thirty were injured. But the state government and the Chief Minister denied that Kar Seva took place or that the structure was harmed, something that we had witnessed with our own eyes. Kar Sevaks had removed bricks from the outer wall. One wall had been demolished. Almost all the frames and windows had been removed. Some breakage was done in the sanctum sanctorum as well. The army was called in by four in the evening, but the area was not handed over to them. Only a flag march was done to restore control. District administration was planning to hand over the Babri structure after getting it repaired. Administration put a restriction on news and pictures of Kar Seva. No pictures of the vandalism of the structure were published. Though ome of them are present in this book.

After breaching strict measures of 24 circles of security, one lakh Kar Sevaks managing to reach the spot was quite shocking. Among them were 20,000 sadhus. Most of the Kar Sevaks had made it there after walking for more than three hundred kilometres through the farms and fields. Among them most were from the states of Andhra Pradesh, Gujarat, Madhya Pradesh, West Bengal, Haryana, Delhi, Rajasthan and UP. They were mostly young. They had started gathering by the banks of Saryu since the early morning of 30 October. Within two hours their numbers had swelled to forty thousand. DIG, G.L. Sharma told me that their number was twenty-five thousand. Six thousand Kar Sevaks had gathered over the one-and-a-half kilometre-long bridge of Saryu, by six in the morning. The administration fired bullets to have them dispersed.

The bullets were fired at three places : first, on those Kar Sevaks who had climbed the domes and those who were digging the foundation. Second, in front of the Nand Bhavan at Manas Bhavan junction; where sadhus were holding the front. Third, at the Saryu Bridge, where bullets were fired in the afternoon. Kar Sevaks had reached via this bridge. They had travelled along the river from Katra town of Gonda district through Durga Ganj and Manjha village. They had been hiding here for the last ten days. Villagers had been taking care of them.

By the evening of 30th October, the pressure had eased off from the Janmabhoomi enclosure. The Police had vacated all the temples of Ramkot. Ayodhya was also sealed. A flag march was held at Faizabad. The locals of Faizabad and Ayodhya were arranging for food and water for the Kar Sevaks. Ashok Singhal made an appeal and said, 'I congratulate the Ram-bhakts on this historical victory of the entire Hindu community. After destroying all obstacles and after the sacrifice of Ram-bhakts, Kar Seva has started today. Those Kar Sevaks who have not been able to reach Ayodhya, should reach Ayodhya and perform two days of Kar Seva before they return to their home.' Kar Sevaks continued to pour in after this statement by Singhal.

On the other hand, to save him from embarrassment and to tell Muslims that the government had not failed in Ayodhya, Mulayam Singh gave a statement, 'No Kar Seva has taken place at the disputed site. No damage has occurred to the mosque. Those who tried to force their entry into the disputed area have been arrested. People should not pay attention to rumours.' The Central Home Minister, Mufti Mohammad Sayeed also congratulated Mulayam Singh Yadav on the courageous disposal of the sensitive Ayodhya issue. Sayeed said, 'despite trying no Kar Seva could begin.' BJP, which was supporting the government, expressed its objection to V.P. Singh. The next day, V.P. Singh summoned Chief Minister Mulayam Singh Yadav to Delhi. All across the country, 35 people had lost their lives in the violence due to this incident and 30 cities were placed under curfew.

Even amidst firings and communal violence, Kar Sevaks kept coming to Ayodhya till 1 November. Kar Sevaks remained adamant about Kar Seva and stayed by the riverbanks, lanes, temples, maths, chhawanis and akhadas. Considering the incidents of 30 October, both sides made amendments to their battle formations. On one side the army was doing the flag march and on the other, foot march of Kar Sevaks was also taking place. The district collector told me that the journalists and other people were restricted from going towards Ram Janmabhoomi as repair work of the disputed structure was being done. Archaeological experts had been called to Ayodhya by the government for the repair. They were helping the army to restore the structure.

After getting injured by police lathis, Ashok Singhal was in the hospital. On the second day he fled from the hospital. After fleeing he gave a statement that the incidents at Ayodhya were the result of the arrogance of the Chief Minister. All this happened while the Home Secretary announced in Lucknow that Ashok Singhal has been arrested and this was broadcast from *Akashwani* and *Doordarshan*. After his escape, the Chief Minister had to say, 'Singhal was never arrested'. He was hiding at a temple next to Kaushalendra Bhavan. Here, throughout the day he was busy making strategies for Kar Seva. At this secret location a meeting was held between Ashok Singhal, convener of Kar Seva Samiti, Saint Vamdev Maharaj and vice-president of Ram Janmabhoomi Mukti

Yagya Samiti, Nritya Gopal Das.

In the morning Nritya Gopal Das and Saint Vamdev addressed Kar Sevaks. It was quite astonishing that *Doordarshan* was broadcasting fake news of their arrest while these three members of VHP were addressing the public and making strategies daily. This made it clear that the government and the administration were completely delusional and misled about the whole situation.

Even after the firing incident and increasing tensions, Kar Sevaks were not ready to leave Ayodhya. Those who performed Kar Seva the previous day returned, but even now thousands of Kar Sevaks were gathered at Mani Ramdas Chhawani, Badi Chhawani, Khaki Akhada and Digambar Akhada. They said that they had taken a vow to perform Kar Seva, and that they could not return without doing so, even if they had to face bullets. Kar Sevaks were gathered across Saryu, towards the Gonda side. It was then that I met Ashok Singhal behind the Digambar Akhada. I asked him, 'how will this blockade end? Kar Sevaks are not leaving. In fact more are coming, while the administration has banned "the darshan".' Ashok Singhal said, 'Government itself wants to incite violence. If Kar Sevaks are gathering they should arrest them and send them to jail. Administration is not arresting them, instead provoking them for violence. We will discuss it with the saints and decide on something. We will begin Kar Seva again from 2 November.'

I had never seen such a fever of Hindutva before. Common people, officers and police personnel, all were suffering from it. In the moments of heightened excitement on 30 October, two uniform clad PAC personnel had started the Kar Seva. When district administration arrested them they escaped and reached Mani Ram Chhawani. These PAC personnel also made a speech to the Kar Sevaks. One among them was Pardeshi Ram of second Gorakhpur battalion. In his speech he said that if Kar seva started again then the whole lot of jawans will perform Kar Seva. This raised an alarm with the district administration. They removed PAC from the inner ring at the Janmabhoomi area.

The deadlock remained. District administration and government wanted to pressure the saints into postponing Kar Seva. For this, constant talks were being held with VHP at the DM and SSP level. Government had placed Ayodhya Municipal Chairman, Avdhesh Das Shastri for this purpose. Avdhesh Das Shastri was from a Congress background and his ashram was close to Raj Sadan. Bajrang Dal chief Vinay Katiyar used to come to this very ashram to talk to the district collector, while police was looking for him to arrest him.

When things didn't work out in these talks, VHP decided to begin Kar Seva again on 2 November. Saint Vamdev announced the decision to Kar Sevaks and they were enthused. They were ready to go to any extent. People were determined to move towards the birthplace on 2 November. Saint Vamdev gave the government a warning, 'If the administration fires upon Kar Sevaks, I will be the first one to lay down my life. We will go for Kar Seva. If they want to stop Kar Sevaks they should make a statutory arrest. Kar Sevaks will surrender peacefully. But the condition is that their arrest should be a statutory arrest. 'Government representatives responded to Vamdev's statement saying the number of Kar Sevaks was so huge that they would be unable to issue warrants for the arrests. Nritya Gopal Das and Vamdev announced that Kar Seva has been stopped by the government. There was prohibition on the Parikrama. Curfew had been imposed unnecessarily resulting in chaos in the daily life of the people. Firing on unarmed Kar Sevaks had created provocation. Sadhus and Saints were to begin Satyagrah against it. Ayodhya was again reeling with the fear of another big tragedy.

It was Kartik Poornima on 2 November. On this day a huge number of devotees gather in the city for a holy dip annually, without any summoning. This time the number was in lakhs. One lakh Kar Sevaks were already in the city. On 2 November 1990, Ayodhya turned into a battleground. Kar Sevaks were in the mood to 'do or die' to break the security cordons. It was estimated that five lakh people will gather on the day of Poornima even though all trains had been cancelled. Somehow people kept pouring into the city. All temples were full of Kar Sevaks and security personnel. The constantly increasing number of Kar Sevaks was unnerving the administration.

Late into the night, the VHP and the saints kept discussing about which group would move forward from which direction on 2 November. Ashok Singhal spoke to the Kar Sevaks who had come from different provinces. He explained to them the administrative encircling of the area. Nritya Gopal Das, Saint Vamdev, Uma Bharti (who had arrived late in the night) and Omkar Bhave were present at the meeting. A few more people were present at this meeting who had lately been opposing events held by the VHP. These people were Lakshman Kiladheesh, Sita Ramsharan and Kaushal Kishore Phalarai.

Government officials were also provoking people. A statement made by Labour Minister of UP, Azam Khan had enraged people. Azam Khan said on 30 October that the harm that was caused by Kar Sevaks on the walls and window frames of the Babri mosque had been repaired. Government would spare no effort to let any miscreant get close to the mosque. Azam Khan was one among the initial convenors of the Babri Action Committee. Azam Khan, who hails from Rampur UP, was often in controversies over his foul statements. The knives of Rampur were quite well known and Azam Khan spoke like one. With a very sharp edge to his tone. 'Bharat-mata dayen hai' meaning Mother India is a witch. This controversial statement brought him to the fore.

There was violence in Ayodhya again on 2 November. Kar Sevaks were determined to reach the Janmabhoomi, and the administration had put forth all its power to ensure that they didn't come near it. There was a sense of disappointment and frustration among the officials over the failure of 30 October. A huge mob moved in from Mani Ramdas Chhawani, Digambar Akhada and from Saryu river side. Police tried to stop the mob, which was closing in from three sides, at Hanuman Garhi. When the mob didn't stop, firing began. SSP Subhash Joshi said that there was no option but to fire, or else the Kar Sevaks would had trampled them and demolished the structure. But the place where firing took place was about two kilometres away from the structure. The Kar Sevaks were unarmed. After firing was heard, the procession, which was coming from Digambar Akhada, sat down on the road and started singing Ramdhun (Ram Bhajan).

I stood against a wall with a colleague J.P. Shukla, because the shots being fired by the police were whizzing past us. Shukla is now retired from *The Hindu*. Shuklaji had an argument with SSP Subhash Joshi. He questioned why the Kar Sevaks were being fired at when they were unarmed and sitting on the road. But none of us were able to do anything. Each one, everywhere was enraged.

After this firing incident, the blood of the Kar Sevaks was all over the roads, temples and Chhawanis. Indiscriminate firing by the paramilitary forces had killed numerous people. Many had been injured. We saw about twenty-five dead bodies lying on the road. By evening, Kar Sevak Samiti released a list of forty dead Kar Sevaks in the newspapers. They too didn't have a count of the number injured.

The administration claimed that Kar Sevaks had reached close to the Janmsthan. This was wrong as the firing incident took place about two kilometres away from the Janmsthan. The administration had another argument for it. They claimed that at first they had attempted to disperse the Kar Sevaks using lathi-charge, then tear gas and when it all failed, police had resorted to firing. But the fact is that administration fired at Kar Sevaks, indiscriminately, when they were sitting peacefully on the road and singing Ramdhun.

After taking a dip in the river for Kartik Poornima, Kar Sevaks and sadhus approached the police barricading. Security forces had already sealed the one-kilometre-long passage to the disputed area. There were police pickets at the beginning of lane openings and close to Hanuman Garhi. Kar Sevaks gathered and stood at these places.

When chased by the security forces, Kar Sevaks sat down at the spot. When the IG of the zone, G.L. Sharma saw that the number was increasing, he told the officers that the directive of the government was clear and that the mob should not be allowed to sit on the road. After this order from the IG, security forces used tear gas and lathi-charge to remove Kar Sevaks. But Kar Sevaks held their ground. Suddenly the forces started firing without any warning. Kar Sevaks were aimed at, chased and shot in the lanes of the city.

The firing operation was being done under the supervision of IG of the zone, G.L. Sharma, SSP Subhash Joshi, Sub-Commander CRPF Usman and Sub-commander of the 58th battalion, Tarminder Bhullar. This operation was so barbaric and ruthless that Kar Sevaks were not even permitted to pick up the injured. Even the police were not helping them. Those injured by the bullets were left on the road, reeling in pain.

Of those who died in this firing incident five were at Dant Dhawan Kund, three at the Akhada, three at Hanuman Garhi, one at Rambagh, three were found at a different house and two bodies were found in front of the police station. Five bodies were carried by Kar Sevaks. They were kept at Char Dham temple of Maniram Das Chhawani.

This indiscriminate firing was done without the permission of the magistrate. After the firing, CRPF had District Magistrate Ram Sharan Srivastava sign the order for firing. The magistrate was restless when the firing was being done. He told the officers, 'I don't understand how many people will be killed like this.' The Magistrate went on leave that night as a protest against being forced to sign the shooting order. Madhukar Gupta, the Commissioner of Faizabad was also not in a position to tell how many rounds were fired that day.

The first shot was fired at 10:30 in the morning at Hanuman Garhi square. After this, the police force moved towards Digamber Akhada. This Akhada had been on the target of security forces for the last few days. This was the centre of all activities. Security forces dragged two brothers, Sharad Kothari and Ram Kothari out of Digamber Akhada and shot them in the head. Right in front of us! Sitaram Mali from Jodhpur had committed the 'heinous sin' of throwing the tear gas bombs in the drain. CRPF personnel placed the gun in his mouth and shot him. Right in front of our eyes! Ram Anchal of Faizabad would just not stop singing the Ramdhun. He was shot in the back and killed.

In the indiscriminate firing, the forces didn't care for the sanctity of the temple or the akhadas. They entered the temples to shoot at the Kar Sevaks. Many rounds were fired after entering the Ramanandi Digambar Akhada. There was terrible panic among the sadhus. Some CRPF jawans were crying while firing. Some had put down their guns and picked up canes. Upon entering an akhada, DIG G.L. Sharma asked the CRPF battalion to return. A CRPF deputy commander, Sampat Singh said in anger, 'Sir, we won't back off now. We have achieved success. Now we will return only after having vacated temples and akhadas.' The DIG moved to the back of the room and the forces began shooting indiscriminately.

People were not moving away even after a warning from the SSP. We thought that our presence would reduce the barbarity, but that didn't happen. Trying to remain safe, we kept close to the walls. Now we were in a lane which connected Hanuman Garhi square to Digambar Akhada. A Kar Sevak from Shriganganagar, his name remains unknown, was shot and fell. He used his blood to write on the road – Sitaram. I don't know if this was his name or if he was remembering Lord Ram. The CRPF personnel shot him in the head even after he was down. After the killings at the Tulsi Square, at 10:45 a.m. police fired at the Kar Sevaks sitting in front of the police station. People had been sitting on the road here and singing Ramdhun for the last one hour. They were being led by the MP from Khajuraho, Uma Bharti and MP from Ahmedabad, Harendra Pathak. Police fired here as well after arresting both. The priest from the temple in front of the police station died on the spot. One sadhu was pouring buckets of water to help those suffering from the effects of tear gas. Security forces aimed and fired at him and he fell off the roof. Kar Sevaks had to hide till they were able to take away the dead bodies of those shot. Vinay Katiyar gave us a list of 40 dead people.

There was dead silence in Ayodhya till late in the evening. There was grief and anxiety everywhere. The whole of Ayodhya was under the siege of police and Kar Sevaks. Saints were shut inside temples. Temple doors were closed. No temple bells were ringing. No evening prayers were being offered. There was sadness everywhere. Curfew was only on paper. People were running around carrying the wounded. Riots had started in other parts of the country as a reaction to the events in Ayodhya. Reports said that 54 people had died in it, other than the people who died in Ayodhya. 24 died in Gujrat, 13 in Bihar, 4 in Karnataka, 6 in Andhra Pradesh and 2 in Rajasthan. 42 cities in Uttar Pradesh were under curfew. Transport to the state had been cancelled. Censorship had been imposed on the news. To stop the spread of tension, evening editions of newspapers were seized in Allahabad, Lucknow and Varanasi.

The people of Faizabad had taken to the streets to protest against the firings. Late at night about one and half thousand people encircled the residence of Commissioner Madhukar Gupta. Children and women were leading this procession. This mob entered the Commissioner's residence. The security there was inadequate. The mob demanded an answer as to why there had been open firing at the Kar Sevaks. What had been their fault? After a lot of pleading, the Commissioner managed to get the people to agree to go back. In the meantime the Principal Development Officer, Prabhash Jha took charge as the caretaking Collector. The reason behind which was that the Collector, R.S. Shrivastava had made an excuse and had taken sick leave the previous night.

No journalist had been able to go to Ram Janmabhoomi in the last three days. The entire area was empty. Kar Sevaks were angry with newspapers. They wanted the death toll of Kar Sevaks to be reported in the hundreds. Mulayam Singh government was worried that incidents of Ayodhya may incite a reaction in other cities. Back then, there were no TV and news channels. That's why the government thought of putting newspapers under vigil and stop the news from reaching people. Newspapers were published at Varanasi, Gorakhpur, Kanpur and Allahabad. But the district administration didn't let copies be distributed. To show their displeasure and as a mark of protest, editors at Lucknow and Banaras got arrested disobeying the government.

3rd November was a very sad morning in Faizabad. When I was about to step out of my hotel Shaan-e-Awadh, I saw a huge number of women going somewhere during this time of curfew. The Commissioner lived next door to my hotel. I was curious. When I reached the road, I saw that all the women were wives of the soldiers and government officials of Faizabad and they were going to the protest against the Commissioner. By the time I reached there these women had entered the residential office of the Commissioner. They were stopped, because there were broken flower pots around the house. They had surrounded the Commissioner. They asked him, 'Why were the unarmed Kar Sevaks fired at?' The Commissioner replied, 'It was a government order.' The women asked, 'Why are you following undemocratic orders of the Chief Minister?' They told the commissioner, 'Stop communicating in this language of bullets.'

An ADM's wife said, 'Why do you force the magistrates to sign orders of firing? If you did that again, no Magistrate will sign it. Those Kar Sevaks, who can be persuaded, can be arrested, from now on. Mr. Commissioner, you will not pressure anyone into giving orders to shoot.' The Commissioner began to sweat at the fury of questions. A wife of an officer said, 'Why do you agree to every undemocratic order of Mulayam Singh?'

Commissioner Madhukar Gupta said, 'What else can I do?'

The woman replied, 'You should tell him the truth. You should refuse to shoot at the saints. Refuse to follow illegal orders.'

The Commissioner said, 'This is the decision of the government. We don't have any role in it. We can take your views to the government.'

The wife of a magistrate said, 'By following all the orders of the Chief Minister, you are turning him into a dictator.'

The Commissioner said, 'But maintaining order is our responsibility. We need your help. You should not pay attention to rumors.'

The wife of an officer said, 'Have some compassion. Remove the governmental blindfold. All the reports in the newspapers are rumours and your government is the only flag bearer of truth! You have killed humanity.' Another woman said, 'Can you fire at your own family?'

Commissioner Madhukar Gupta said, 'They were wrecking buses. Pelting stones.'

One woman said, 'Buses can be repaired. But can you bring back children and husbands of the women who have lost them?'

The Commissioner was speechless. Officers' wives screamed and asked, 'Why were canes not used? What was the readiness of your police force? Just because of one statement of the Chief Minister that not even a bird can pass through, you people started shooting unarmed people to please him!'

Madhukar Gupta was the son of Ashok Singhal's maternal uncle. The mob had Ashok Singhals' sister in it as well. She said, 'Will you stop only after having your brother killed.'

Later Madhukar Gupta also became the secretary at the centre.

The kitchens at the officers' residence remained cold that day, because the wives were sitting at the Commissioner's house. They wanted a written assurance that there would not be any more firing. While this ruckus was going on at the Commissioner's residence, wives of the army personnel took out a procession from the camp. The procession went through the entire town. Principals of colleges, teachers and lawyers also joined this procession when it passed through the city and by the time it reached the Commissioner's residence, the number was in thousands. The children and women were carrying placards which read, 'Stop killing unarmed Kar Sevaks', 'Don't become General Dyer'. To keep the increasing anxiety in check, the Faizabad-Lucknow road had been closed because the Commissioner's house was on this road. The Commissioner escaped from the back door of his house.

Now the government was facing the difficulty of evacuating Ayodhya of Kar Sevaks, because the firing that happened the day before had made the situation worse both at Ayodhya and in the other parts of the state. The government was also looking for a way out of the situation it had created due to its own misdeeds. Chief Minister Mulayam Singh Yadav wanted the VHP to announce a postponement of Kar Seva and ask the Kar Sevaks to return to their homes. But VHP was adamant that Kar Sevaks, who were on their way to Ayodhya, could only be asked to return after they had had darshan of Ram Lalla. The VHP was of the view that those Kar Sevaks who had taken the risk to come all the way from far-flung areas should at least be allowed to have darshan of Ram Lalla. Only then could they be asked to go back.

To get help in getting Kar Seva postponed and to send away the Kar Sevaks from Ayodhya, Chief Minister Mulayam Singh Yadav started looking for contacts in the Sangh. Kaushal Kishore was one such person in the Sangh who was close to him. Mulayam Singh spoke to him and sent him to Ayodhya on a government flight. He asked him to somehow get the Kar Seva postponed. Kaushal Kishore arrived straight at Maniram Das Chhawani after landing at Faizabad. The temple of Char Dham of this Chhawani was an impregnable fort of this movement. Kar Sevaks had gathered here. Speeches were being delivered at the time he arrived.

Kaushal Kishore reached and unilaterally announced the postponement of Kar Seva. In an environment of tension and anger, Kar Sevaks chased him away. Vinay Katiyar intervened to save him. Katiyar asked, 'Amidst the tragic and depressing firing, who took this one-sided decision and when?' Kaushal Kishore told him, 'How will the deadlock break? After so much of bloodshed it will be best to postpone the Kar Seva.' Vinay Katiyar replied, 'I have only been asked to follow instructions from Ashok Singhal and Moropant Pingle. Kar Sevaks are enraged; they won't listen to you and me. You talk to Moropant Pingle.'

Kaushal Kishore went to Moropant Pingle. Pingle also said, 'How can we announce unilaterally. Vinay Katiyar is right. Vinay Katiyar will be the one to decide about Kar Seva. Who has given you the authority?' Everyone was shocked with this changed position. Later Ashok Singhal, Vinay Katiyar and Moropant Pingle decided that the government should first give permission for darshan, even if it gave permission to smaller groups at a time to have darshan. Only then would they announce postponement of the Kar Seva. Kaushal Kishore called Mulayam Singh and informed him of the decision.

The difficulty that Mulayam Singh Yadav faced was that he had to put a stop to the darshan, because the damage done to the structure on 30 October was substantial and he didn't want fresh pictures of the damage to be made public. He didn't want to open the premises for visits before it had been repaired. But the government had to give in. They opened the disputed area for darshan. Kar Sevaks were allowed for darshan and Kar Seva was postponed.

VHP announced the postponement of Kar Seva but also said that Kar Sevaks who were stuck enroute should reach Ayodhya and be part of Shri Ram Maha-Yagya. They were asked to go back after seeing Ram Lalla. Shri Ram Maha-Yagya was to go on till 7 November. VHP announced that ashes of the martyred Kar Sevaks will be sent to many parts of the country. Condolence meetings will be held. Processions with the ashes will be taken out. How could the government stop this? This would create an anti-government public opinion across the country. The state government ended the deadlock by agreeing to their demands.

After an agreement with the state government, the movement of Kar Sevaks started again. A condolence meeting was held for the people who died at Ayodhya. At this memorial service, all of Ayodhya was bowing to two Kar Sevaks. People thronged the river banks of Saryu to be part of their funeral. The bodies of the two Kothari brothers were placed on the pyre and shouts of 'Amar-Ho' meaning 'live forever' were echoing everywhere. Ram Kothari (23) and Sharad Kothari (20) were pulled out of a house and shot dead by the security forces on 2

November. It was because these brothers had raised saffron flags on the domes of the disputed structure on 30 October. For many generations their families had been living in Kolkata. These were the only two sons of their father Hiralal Kothari who had an unmarried daughter as well. Hiralal Kothari was in deep shock. His elder brother Dau Lal Kothari came to Faizabad. He performed the last rites for the bodies. In a choked voice, Dau Lal said that the sacrifice of the sons would not go in vain. But what could he tell the mother of Sharad and Ram? He broke down whenever he thought of it. Until then the mother had not been told about the sacrifice of her sons.

Dau Lal ji said that he had received the news on the very day it had happened. By four o'clock he knew that the boys were no more. After raising the flag on the disputed structure on 30 October 1990, under the leadership of Vinay Katiyar, both brothers moved towards Digambar Akhada from Hanuman Garhi. When the police started firing, both turned around and hid in a house. It was then that a CRPF inspector pulled Sharad out of the house, made him sit on the road and shot him in the head. When Ram saw what was happening to his brother he rushed out to save him. A bullet from the inspector went through his throat. Both died on the spot.

Both the brothers had left from Kolkata on the night of 22 October. They had stopped at Banaras. The government had cancelled all trains. So they took a taxi and came up to the town of Phoolpurin Azamgarh. The roads were blocked from here on. They began walking on 25 October and after having walked about 200 kilometres reached Ayodhya on 30 October. Sharad was the first person to reach the disputed site on 30 October. He was the one who climbed the disputed structure and raised the flag. That day they were beaten with canes and chased by the CRPF. Sharad and Ram Kothari were now a part of the story of the temple movement. Their tales were being told in Ayodhya.

The results of Kar Seva brought Hindu sentiments to boiling point. Sharad Kothari and Ram Kothari had become extreme symbols of devotion for the sake of Ram temple. The firing on the Kar Sevaks resulted in Mulayam Singh losing his political ground. Ram devotees deposed the government. The demolition did not just happen on the ground, but also in the hearts of the people. No one had assumed the severity of their actions.

This shooting incident caused a country-wide reaction. Prime Minister V.P. Singh lost his government within seven days. The tide of 'Hindutva' that we saw later had its seeds sown that very day. In November itself a new government was formed at the centre under Chandra Shekhar's leadership. Chandra Shekhar was a plain-speaking socialist. His government had the backing of the Congress. The new Prime Minister again started to look for a solution to Ayodhya. He gave the responsibility of talking to both the sides of the dispute, to his union state minister, Subodh Kant Sahai. A committee was formed that had eight specialists from both sides. This committee also had Sharad Pawar, Bhairon Singh Shekhawat and Mulayam Singh. Both sides, Ram Janmabhoomi and Babri Mosque representatives, brought forth the historical evidence to strengthen their claims. The committee met six times. At one point it felt as if the committee was close to finding a formula. People began to hope. But in March 1991, the immature leadership withdrew their support from the Chandra Shekhar government, that too upon the baseless accusation that a government agent was spying on Rajiv Gandhi. The result of this was that the Ayodhya issue remained as it was and the country was once again in need of a general election.

Chapter 4

LAYING THE FOUNDATION

The spring of 1988 was like a political autumn for the Rajiv Gandhi government.

The tenure of 'Mr Clean' now had stains of controversies. He was accused of corruption in a major weapons contract political scandal with Sweden's company, A. B. Bofors. Sweden radio broadcasts accused Rajiv Gandhi in the scam and the person closest to him, who was also the Finance Minister in his own government—Vishwanath Pratap Singh publicized it. After this, Rajiv Gandhi kept getting into controversies. Under these circumstances, politics took a new turn in June 1988 during the Allahabad by-elections. Congress lost to V.P. Singh. The stains of corruption on Congress darkened. Independent India's strongest party with 415 MPs was moving towards instability.

Suddenly VHP became active whereas Congress was being attacked from all sides. VHP called the third dharmsansad in Allahabad in February 1989 in the Hindu month of Magh. Devraha Baba was also present at this dharmsansad. This dharmsansad happened under the leadership of Paramhans Ramchandra Das and announced that the foundation of the Ram would be laid on 9 November 1989 in Ayodhya.

The dharmsansad approved outlay of the proposed temple which was to be built in Nagar Shaili with an investment of ₹25 crores. 9 November 1989 was Devosthani Ekadashi. It is believed that the Gods rise after four months of sleep on this day. Many gather in Ayodhya on this occasion for a bath in the Saryu river and to take a round of Ayodhya. According to mythological beliefs, Ayodhya's circumference is 14 miles. So people come to Ayodhya and take a complete round of it. The place decided for the foundation fell in the disputed area. But VHP said that they did not consider it disputed. So 9 November 1989 was decided upon for 'bhoomipujan' or worshipping the land and 10 November for placing the founding brick. To give the campaign a comprehensive shape, the saint community planned to bring a brick from every village of the country for the temple. Bricks from three lakh villages had to reach by 5 November 1989 for the foundation. There could not be a better show of rising Hindutva than this. BJP, at this time, was a party with merely two MPs. It took advantage of the opportunity and supported this campaign in its national executive meet on 11 June in Himachal Pradesh's Palampur. Ram Janmabhoomi's issue was included in BJP's agenda for the first time. The country's atmosphere was getting heated. Both sides got into fiery, provocative speeches. Prime Minister Rajiv Gandhi could not understand what needed to be done. As a person he was outright and simple. He was surrounded by a set of advisors. At that time, he did not have his own opinions. His advisors told him that keeping the majority Hindu sentiment in mind, they should get the foundation laid. Before BJP grabs this opportunity, he must make the first move and cease the agenda of Hindutva. Lok Sabha elections were to happen by next year in March. Rajiv Gandhi's personal assistant R.K. Dhawan told me in an interview, 'He was told that after getting the foundation laid, get elections preponed and start the election campaign from Ayodhya.' Later this actually happened. Rajiv Gandhi started his campaign from Ayodhya and repeated Congress's commitment towards 'Ramrajya' in his speech. At that time, the writer of Rajiv Gandhi's speeches was Mani Shankar Aiyar. But Aiyar said that there was no mention of Ramrajya in the speech written by him. Rajiv Gandhi had probably added this under pressure of the general public sentiment so that he could gain from it in the elections, because he had understood that elections are fought and won on emotions in India. The announcement of Ramrajya by Rajiv Gandhi in the very beginning of the campaign was made with a motive behind it. During campaigning, everyone explained the meaning of Ramrajya according to their mindset. People looked at it as the changing stand of Congress. Leftist friends said that this is Congress's 'soft Hindutva'. The term Ramrajya has been used for a better political arrangement earlier as well. Mahatma Gandhi used it most of all during the war of independence. While talking about his Ramrajya Mahatma Gandhi used to say,

'For me, Swaraj (independence) and Ramrajya (Ram's rule) is one thing. How will such Ramrajya be established? When will that find an existence? We will call it Ramrajya when the country's ruler and its people, both are honest. When both have a clean heart and intent to sacrifice. When both remain disciplined and in control despite the worldly pleasures. When the relations between them are as deep as father and son. That is Ramrajya. This is also the true definition of democracy. The democracy I believe in is inherent in Ramrajya. How did Ramchandra rule his kingdom? Today, rulers feel that ruling is their birth right. They don't even recognize the voice of the people's thoughts. During Ramrajya, all were equal. The people were free from all kinds of fears. They loved each other and were honest. There was no need of a magistrate to punish a criminal then because there was no crime.' (*The collected works of Mahatma Gandhi*, Number XXXV, 489-90)

There was a similarity between Gandhi's and Tulsidas's 'Ramrajya'.

'दैहिक दैविक भौतिक तापा। राम राज्य सपनेहु नह व्यापा।।'
"*Daihik daivik bhautik taapa, Ram Rajya sapnehu nahi vyapa*"

It means that no one could even think of any physical, divine or materialistic issues during Ramrajya. But VHP had used this term so often during the Ram Mandir campaign that by then, Ram had lost its real meaning and become an identity of the Ram Mandir movement. That is how Rajiv Gandhi's opponents took 'Ramrajya' away from him. He was also accused of encouraging the divisive feelings in Hindus. Amidst it all, Rajiv Gandhi decided to bring forward the elections. The date of laying the foundation of the temple was already decided as 9 November 1989. The date of elections was also decided as 22 and 24 November 1989. This meant that the election campaigning and journeys of getting bricks from other places were to happen at the same time.

There was a lot of speculation around elections. What would happen? No one in the Congress party knew the answer to that. The foreign minister at the time, P.V. Narasimha Rao writes in his book *Ayodhya 6 December, 1992*—'It was 16 October 1989. At around 8 in the morning, when I was reading the newspaper, I suddenly got a call from the prime minister's residence. I was asked to meet the PM at 9:30. I found it a bit weird. But then I thought that a young prime minister can call his foreign minister at any time, because anything can happen at any point around the world that needs immediate attention. So I reached 7, Race Course road on time.

'Rajiv Gandhi was already busy talking to some of his close associates. In a few minutes and in an unexpected manner, the secret was out. Rajiv came and said to me—"You have to lead the Indian delegation at the Rashtramandal Shikhar Sammelan starting in Kuala Lumpur from tomorrow in my place. My tour has been cancelled. Today we are going to announce the date for the Lok Sabha elections. Elections are likely to take place around 20th of the next month. There is no time and I have to get busy with the election work now".

Narasimha Rao writes, 'From the Prime Minister's tone, I felt that this is his final decision. I was the main member of CCPA (the cabinet formed for political related work) then. But I felt that this decision was taken without consulting CCPA. I was worried that I would have to start election campaign from my constituency Ramtek also early, the same constituency from where I had won with a huge majority in 1984. But this time, I was finding the contest tough. This was not a personal feeling. I was feeling like this because of the situation that existed. Even though I was getting support from the public and Congress workers just like before.'

Narasimha Rao writes, 'I returned to India soon. Perhaps a few hours early. Because I had exchanged my return with a prime minister who had understood my election related priorities. Few hours after submitting report of Shikhar Sammelan to the prime minister, I started for Ramtek.' Ramtek is at the border of Maharashtra and Andhra, next to the Ramgiri mountain range where Lord Ram is said to have rested while going to Panchvati.

'Few months back, the Prime Minister had formed a cabinet to keep an eye on the worsening situation of Ayodhya and if possible, to find a better solution. I was appointed as the chairman of this committee. Although later it just became one of the many committees. I was expected to take a decision in Delhi and convey it to Lucknow. But it became clear to me in the very first meeting of the cabinet that we cannot reach a conclusion without including Lucknow. So we suspended the meet and requested the UP CM to participate in the next meet. But for some reason, the next meeting of the cabinet could never take place and I had to leave the matter there only.'

Narasimha Rao talks about the anxiety in the Congress leaders and workers regarding Ayodhya. 'Congress candidates and workers had their doubts regarding Ayodhya since many years, because of which they were anxious. We were in a shock and dilemma seeing politicization of the long-standing religious conflict for the first time.'

After 1985, BJP started working on the agenda of Hindutva. Congress refuted it in the name of secularism. The Congress's stand against the BJP was changing to its stand against Hindutva. This was where the Congress got caught in BJP's agenda.

The former Prime Minister describes the state of mind of the Congress party at that time, 'Being in power, despite feeling strongly for the religion, we will be seen as non-secular if we expressed it. As a result, BJP became Hindu religion's saviour and the only trusted party among general public.'

I have not understood till today why Congress did not understand what Narasimha Rao was saying. How can any secular country remain alive after hurting the religious sentiments of the chief religion? In a country where religion dominates most parts of the life of its people, how can one keep people under the influence of pseudo-secularism for decades? This thought probably led to Congress leaders playing a role in Ayodhya during the Rajiv Gandhi tenure. But looking at the election time and its needs, the unsual role the state government had to play had an opposite impact. Narasimha Rao writes, 'BJP at least had the support of VHP and RSS, who were spporting the demands and sentiments of Hindus. But in Congress, the UP chief minister and one of the important union ministers (who was close to Rajiv Gandhi) got into a competition to capture Ayodhya. Congress had a very different take on this matter initially. Then it got involved in the foundation process completely. This affected the party's friends. When locks of the temple were opened in 1986, the mindset was that Congress got it done, even though it was due to the court's order. This created a lot of furore.

Congress was embarrassed in front of the Muslims and the credit for it went to the BJP. So basically both Hindus and Muslims moved away from Congress for different reasons.'

Narasimha Rao believed that compromising with VHP was like compromising with anarchists to remove anarchy. Narasimha Rao himself was very affected by the *Ramshila yatras*. He writes—'Being an MP from Ramtek, I got a chance to witness the *Ramshila yatras that* were crossing the national highway that ran through Ramtek Lok Sabha constituency. These *shila yatras* or brick rallies were coming from the south Indian states. When I would go on a round in my constituency and cross the national highway, people travelling in trucks would recognize me and stop. They would stop my car and talk to me for a little while. Through these interactions, I had deeply understood public emotions regarding Ram Mandir. I also got an idea of the kind of tough times candidates of the Congress party will have to face when politicization of Ram Janmabhoomi will end with a definite programme.'

Then why did Rajiv Gandhi perform such a somersault? Congress men were also fighting this question constantly. I got the answer from Samajwadi party's leader Madhu Limye. After quitting politics, Madhu Limye would only spend time reading and writing in his official residence at Satyamarg. If you had to solve a political mystery, there was no one better than him to go to. He would serve you tea along with the solution. He told me, 'How can you neglect religion? Soviet Union neglected religion for 70 years and the result is in front of us.'

'Before Gorbachev resigned from power and disintegration of the Soviet Union took place, *Moscow News Weekly* conducted a free voting survey in which most said that they have faith in the orthodox church. They voted for Lalsena in the second place and communist party in the third. The same way Voltaire and Russo's France along with the French could not ignore Christian sentiments. Japan also could not neglect the Buddhist land. So then, how can Rajiv Gandhi be an exception?'

This was the logic behind the situation. Now let's return to our story. On one hand, Rajiv Gandhi was preparing for the Lok Sabha elections and on the other hand, VHP and BJP were preparing for laying the foundation for Ram Mandir. After the Bofor scandal, Rajiv Gandhi had lost both his trustworthiness and his poularity. He was facing a great challenge from the alliance formed between his former finance minister Vishwanath Pratap Singh who had left the party, his maternal cousin Arun Nehru, Arif Mohammed Khan who had resigned from his government, Vidyacharan Shukla and others. On the other hand, BJP was a party with just two MPs, who was looking for an issue to win the elections. VHP and RSS were warring over Ayodhya from the start. But as a political party, BJP had not touched upon the issue. Just before elections, BJP's national working committee's meet took place on 11 June 1989 in Himachal Pradesh's Palampur. The Ram Janmabhoomi issue came up for the first time in party's agenda there. In the working committee's meeting, BJP passed a resolution and demanded that Ram Janmabhoomi be handed over to Hindus. The Palampur resolution said–

'Bhartiya Janta Party's national working committee is serious on the ongoing Ram Janmabhoomi dispute. The party is worried about the insensitive and indifferent attitude of political parties, especially that of Congress towards the issue and the about the betrayal to the majority population of the country which is Hindus.

'The party believes that according to all the available evidence, Mughal emperor Babur came to Ayodhya in 1528. He got all temples demolished around the area that is believed to be Lord Ram's birth place. Babur got a mosque built there. Since then, Hindus have been waiting for reconstruction of a temple there, which they consider very holy. During the war of independence in 1857, Muslims had agreed to the claims of Hindus on Ram Janmabhoomi, but the English played the divide and rule politics and the matter got worsened. Although despite all this, the efforts of making Muslims understand that they must drop their claim on this land and respect sentiments of Hindus continued. Even then the land got stuck in a long legal battle.'

'BJP believes that this is a conflict a court cannot resolve. Courts can resolve disputes over posts and ownership. But a court cannot pass judgement on whether Babur actually attacked Ayodhya, got the temple demolished and built a mosque in its place. Even when a court has given a verdict on such matters, it has never been able to undo history's barbarity. In 1885, British judge Colonel A.E.F Camier's response to the public appeal filed in this matter said—"It is very unfortunate that a mosque was built in a place that is specially pious for Hindus. But this happened 356 years ago. Now it is too late to find a resolution to the matter". (18 March, 1986, Civil appeal number 27/1885, district court, Faizabad)

The current dispute was born out of court's two different decisions. First, the verdict of 1951 and second, the 1986 verdict. On 3 March 1951, Faizabad's civil judge had this response on Gopal Singh Visharad vs. Jahoor Ahmad and some other matters—At least Muslims haven't treated the area as mosque since 1936, nor have they prayed there. But Hindus pray and perform rituals on the disputed land. After this on 1 February 1986 Faizabad's district judge gave reference of the 1951 verdict and ordered that 'Hindus have had the right to pray here for the last 35 years without any hindrance. The two gates that were locked in 1951 in the name of law and order, should be opened.' (Civil appeal number 6/1986)

The 1951 order had made people furious. Till then, unlike today the sweet word in the name of secularism was not invented. It is to be noted that during the same period, the Indian government led by Pandit Jawaharlal Nehru and Sardar Patel with the backing of Mahatma Gandhi had passed a similar decision of barbarity. This is when the decision of reconstruction of the Somnath temple in Gujarat was taken. When the archaeological department suggested to declare it as a protected monument (a similar suggestion is being promoted regarding the Ram Janmabhoomi these days), the home minister, Sardar Patel officially wrote in the government files—

'The feelings of Hindus for this temple are strong and massive. In the current times, it seems difficult to pacify Hindus without restoring the statue in the temple. 'When Jyotirling was duly established in Somnath, the country's president Dr Rajendra Prasad had taken part in that ceremony.

Although by the time the second court order came in 1986, secularism had become a reason for Hindus' resentment and this word had become synonymous with Muslim appeasement. The Muslim League lobby had taken up an aggressive outlook. This lobby's campaign against Supreme Court's decision in the 1985 Shah Bano case benefitted them a lot. An anxious government had to amend the criminal law. They had to constitutionally cancel the Supreme Court's order. After tasting success, this lobby formed a Babri Masjid Action Committee and attacked Faizabad court's decisions. To go against the decisions of court, they went to the extent of boycotting Republic Day. In a rally organized by this lobby in front of the Parliament House, a threat of violence was given if these orders were not taken back. It is important to note that most members of the Babri Action Committee were from Congress. This was BJP's Palampur resolution.

With this resolution, BJP not only took the Ram Janmabhoomi on its agenda, but also declared that the court cannot pass any judgement on it. This was a question related to faith.

The point where VHP had announced the laying of foundation on 9 November 1989, was the *Singhdwar* of the proposed temple. According to this map, the proposed temple's *garbhgrah* (sanctum sanctorum) was also at the same place, which was the disputed site's main dome. This means that if the government lets the foundation get laid, the disputed structure's *garbhgrah* would be the temple's *garbhgrah*. So in this context, the place where foundation was to be laid was disputed. This means that in the map of the proposed temple, the temple's *garbhgrah* is exactly where Babri Masjid's *garbhgrah* is said to be. The temple's *Singhdwar* foundation was to be laid 192 feet away from this *garbhgrah*. The proposed temple was to be 270 feet long, 126 feet wide and 132 feet tall. The UP government went to the high court against the proposed foundation. On 14 August the High Court ordered to maintain status quo. But no ban was put on laying the foundation or on worshipping the founding. The ceremony and rituals of purifying the founding brick by VHP started from 30 September all over the country. This was the first day of Sharadiya Navratra. 22 states in the entire country were divided into 11 areas. One brick from every village was to be purified. The plan was to then keep the holy brick in a chariot, take it to the district and state headquarters and then to Ayodhya. By 5 November, all bricks were to reach Ayodhya. These bricks made from the local soil, were wrapped in a saffron cloth and placed on the chariot. One brick was worshipped by thousands of people.

Bricks coming from Madhya Pradesh, Maharashtra and South India were joining the rallies after crossing Allahabad and Jhansi districts. Similarly, the ones coming from Haryana, Punjab, Rajasthan were to reach Ayodhya via Meerut, the ones coming from Kashmir and Himachal Pradesh were to reach Ayodhya via Muradabad, Bareilly. After 600 small Ram *shilayatras*, 5 big *shilayatras* were planned for Ayodhya. The state government had given orders to all district magistrates that these must not be stopped at any point. But at the same time they were also asked to ensure that the rally does not wander unnecessarily. An understanding, regarding the *shilapujan* and *shilayatras*, was reached between Uttar Pradesh's chief minister Narayan Dutt Tiwari and VHP. The government gave permission for the foundation programmes. A compromise also took place between both parties in which Home Minister Buta Singh was also present.

Uttar Pradesh's chief minister had a meeting with the representatives of VHP on 24 September 1989 in which the home minister was also present. In this meeting, VHP's plan of organizing *shilapujan* in different parts of the country was discussed. The whole process of transporting the collected bricks to Ayodhya by 9 November 1989 and all aspects of laying the foundation were discussed in detail.

The following were agreed upon after the meeting—

1. VHP will give information pertaining to the route of the *shilayatra* to the district administration in advance. At the same time, it will accept the administration's decision if it wanted to change the route in the interest of the public.
2. VHP leaders will not use any provocative slogans that may disturb peace.
3. Till wherever possible, the holy bricks will be taken in trucks and the route of the trucks will be decided after discussing with the related district administration.
4. VHP's senior and responsible office bearers will take the responsibility of leading the rally and will fully support the local administration.
5. The place where the holy bricks were supposed to be collected

and kept in Ayodhya will be decided after discussing with the district administration.
6. VHP will follow the orders given by the Lucknow bench of the Allahabad high court on 14 August 1989, in which it is said that all parties will maintain status quo in the matter and will not make any change to it so that peace and social harmony is ensured.

The below mentioned officers will be in touch with the Uttar Pradesh government and cooperate—

Dau Dayal Khanna, 2. Shrichandra Dikshit, former DGP (U.P.) 3. Omkar Bhave 4. Suresh Gupta, former vice chancellor, 5. Mahesh Narayan Singh, Ayodhya.

This agreement letter was signed by Ashok Singhal, Avaidhyanath, Nritya Gopal and Dau Dayal Khanna.

VHP planned to divide the entire country in two parts and transport the holy bricks to Ayodhya through five chief shilayatras. The first main yatra or rally began on 5 November by the name of 'Chitrakoot Yatra' that started from Banda and reached Ayodhya via Fatehpur, Raebareli and Jagdishpur. The second rally started from Lalitpur on 4 November by the name of Brahmawatwas was to reach Ayodhya the next day on 5 November via Jhansi, Urai, Kanpur, Unnav, Lucknow and Barabanki. Other smaller shilayatras from Itawa, Farrukhabad, Hamirpur, Sitapur, Hardoi, Lakhimpur and Biswan were to join this main rally at different points. The third shilayatra named 'Gorakhnath' was to start on 5 November from the Gorakhnath temple in Gorakhpur and reach Ayodhya via Sahajnawa, Mahanghar, Khalilabad, Muderwa, Kaptanganj and Harayya. It included the smaller shilayatrasof Padrauna, Devariya, Maharajganj, Siddharthnagar, Balrampur and Behraich. On 5 November, the fourth main rally had to begin by the name of 'Kashi Yatra'. This reached Ayodhya via Varanasi, Jaunpur and Gosainganj. This included the smaller rallies of Sonbhadra, Gazipur and Baliya. The fifth rally called 'Prayagraj' reached Ayodhya via Pratapgarh and Sultanpur. This had bricks from Doaba and Gangapar.

The Ram Janmabhoomi 'mukti' or freedom campaign had been

running in Ayodhya for the last four hundred and fifty years. But one person had taken this campaign to every village and household through 'Ramshilas' in one move. This person always remained backstage. His mind always worked on how more and more people could be emotionally attached to the campaign. This unforgettable person who gave the Ayodhya campaign life was Moropant Pingle. He was the actual strategist of the campaign. The way he got the entire country to worship Ramshilas and established a connection between them and the holy bricks was an innovative experiment. About three lakh bricks were purified and worshipped in the country. Then moving from the village to the tehsil, district and then the state headquarters, about twenty thousand shilayatras left for Ayodhya. About six crore people worshipped the Ramshilas. Shilas or bricks from forty places reached Ayodhya. The first shila was worshipped in Badrinath. Every person who worshipped it also offered ₹1.25. So about six crore people got directly and emotionally attached to Ayodhya's foundation. Ayodhya had never seen such an intense campaign before. The Gau-raksha (protecting the cows) campaign was also not as intense.

Moropant Pingle, the man responsible for taking the campaign to each and every household was a Brahmin from Maharashtra. A very simple and humble man, Pingle was a graduate from Nagpur's Morris College. Whenever he met me in Ayodhya, he would only say one thing, 'I have to make this campaign India's biggest campaign till now.' He was behind all initiatives like shilapujan, shilanyas, charan paduka, Ramjyoti yatras. But he always worked behind the curtains.

'Shilapujan' had created a tide in the entire country. Every village donated bricks for the Ram Mandir. A sum of ₹1.25 was asked to support the campaign from every family. The Indians living in villages resolved to make it happen. All the saints and priests in the country became part of it. The villages that donated bricks were dedicating their lives for its honour. Moropant Pingle had taken the dream of building Ram Mandir from Ayodhya to the entire country. This was the reason why Moropant Pingle was known as the field marshal of the Ram Janmabhoomi.

The 1984's Ram Janki Rath yatra was like the departure point for the Ayodhya campaign. Moropant Pingle was the coordinator and governor of this rally. Seven chariots were taken out in Uttar Pradesh and Bihar. Ram was shown in captivity in these rallies. This was the live picture of Ram's situation in Ayodhya. These chariots provoked the silent Ram followers towards rebellion in the Hindu belt. They were so overwhelmed with feelings that they would do anything for Ram.

But this wasn't the first time. Once before as well, Pingle had stirred everyone from East to West and North to South India to execute a mission.

Recorded in history, the year 1982-83 is witness to his managerial skills and capabilities. During this time, there was a plan of conducting a nationwide 'Ekatmata Yatra' or a 'Rally of Unity'. Three rallies were planned throughout the country. The motive behind these rallies can be understood by knowing their routes. While the first rally was from Haridwar to Kanyakumari, the second went from Kathmandu's Pashupatinath temple to Rameshwar dham and the third from Bengal's Gangasagar to Somnath. There were some symbols decided for these. Gangajal was carried along for worshipping Mother Ganga and Mother India. So Mother India's picture was one of the main symbols. Hundreds of smaller rallies joined the main rallies on the way. Three such rallies had to cover about 50,000 kilometres. After that they had to enter Nagpur at a specific time. This was unbelievable in those times of limited resources. But this miracle did happen. Behind this also was Moropant Pingle's sharp sightedness. More than six and a half crore people from all over India participated in these three rallies. Moropant had reached Nagpur even before the rallies. Like the other citizens of Nagpur, he also witnessed the rallies enter the city. The feelings these rallies of unity generated became the basis of combining Ayodhya with the tide of Hindutva. Moropant Pingle was groomed by the founding Sarsanghachalak of RSS, Dr Hedgewar. This was Moropant's way of functioning—to be in the role of a manager and never taking any credit; creating everything, but staying away from everyone's attention. But who can stop history? His name is marked in it.

The purified bricks started reaching Ayodhya from 5 November. There were about three lakh bricks from all over the country on the way to Ayodhya. The bricks were worshipped in three lakh, sixteen thousand villages. To get these bricks, the district administration had arranged for forty thousand cars in Ayodhya. The government had set up ten temporary police stations to ensure that nothing goes wrong in the shilayatras. The government was helping in getting these yatras to Ayodhya, but was silent on where the foundation would be laid. VHP had captured a five feet wide and seven feet long area in front of Babri Masjid and planted a flag there. The Babri Masjid Action committee appealed against it in court and said that the place where VHP has put a flag is disputed. The state government also said the same to the court. On the other hand, all non BJP parties passed a resolution in Lok Sabha on 13 October and told the government not to give permission of laying the foundation. Babri Masjid Action Committee claimed that plot number 586, the plot on which foundation was to be laid, was registered as a graveyard in the documents. In the meanwhile, Justice V.M. Tarkunde filed a writ petition in court and demanded a ban on shilapujan and shilayatras. But the Supreme Court dismissed the petition saying that conducting a religious rally is the fundamental right of people.

VHP claimed that plot number 586, the place where they had put the flag is under them. In the municipal corporation's record, this land was registered with Dharamdas. Baba Dharamdas had handed it over to Ram Janmabhoomi Trust in April 1986. The office of the Trust was established and had been functioning from 1986 here. Dharamdas had had this land since 1943. Even if the court's order of maintaining status quo was accepted, it was only for the temple's bhavan which was the disputed structure and receivers were deployed there.

Ram Janmabhoomi Trust's acting chairman, Ramchandra Paramhans declared that the place decided by VHP for laying the foundation will not be changed. His argument was that how could the land be in dispute when he had got the land registered in the name of the Trust? If the government considers this as the land of *Najool*, then it is also their responsibility to prove it.

The state government wanted the foundation to be laid, but at a different location. The government offered to get VHP the land next to it. VHP dismissed it completely and asked Devraha Baba to interfere because he was playing the role of a mediator between Prime Minister Rajiv Gandhi and VHP on the issue of foundation. At that time Rajiv Gandhi was under pressure of the circumstances. All his associates had left him. He was not able to understand what to do. Someone told him to contact Devraha Baba. Devraha Baba was a divine man. No one knew his age. He did not live on land. He lived on water, atop a 12 feet high scaffolding. This ascetic had scaled the Himalayas. He lived naked all his life. He lived near Lar road in Devariya district and belonged to Maeek. He was a devotee of Ram. That is why he would spend most of his time at the banks of Saryu and Ganga. His blessings were considered very impactful. When Rajiv Gandhi's mother Indira Gandhi had a problem, she would also go to Baba only for a solution.

Rajiv Gandhi went to meet Baba in Vrindavan on 6 November 1989. Baba said, 'The temple should be built. You get the foundation laid. But make sure that the place of laying the foundation is not changed.' It is said that this was the moment when Rajiv Gandhi diligently started working towards getting the foundation laid. The next day baba called VHP's leader Shri chandra Dikshit. He said to him, 'Relax. I have asked the prime minister to lay the foundation at the same place where you people have planted the flag.' So the decision of where the foundation would be laid was taken in Vrindavan and not in Lucknow or Delhi, with the blessings of Devraha Baba. Rajiv Gandhi's messenger, Lok Sabha chairman Balram Jakhad remained in touch with Baba constantly. What happened later in Ayodhya was the same as decided in these meetings. Both parties had blind faith in Baba and were following him.

Ram Janmabhoomi Trust's managing trustee Ashok Singhal told me, 'Devraha Baba is a religious leader who guides us in every step.' Baba said to Rajiv Gandhi on 6 November that he should support the VHP's demand of building the temple. The events that followed made it clear that Rajiv Gandhi did what was told by the Baba. On the first day of laying the foundation, Baba rejected the official suggestion of changing the foundation spot even though some leaders of VHP had agreed to change the location. This is what Vinay Katiyar said:

'Till the last minute, government wanted to move the foundation location to plot number 576. There was no dispute over this plot. This place was seven yards away from the original place. On 5 November, some senior officers had taken a round of the area to get this done. This plot was on lease with Ramkripal Das. He made an offer to give his land for laying the foundation. There was a bathroom and a wall there that was razed to lay the foundation. On 6 November, the state government had filed an application in court and asked if plot number 586 fell in the ambit of the disputed land. To this Allahabad high court's special division bench had called the land on which VHP was going to lay foundation disputed. The bench had said in their decision that the land on which VHP had planted the flag is disputed so status quo should be maintained there.'

A member of the bench and acting chief judge, K.C. Agarwal, justice U.C. Shrivastav and justice S.H.A. Raza said in their decision, 'We clarify that the order passed on 14 August 1989 was about the entire outlined land that included plot number 586.'

So the court made it clear that this plot also falls in the disputed area. There was no room for doubt now. Now the question was, that if the government knew about the status of the plot, why did it ask the court? Administrative officers said that one reason for this was to create legal pressure on VHP to change the location of the foundation. If VHP agreed to this, there was no problem at all. Then the foundation and Mahayagya could be easily done on the non-disputed land. Even the Babri Masjid Action Committee would not have had any objection if the foundation was laid at that place. In this way, the government would have been able to make both Hindus and Muslims happy and their happiness meant votes.

But this divided the leaders of VHP. Devraha Baba called Ashok Singhal and former police Inspector General, S.C. Dikshit to Vrindavan. Singhal told, 'Devraha Baba clearly said that we must lay the foundation at the decided place only. He also said that Rajiv Gandhi is also ready to do it there. He has assured me of it.'

The government was torn between the High Court's decision and Devraha Baba's order. Prime Minister Rajiv Gandhi sent Home Minister Buta Singh to Lucknow the next day early morning on 8 November, because an agreement could be not reached between Prime Minister Rajiv Gandhi and Chief Minister Narayan Dutt Tiwari on the issue of laying the foundation. Despite having the image of an obedient and yes-man kind of a leader, Chief Minister Narayan Dutt Tiwari wasn't ready for laying the foundation. This was the same Narayan Dutt Tiwari who was infamous for being that obedient that he is said to have picked up Rajiv Gandhi's brother, Sanjay Gandhi's slippers during emergency. Despite this, he wasn't listening to Rajiv Gandhi in this matter. The meaning was clear. He was looking at the damage the Congress party would face if the foundation was laid. On 6 November, after the High Court banned the laying of foundation, Rajiv Gandhi wanted the state government to convey to the High Court that the chosen place for laying the foundation does not fall in the conflict zone. Narayan Dutt Tiwari wasn't ready for this.

Elections had been announced. Narayan Dutt Tiwari would go out to campaign every day. That very night of 6th November I got a call from Narayan Dutt Tiwari. He said, 'I am traveling to Jhansi for a public gathering tomorrow. Will you come along?' I agreed. I thought I would be able to accomplish two things in one go. One, I would get to know the public's mood about what's going to happen in the elections in the CM's rally in Bundelkhand. Secondly, by talking to Narayan Dutt Tiwari, I would also get to understand what's actually happening on the laying of the foundation front.

I reached the CM's house located at Kalidas Marg at 9 a.m. We had to go to Jhansi in a helicopter from Lucknow. The CM's personal secretary Kailash Pant asked me to wait in a room and told me that the CM was talking to someone. After that, he would leave for Jhansi. Some time passed. Half an hour passed. Soon one hour had gone by. When it was almost two hours, I asked Kailash Pant what the matter was because Narayan Dutt Tiwari was a punctual man. Kailash Pant requested me to wait and said that the matter was serious. I kept waiting in that room and suddenly I saw Narayan Dutt Tiwari walk out of the house. I felt a little strange. He wasn't like this. He would stop upon seeing me. He would ask me if all was well, invite me to eat and even inquire about my parents. This had always been a habit with him. But today, his behaviour wasn't the same. After some time, I was called by him. He was waiting for me in the portico. I quickly went. I was asked to sit next to him. The car left for the airport. He didn't even respond to my greeting properly. His face was red with anger. I was waiting for him to speak up. But he did not say anything. I was wondering what had happened to him. So I asked him. Had something been decided on laying of the foundation? He said resentfully, 'Ask Buta Singh. He has come to get it done.'

After speaking to him a while longer, I came to know that Buta Singh had arrived early that morning in a BSF plane. His meeting with Narayan Dutt Tiwari had been going on. Buta Singh wanted that the decision given by the High Court the previous day i.e., that the decided place for laying the foundation falls under disputed land and foundation could not be laid there, should be challenged by the state government. He wanted the state government to tell the court that VHP was laying the foundation there which meant that that particular area in plot number 586 was not disputed. Only then will the road to laying the foundation open up. Later it was decided that after giving the layout of the area, Faizabad's district magistrate would give a statement that the point decided for laying the foundation was not disputed. After a meeting, Faizabad's DM was given instructions to do as decided. Pandit Narayan Dutt Tiwari was upset about this very thing. Contrary to his nature he was adamant to not fall in line with Delhi's advice. Later history proved him right.

By the time we returned in the evening, Buta Singh had had a talk with the VHP leaders. Also, DM at Faizabad had identified that the foundation-laying spot was not disputed. With this announcement he had quelled all the uncertainties regarding foundation-laying. Now there was no legal hindrance in laying the foundation. District Magistrate Ram Sharan Srivastava told me about the intention of the government. He said, 'Yesterday the map attached with the order of the High Court didn't have the spot of the foundation-laying.'

To stop the foundation-laying, the next day Babri Action Committee called for an emergency meeting at the Taat Shah Mosque in Faizabad. To stop the laying of the foundation, Action Committee leader Syed

Shahabuddin reached Faizabad. Janmorcha leader Vishwanath Pratap Singh had also reached Ayodhya for the same. After reaching Ayodhya, he asked Rajiv Gandhi if the government had approved the plan proposed by the VHP. That very day, CPI (M) rallied against laying of the foundation. CPM had a good hold in Faizabad. Mitra Sen Yadav of CPM was a member of parliament from this place. The priest of the Ram Janmabhoomi Temple, Baba Lal Das was also a CPM card holder.

When the Congress party was soft on the issue of foundation-laying, senior Congress leader Pundit Kamlapati Tripathi began to oppose the foundation-laying. Kamlapati was a pooja-paathi or the praying-ceremonial Brahmin leader. He announced that if VHP were to use a spade to dig for the temple at the Mosque site, then the first blow of the spade will have to be upon his body. He announced that he will go to Ayodhya on the day of the foundation-laying. He wrote a letter to Prime Minister Rajiv Gandhi to declare the site a national monument. In his letter he wrote—'My understanding is that if the Ram Janmabhoomi-Babri dispute escalates any further, it will not be good for the country. In my opinion, Babri Mosque and Ram Janmabhoomi should be declared a national monument. I request Hindu-Muslim to accept this.' He further wrote —'Any solution through the court seems impossible in this matter. If the verdict goes against any one party, it is impossible that it will be acceptable to the other party. If this dispute continued, it will increase the risk of dividing the country.' Both, Chief Minister Narayan Dutt Tiwari and Prime Minister Rajiv Gandhi requested Pundit Kamlapati Tripathi to not go to Ayodhya, but he did not listen. He went to Ayodhya.

During those days Pundit Kamlapati Tripathi was angry with Rajiv Gandhi. Rajiv Gandhi had sidelined him. So, it was believed that he took this stand to put Rajiv Gandhi in an awkward position. This attitude of Kamlapati Tripathi pleased a certain section in the Congress. After a few days when his son, Lokpati Tripathi met me during the elections, he said, 'Babu's stand is benefitting the Congress in the elections. Muslims are moving away from Vishwanath Pratap Singh and coming towards the Congress.' Elections were held in 20 days from that day. The country had a new Janta Dal government. Congress got only 15 seats in UP.

After a few days I met Lokpati Tripathi again in the secretariat. After exchanging pleasantries, I asked, 'What happened Pundit ji? You were saying that Babuji's stand will benefit the party.' Lokpati fretted and said, 'My Babu, "the grandson of Babur", wanted to build the Mosque and the party got defeated...' Lokpati was a blunt leader. But I didn't like the comment he made about his father. This showed his helplessness. After this, he also never won any election.

Eventually the time came to lay the foundation. On 9 November 1989 at 9:33 a.m., in the Purva Bhadrapada Nakshatra, the prayer for foundation-laying was performed. Amidst the blowing of the conch shells and chants, digging for the foundation started. It was at the same spot in the proposed map where the main entrance was to be. Swami Vamdev did the *bhoomipujan* or prayer for the land. First strike of the spade was by Mahant Avaidyanath. One by one, Paramhans Ramchandra Das, Swami Vamdev and Satyamitra Nanda Giri, all dug the ground. The Nav-Grih, Gaur-Ganesh, Ashta-Digpal, Nag-Pujan, Varun-Pujan and Vastu-Puja were performed by Pundit Mahadev Bhatt and Pundit Ayodhya Prasad.

Afterwards, Nritya Gopal Das, Ashok Singhal, H.V. Sheshadri, Swami Chinmayananda, Ramandacharya-Ramanujacharya and Dharam Das also participated in the digging for the foundation. The place of the foundation-laying belonged to Dharam Das. The district administration said that about eight lakh people had gathered in Ayodhya on this day.

Foundation laying took place the next day, on 10 November 1989 at 1:40 a.m., in Uttara Bhadrapada Nakshatra. A Harijan form Bihar, Kameshwar, placed the first brick of the temple. This first brick had come from Bangladesh. It contained ashes from 56 yagnas. Seven more such bricks were worshipped before laying the foundation. It was done amid recitation of Gurugranth Sahib, Jain-Buddhist prayers and the calls of 'Mandir yahin Banayenge' meaning, we will build the temple right here. Snakes made of eight metals were put in the foundation. Hosts of the yagna were Shrish Chandra Dikshit and Badri Toshewal. After the first stone was placed by a dalit, Mahant Ramchandra Paramhans of Digambar Akhada placed five more stones in the foundation.

The foundation laying was considered a fraud by the Muslim

community. A march was taken out in the morning by them from Faizabad's Taat mosque. The march against the foundation-laying was under the banner of Babri Masjid Sangharsh Samiti. Their intention was to go up to Ayodhya, but after a short distance, police asked them to return. When they refused, they were arrested. No resistance was posed in the arrest. The arrest was led by convener, Mohammed Azam Khan, Zafaryab Jilani, Muzzaffar Husain Kichauchvi. People from all over the country especially from Aligarh had participated in the march. They held placards which said—*Rajiv Gandhi Hosh me aao, Shilanyas par rok lagao*, meaning, 'Come to your senses Rajiv Gandhi and put an end to the foundation-laying'.

Later the Ulemas and Babri Masjid Action Committee leaders said, 'The foundation-laying has taken place at a cemetery and the mosque is safe. So there is no need for any martyrdom and it will have to be seen that this government is ousted, which had kept us in the dark and got the foundation laid.' According to them, with this act, the government had acted illegally, immorally and it was a contempt of the court. This had resulted in lack of trust in the government among the secular people. The Samiti stated that plot number 586, where the foundation had been laid was disputed and that the land belonged to the cemetery. Government had lied to the entire nation and got the foundation laid under tight security in a manner that seemed like some government programme. The Samiti asked the government to clear its stand. Babri Action Committee appealed to the people to teach a lesson to Congress so that no other government in future would dare play with the communal forces.

But all this made no impression on Rajiv Gandhi. He wanted to take the credit for laying the foundation. In an election campaign at Nagpur, he said that the credit for a peaceful foundation-laying goes to his party. He said that the steps taken by his party and the government, after the court verdict, helped remove tensions in Ayodhya.

The condition of the permission for the foundation laying was that it would be symbolic and no permanent structure would be erected. This was to be till the time both communities reached an agreement. Under pressure from the people, VHP announced that it will resume construction right after the foundation was laid. This plan included expansion of the temple towards the disputed structure. So the state government stopped construction on 11 November. VHP postponed construction announcing that the new dates for construction will be announced on 27-28 January at a religious congregation in Allahabad. Till then priests and saints will try to depose the government in forthcoming elections, the government that had stopped the temple construction. It meant that both parties were now engaged in getting the government removed. Rajiv Gandhi didn't gain anything out of it.

Babri Action Committee announced that a lesson needs to be taught to the present government for laying the foundation and VHP announced that the Congress government should be removed for stopping the temple construction. Congress was ousted in the elections held after 20 days although it was still the single largest party in Lok Sabha. V.P. Singh joined hands with both—BJP and Left parties and formed his (Janata Dal) government at the centre. Rajiv Gandhi's inexperience had angered both the parties, and V.P. Singh's jugglery of the support he took of those who opposed and those who supported the temple construction helped form his government. The Hindu card played by Rajiv Gandhi didn't work. Muslims went away but the Hindus didn't come to his fold. All his efforts—getting the foundation laid, holding the first gathering at Ayodhya, seeking blessings of Devraha Baba to create a Hindu wave—came to nought.

Foundation laying in Ayodhya resulted in a change of throne at Delhi. It changed the politics of the country. It was the first time that a complete shake-up in politics of the country was witnessed. By aligning with the foundation-laying, BJP had jumped to 85 seats from being a 2-seat party. V.P. Singh, aided with his anti-corruption image and opposing the foundation-laying at Ayodhya, had become the Prime Minister. Janata Dal got 143 seats under his leadership. Rajiv Gandhi's Congress that had created history by winning 415 seats in the previous elections had shrunk to merely 143 seats. Rajiv Gandhi was watching the entire game of foundation-laying from the pavilion, but BJP took all the credit for it. Hindus didn't come with the Congress. Muslims didn't stay with them. But Congress failed to learn any lesson from it.

After Rajiv Gandhi, Narasimha Rao also tried to deal with the Ayodhya issue in a similar fashion, with the help of the Hindutva factor. But whoever tried to take refuge in the blizzard of Ayodhya got buried. He, who was vocal, shined. Even though the Ram temple could not be constructed over the foundation that was laid, it helped erect a magnificent palace of Hindutva politics.

Chapter 5

LIBERATION OF RAM LALLA

Ayodhya's aggression was resting behind a locked door. The lock opened and fire broke out. This fire first started burning Ayodhya and later spread through the entire country like a forest fire. This fire left behind it a burning question. Who was behind the unlocking of the Ram Janmabhoomi, Congress or BJP? Was it Rajiv Gandhi or VHP? This question is still burning. How did the lock open? Who were the people behind it? And who are the people who have not come out into the open yet? Did the government at the time make a bigger mistake in trying to take people's minds off the other mistake they had made? What happened that day? This is a mystery till date. No one had any clue about such a big decision being taken. If the lock had not been opened, the foundation would not have been laid at the disputed site. If the foundation had not been laid, there would have been no demolition.

This means that the roots to the demolition in Ayodhya lay in the lock being opened. After analyzing the gains and losses from it, opening of the lock of the temple gate was a strategic move by the prime minister at the time, Rajiv Gandhi. Don't be surprised. This is history's bitter truth!

Why and how did all of this happen? This also makes for an interesting story. This decision divided the country communally, once again, since partition. Religious hatred went deep inside us. We witnessed this double-faced politics very closely. This incident took Indian politics and society to a point where Hindus and Muslims are still fighting. It was an immature decision by Rajiv Gandhi to appease majority after the Shah Bano case. It seemed as though it was the only way out for the government to shift people's focus from the anger that was there against his government for surrendering to the Muslims. It culminated with the demolition that took place in Ayodhya.

The votebank politics at the time, forced Rajiv Gandhi to get the temple gates unlocked. But he was unaware of its far reaching consequences. This failed strategy left Congress hanging in the middle of nowhere. Muslims became angry because the lock was opened and Hindus were on BJP's side to get the temple constructed. Congress got nothing. Congress is still dealing with this issue. Have you ever heard of a court order being implemented in mere forty minutes in Independent India? On 1 February 1986 Faizabad's district judge ordered the lock of the disputed structure in Ayodhya to be opened and the state government gets it implemented in merely forty minutes! The court's verdict came at 4:40 in the evening. At 5:20 p.m., the disputed structure was opened. Umesh Chandra Pandey, the lawyer who filed the petition for opening it also says, 'We did not have an idea that everything will happen so fast.'

Doordarshan's team was already present there to cover the whole event. At that time there was no other news channel in the country except for *Doordarshan*. The whole event was telecast on *Doordarshan* that evening and all of India watched it. At that time, Faizabad did not have a *Doordarshan* centre. The camera team had gone from Lucknow. It takes three hours to get to Faizabad from Lucknow, which meant that the camera team was sent in advance. The script of this event was written in Delhi. Ayodhya only provided the characters. Such a big plan was being executed in Faizabad, but the UP government had no clue of it, except for Chief Minister Vir Bahadur Singh who had been told to keep in direct touch with only Arun Nehru regarding Ayodhya. After Vir Bahadur Singh resigned from the CM post, I had a long discussion with him over this. According to him, the whole situation was being managed by Arun Nehru after consulting Rajiv Gandhi. "Yes, I was definitely told that the government will not give an affidavit in court. But Faizabad's collector and police superintendent were to appear in court and say that the administration will have no objection if the lock is opened." Vir Bahadur Singh told me that Faizabad's commissioner was getting orders directly from Delhi and Delhi asked them to do whatever it takes to ensure that the application to open the lock is passed. Arun Nehru told Vir Bahadur Singh to get the court's decision implemented immediately. Vir Bahadur was so full of confidence at this because Rajiv Gandhi had given him direct orders, otherwise a decision being taken in merely two days on a matter that was pending for 37 long years, that too without hearing from related parties, was not possible.

Faizabad's district judge Krishna Mohan Pandey made the verbal testimonies of District Magistrate I.P. Pandey and SSP Karamveer Singh the basis of his decision to unlock, in which both had said together in one tone that neither does the administration object to opening the lock nor will it disturb the law and order. Indu Prakash Pandey later became Uttar Pradesh's additional chief secretary(economic affairs) and Karamveer Singh became the state's Director General of Police. Thus both had reached the top of their respective departments. In such adverse circumstances, this direction by the district administration could not have been without the will of the government. The important thing was that Umesh Chandra Pandey, on whose application the lock had been opened, wasn't even a litigant in the Babri case. And the person who was the actual litigant wasn't even heard by the judge.

Nobody knew on whose orders, when and why was Ram Janmabhoomi actually locked. Such an order is nowhere to be found. Locals say that the lock was put in 1971 and that nobody had put a lock in 1949. The legal aspect of the whole matter was that the place was under a 'receiver'. In 1949, the court had confiscated this property and made Faizabad's Priya Dutt Ram the receiver. Ram Lalla's food was prepared in the kitchen on the Ram platform. After this, the guard would unlock the disputed building. In 1971 receiver Priya Dutt Ram died. Then a dispute started between the new receiver and Nirmohi Akhada. Court appoints a receiver when there is a property dispute between two parties. The receiver looks after the property till the dispute is resolved. Police interfered in the dispute between the new receiver and Nirmohi Akhada. They locked the place and kept the key with themselves. The guard present at the location changed and the key was handed over to the new guard. There were two gates there. One was always open for prayers and to offer food to idols. This practice went on for a long time. Basically, this place was never ever locked up completely.

On 28 January 1986 Faizabad's magistrate, Hari Shankar Dubey dismissed the application by a lawyer called Umesh Chandra Pandey to open Ram Janmabhoomi's lock. After merely two days, Umesh Chandra Pandey filed another application in the ongoing case number 2/1949 in the court of Faizabad's district judge. The very next day the District Judge took the opinion of the District Magistrate and Police Chief into consideration. Instead of filing an affidavit in the matter, both these officers verbally said that nothing would go wrong by opening the lock. They also said that law and order would not be disturbed by doing so. This was actually a decision made by the centre being forced through the district administration. It was the will of the Central government that was being implemented by the state government and district administration. This statement made by both the officers helped the judge to take a decision.

Mushtaq Ahmed Siddiqui, the lawyer who represented Muslims' legal stand on Babri Masjid, requested the court to hear him out regarding this petition. The judge agreed. But the judge gave his verdict at 4:40 p.m. without hearing him. The decision said, 'the permission to appeal is granted. Defendants are ordered to unlock gate number 'O' and 'P' immediately. Defendants will not pose any problems for applicants and people of their community while they offer prayers and make visits.' This building had two gates. The district administration had named them O and P for their convenience. To understand these two gates, you can take a look at the map published in this book.

After this decision taken by the District Judge, the DM and SSP dropped the District Judge to his place. His security was heightened. Then within forty minutes, the lock was broken in the presence of the police and prayers and devotional songs began there. Let's take a look at the government's intention. If the court had given this decision, what was the duty of the administration? Could such a sensitive decision be left only to the court or law? Wasn't it the district administration's duty to take the state government into confidence? They did not do it because they were getting orders from both the governments. Now the question arises whether there was only merit behind this or something else? You will be shocked to know that there was emotion, faith and a monkey in the form of God behind it!

Faizabad's then district judge, Krishna Mohan Pandey revealed this while talking to us. Krishna Mohan Pandey writes in his autobiography published in 1991—'The day I was writing the order for opening the lock, a black monkey kept sitting on the roof of my court holding a flag post all day. The people who had come to the court to listen to the verdict kept giving him fruits and peanuts. But he did not eat anything. He kept sitting quietly. He left only after I gave my verdict. When the DM and SSP dropped me to my place after I gave the verdict, I found the monkey sitting in the balcony of my house. I was surprised. I greeted him. He was a divine power.' Overwhelmed by his devotion, the judge made the decision of having the lock opened. Applicant Umesh Chandra Pandey tells us that he could not sleep that night because of excitement. They spent the whole night singing devotional songs at the Janmabhoomi and went home only next morning.

Judge Krishna Mohan Pandey was a religious man. He lived in Lucknow's New Hyderabad colony after retirement. I often met him in the evenings while taking a walk near the Gomti dam. He talked a lot about religion and spirituality. He told me about the theory of the monkey and divine inspiration behind his decision in detail. He also mentioned that the thought of respect for the divine inspiration gave him a lot of inner satisfaction. Born on 28 March 1932, Krishna Mohan Pandey started his career as an additional judge in March 1960. He had graduated from the Kashi Hindu University in law. He was also a 1959 PCS (judicial) topper. After serving in multiple district courts at different positions; he became Faizabad's District Judge on 17 August 1985. But after he gave this decision, he was made the chairman of a somewhat less important department, the State Transport Appeal Authority. When K.M. Pandey was being considered for the position of a HC judge, the V.P. Singh government blocked it. Unfavourable comments were written in his file. Mulayam Singh Yadav also opposed him. After this, Chandra Shekhar became the PM and Dr Subramanian Swamy became the law minister in his government. The Chandra Shekhar government reopened K.M. Pandey's file. According to Subramanian Swamy, former PM V.P. Singh and a poweful official of that time, Bhurelal, were against promoting K.M. Pandey to the post of a HC judge. Considering Muslims to be his crucial vote bank, even UP's CM at the time, Mulayam Singh Yadav was not in favour of him becoming a HC judge. Hence the state government wrote in K.M. Pandey's file that he had made the controversial decision of unlocking Babri mosque in 1986 and so he should not to be considered for the post. But Subramanian Swamy kept trying to convince Mulayam Singh and at last, he suceeded. Subramanian Swamy says that Mulayam Singh had two to three tasks stuck in Mr. Swamy's ministry, that he wanted to get done through the centre. Seeing Swamy so active on this front, Mulayam Singh started feeling that he will get K.M. Pandey the position of a HC judge at any cost. At last, on 24 January 1991 K.M. Pandey was made a judge at the Allahabad HC. But within a month, on 22 February 1991, he was transferred to the Madhya Pradesh HC. Subramanian Swamy says that he told K.M. Pandey that if he stayed in Allahabad, Azam Khan and Mulayam Singh's other aides would unnecessarily keep creating problems, and in such a case it was better for him to move to the Jabalpur HC. Later on 28 March 1994 Justice K.M. Pandey retired from Jabalpur HC.

You must all read K.M. Pandey's historic decision. So I am putting his verdict as it is here–

This is an appeal against the order dates 28.1.86 passed by Hari Shankar Dubey, Munsif, Sadar, Faizabad in regular suit No. 2/50.

The Brief facts of the case are that in suit 2a/5 the appellant filed an application (422/C) to the effect that the defendants 6 to 9 should be directed not to impose any restriction or hurdle in the darshan and *puja* etc. offered by the applicant and other members of the Hindu community in general of the idol of Bhagwan Shri Ram Chandraji and others in the premises in question by closing the entrance gate of the said place or by putting locks thereon. Defendants 6 to 9, who are State of U.P., Deputy Commissioner, Faizabad, S.P., Faizabad and City Magistrate, filed an objection alleging that they have no intent to interfere in the idols in question as directed by the Court's order on 3.3.51. They only resisted the petition on the ground that they have the power vested under them to adopt such measures as are necessary to maintain law and order and this right cannot be curbed in any manner. The learned Munsif did not give any relief to then petitioner on the application and even did not pass any order in this case because the record of the leading suit No.12 of 1961 were pending in the Hon'ble High Court and consequently he found himself unable to dispose of this application. The main ground is that any order passed in this case will be passed in the file of the leading suit and that since the records of the leading suits are not available, he did not pass any order. It amounted to a refusal of the prayer and consequently this appeal has been preferred. The appellant has only arrayed defendants 6 to 9 of suit no.2 of 1950 as party in the appeal. He says that he has grievances against other defendants and consequently he has not arrayed them as party.

The last order passed on the point of interim injunction in this suit is dated 3.3.51. By this order the Civil Judge has said that the injunction order dated 16.1.50 as modified on 19.1.50 shall remain in force. On 19.1.50 the learned Court passed an injunction order to the effect that the opposite parties are hereby restrained by means of a temporary injunction to refrain from removing the idol in question from the site in dispute and from interfering with puja etc. as at present carried on. This order passed by the learned trial court stands even today and the appeal against the injunction order issued by Trial court in suit No. 2 of 1950 stands confirmed by the Hon'ble High Court.

The only point of consideration in this appeal is as to whether the respondents should be directed to remove the lock which is said to be the main hurdle in offering prayer and in the free flow of pilgrims and devotees inside the premises.

I issued notices to the district Magistrate and the SSP Faizabad, in this case. Both of them have been examined by me in court. The District Magistrate has very clearly stated that the idol installed in the disputed premises is visible from outside. The outer gate has no doors. Inside the main gate there is an enclosure made of grills and two doors have been placed in the inner enclosure. They are P and O shown in the site plan paper No. 136/5 of suit No.2 of 1950. In both the gates the locks were placed and who passed orders for that. No records are available on this point as to who had taken a decision to put locks at the gates O and P. The priest is allowed to go inside through the gate O for performing puja and *bhog*. The lock of the gate P is not opened.

There are other idols inside the temple besides the idols as shown in the map. Most of these idols are visible from outside when the puja is performed there. Besides the priest other persons are allowed to enter the premises under the City Magistrate.

For the last 35 or 36 years no member of the other community has offered any *namaz* prayer. They are not allowed to enter this place. There are idols outside the line 'H.J.' and inside the outer wall offerings are made and puja is performed there. Since 1951 no riot or no law and order problem has arisen at this place. The gates O and P have been locked only to see that the idols are not removed from inside the premises and the locks are also kept to honour the Court's injunction order. The District magistrate further says that there are other ways to protect idols and maintain law and order besides closing the gates O and P. He clearly admits that if the locks at the gates O and P are opened even then there are other ways to maintain peace and to protect the idols kept inside the premises.

The SSP, Faizabad, Shri Param Veer Singh was also examined by me. He has said that police force is retained at the disputed premises. He keeps police in other temples of Ayodhya also for maintaining law and order, particularly on the occasion of festivals. He has stated that whether the locks of Gates O and P are kept close or not, the law and order situation can be kept under control with success. The security and the law and order of that place is not maintained on account of the locks of the gate O and P. The following statement of the District Magistrate is very relevant: '*O and P gate par tala band karne ke alava aur bhi tarike se moortiyon ki suraksha ki vyavastha ki jaa sakti hai aur shanti vyavastha kayam rakkhi ja sakti hai*'. Likewise the following statement of the SSP Faizabad clinches the whole matter; '*O ya P taley rahen ya na rahen main vahan ki Raksha vyavastha safalta purvak kar sakta hun. Vahan ki suraksha O ya P gate ka talon se hi nahi hai. Mujhe avashyakta parne par vahan suraksha kayam karne ka adhikaar rehna chahiye*'. Thus it is clear that it is not necessary to keep the locks for the gates O and P for the purposes of maintaining law and order or for the safety of idols. This appears to be an unnecessary irritant to the applicant and other members of the community. There does not appear any necessity to create an artificial barrier between the idols and the devotees. It appears that opposite parties have remained a prisoner of indecision for the last thirty-five years. Somebody in his wisdom thought it fit to put locks at the gates O and P at any point of time and nobody has cared since then to see as to whether there is any necessity to retain the locks or not.

After having heard the parties it is clear that the members of other community, named Muslims, are not going to be affected by any stretch of imagination if the locks of the gates O and P are opened and the idols inside the premises are allowed to be seen and worshipped by pilgrims and devotees. It is undisputed that the premises is presently in the Court's possession and for the last 35 years Hindus have an unrestricted right of worship as a result of the courts orders of 1950 and 1951 (19.1.50 and 3.3.51). If Hindus are offering prayers and worshipping the idols, though in a restricted way, for the last 35 years, the heavens are not going to fall if the locks of the gates O and P are removed. The District Magistrate has stated before me today that the members of the Muslim community are not allowed to offer any prayer at the disputed site. They are not allowed to go there. If this is the state of affairs, then there is no occasion for law and order problem arising as a result of the removal of locks. It is absolutely an affair inside the premises.

The present appeal is against an order on an application which purpots to be under Order 39 as well as under Section 115(s) C.P.C. There is no justification for retaining locks after the positive statements of the District Magistrate and the SSP Faizabad that the law and order situation can be very well kept under control by other means as well and for that it is necessary to keep the locks on these gates. Consequently there is force in the Appeal.

The appeal is allowed. The respondents are directed to open the locks of the gates O and P forthwith. They shall not impose any restriction or hurdle in the darshan and puja etc. of the applicant and other members of the community in general. However, the respondents are free to take independent decision to control any law and order problem according to the needs of the situation and to regulate the entry of the pilgrims. Cost of the appeal shall abide the results of the suits.

[From *Indian Bar Review*, Vol. XVIII(2), The Bar Council Of India Trust, 1991, pp. 245-48.]

On 30 September 2010 Allahabad HC gave its decision in the Ayodhya case. HC declared Faizabad District Judge K.M. Pandey's verdict on opening the lock, wrong. It also held this verdict responsible for the demolition of the disputed structure. Justice S.U. Khan who was part of the bench of three judges at the Allahabad HC mentioned that incident in his verdict and wrote:

'Everything before 31 January 1936 was exactly the same way as it was post 23 December 1949. Two or three saints would go there, offer prayers and give permission to the general public to pray from outside the grille beside the wall. On 23 December 1949 after establishment of the statue inside the mosque, Faizabad's then DM K.K.K. Nayar sent a report to the state government at 5p.m. and 7:20 p.m. on 25 December 1949 and on December 27 1949 at 9:30 AM. He wrote in his report that the saints and Hindu devotees there had agreed that till the time the civil court's verdict did not come in the case, only two three saints would go inside, do the prayers and perform daily rituals. All other devotees would pay a visit from outside only. HC said in its verdict that a person named Umesh Chandra Pandey, who was neither a party in the Ayodhya case nor a party's lawyer, filed a petition on 25 January 1986. He asked for permission for the devotees to go inside and offer prayers and demanded that the lock on the grille next to the wall be opened. When, in this matter, HC had called for all related files in the main case i.e., lawsuit number 4, it wasn't even reasonable for the district judge to hear this case.'

This was 25 January 1986 when Umesh Chandra Pandey had filed a petition in the munsif court. This was the same court where the title case related to the Ayodhya matter was being heard. The munsif judge said in his order on 28 January 1986 that because the related files were in the HC, Umesh Chandra Pandey's petition will be kept under consideration till the next hearing. The munsif court had not given its final verdict. It had only given a date for the next hearing. But Umesh Chandra Pandey challenged this order by the munsif magistrate on 31 January 1986 in the district court.

State government, deputy commissioner, city magistrate and SP, Faizabad were only made party in the petition to the district judge. These people were party numbers 6, 7, 8 and 9 in the main case. This was because in Ayodhya's main case, all the names from party numbers 1 to 5 were dead and there was no one else to represent them. Mohammed Hashim, who was related to this case, also knew about the petition by Umesh Chandra Pandey. Mohammed Hashim appealed to become a party in Umesh Chandra Pandey's petition, which was opposed by Umesh Chandra Pandey. District Judge K.M. Pandey dismissed Mohammed Hashim's appeal that very day on 1 February 1986 and appoved Umesh Chandra Pandey's petition.

The High Court wrote in its verdict that after the verdict of allowing opening of the lock by Faizabad's district judge, this conflict had become even bigger and had spread at an international level. Before this, people outside Ayodhya and Faizabad did not know much about these cases. According to the High Court, the demolition on 6 December 1992 was a result of the happenings after the verdict of 1 February 1986. The High Court also accepted that K.M. Pandey's verdict had many faults like:

1. When the munsif court had not given any verdict on 28 January 1986 and had only given a future date of hearing, there was nothing to file a petition against, to the district judge.
2. The Ayodhya case's files were in the High Court. In such a case, whether it's a munsif court or a district judge, they cannot give a verdict.
3. The appeal asking to make Mohammed Hashim party in the case was dismissed wrongly, after which there was no one left to oppose Umesh Chandra Pandey's petition. The DM and SP in a way only supported Pandey's petition.
4. Despite Mohammed Hashim being related to the Ayodhya case, his appeal to become party in the case was dismissed on the basis of being unnecessary. On the other hand, Umesh Chandra Pandey had nothing to do with the case. Despite this, his petition was approved.
5. The District Judge did not give any reason as to why the decision

on Umesh Chandra Pandey's petition was taken in such a hurry. An appeal was filed on 31 January 1986 and the verdict was given the very next day.
6. It seemed as if justice was being done but the district judge ignored the other principles.
7. This verdict shook the confidence and faith of the people related to the case and this was the most unfortunate aspect of the case. The impact of the verdict could not be undone.

The news of unlocking of the mosque spread like fire in Ayodhya. Prime Minister Rajiv Gandhi got this news on his Maldives tour. He was preparing his speech before dinner. His associate Mani Shankar Aiyar told us that he broke the news of opening of the lock to the PM.

His face was blank. It seemed he had an idea about it already. But he did not react at all. The Muslim community was feeling cheated with this decision. Communal tensions started rising in the entire state. Chief minister Vir Bahadur Singh remained unnerved. It seemed he knew nothing. But UP's governor, Mohammed Usman Arif was losing his temper. When Vir Bahadur Singh quit as the CM of UP and became Minister of Communications in the Rajiv Gandhi government, he would narrate this incident with a smile. He said, 'I also did not have knowledge of the whole matter. I only knew that Arun Nehru is managing it. The then governor Mohammed Usman Arif was only creating problems for me.'

A number of Muslim organizations were constantly putting a lot of pressure on Governor Mohammed Usman Arif to do something. They had all their hopes pinned on him now. Vir Bahadur Singh told me, 'The governor was putting pressure on me to issue a prohibitory order and inform the court that enforcing its order was not possible. This would provoke violence. When I did not say anything clearly, he was adamant on going to Ayodhya. I was continuously avoding him. I was getting calls from him at my office in every little while. Later, I stopped taking his calls. The issue in front of me was that I didn't know what to tell him. What was I doing and what had I done so far? Till the time it was decided in Delhi what stand to take, I didn't know what to say to him. So I was avoiding facing him and I just kept telling him that I was looking into the matter and would give him a detailed report. After some time I would also tell him about Delhi's stand.'

Vir Bahadur tells us that he avoided him till that evening. In the evening, the Governor sent a message that if the CM was not coming to Raj Bhavan then he himself would come to the CM office. Vir Bahadur Singh requested the Governor over many phone calls that he must stick to the protocol and not jeopardize his position. He told him that he would come and meet him. 'I knew that the governor wanted to go to Faizabad to appease the Muslim community.' His going there would create huge problems. The matter would flare up because by then, protests by Muslim leaders and lawyers in Faizabad had begun. Vir Bahadur Singh says that he somehow convinced the governor to cancel his trip to Faizabad. But seeing his impatience, Vir Bahadur became careful. He gave instructions to his secretary to say that the jet is under maintenance if Raj Bhavan asked for a government jet. Vir Bahadur Singh was a clever politician. He was being careful because he understood what High Command wanted. Vir Bahadur knew that this was the Prime Minister's new tactic to handle Hindu fundamentalists.

Rajiv Gandhi was under immense pressure because of the tense situation in the country. Communal tensions were high. The Hindu Muslim divide was increasing with each day. An incident at Meenakshipuram, two thousand kilometres away from Ayodhya, added fuel to the whole matter. The Hindu community became agitated. This tension started in Tamil Nadu's Meenakshipuram in 1981 in a case of religion change. Four hundred had families collectively converted to Islam. Most of these were backward castes of Hindus. Hindu leaders saw this as a threat to their religion and they reacted. On Prime Minister Indira Gandhi's initiative, an all party delegation submitted an inquiry report of the incident. Later, there was a debate in the parliament over this. RSS conducted a national meet in Bangalore and discussed how to get unity among Hindus. In this very meeting, the then province publicist Ashok Singhal gave a lively speech and presented a plan on finding solutions. This was also a reason why Balasaheb Deoras freed him from Sangh work and chose him for Jagran. 'Virat Hindu Samaj' was created in Delhi with the efforts made by Ashok Singhal. Dr Karan Singh was made the president. This platform organized a 'Sarvpanth Hindu Sammelan' or all rights Hindu gathering at the Ramleela ground which was successful. But this caused communal disharmony to an extent that there were fights and tensions throughout the country even on trivial matters. In UP's Moradabad, there were riots after Eid's namaz. At that time, Congress used to put camps at the namaz spot to look after Muslims. In Moradabad, Congress's Dau Dayal Khanna was arranging this camp in Moradabad. Dau Dayal Khanna had been a minister in the UP government. Then there was chaos and disorder at the namaz area because of a rumor of a pig in the area. Rowdy elements from the Muslim community attacked Khanna and the other Congress members. Dau Dayal Khanna and Moradabad Congress president went to Prime Minister Indira Gandhi to tell her about the Moradabad incident. At that time Khanna wasn't at a level where Indira would give him an answer. Khanna returned hopeless and disappointed. But he was looking for an opportunity to avenge. Around the same time, Ashok Singhal became the Joint General Secretary of VHP. Virat Hindu Samaj remained active till the end of 1983. It is believed that they had the backing of Indira Gandhi. Dau Dayal Khanna and Shrish Chandra Dikshit were seen on the platforms of Hindu Jagran those days. Khanna was trying hard that RSS raises the question of Ayodhya. He was often heard talking about the same thing at every function with Professor Rajendra Singh. He was successful. Ashok Singhal was also of the same opinion. The first step was taken in this direction with the organizing of dharmsansad. In the name of dharmsansad, about 500 saints gathered in New Delhi's Vigyan Bhawan to discuss a way forward in light of the Meenakshipuram event and the situation in the country at large. This was April 1984. VHP, founded in 1964, was behind this first dharmsansad. It was formed by RSS chief Madhav Sadashiv Golwalkar (Guru ji), Swami Chinmaynand (Chinmay Mission), Gujarati writer Keshavram Kashiram Shastri, Bhartiya Vidya Bhawan founder and writer Kanahiya Lal Manilal Munshi and journalist S.S. Apte, together, in Mumbai in 1964 on the day of Janmashtmi. More than 70 representatives came to attend the meet from around the world. These included Master Tara Singh, Gyani Bhupendra

Singh (Shiromani Akali Dal), Sant Tukoji Maharaj, Swami Shankaranand Saraswati, Sushil Muni (Jain saint), V.G. Deshpande (General Secretary, Hindu Mahasabha). The aim of the new organization was Hindu unity and its social spiritual awakening.

The people behind this dharmsansad were VHP Joint General Secretary Ashok Singhal and the person who always stayed behind curtains, Moropant Pingle. Ashok Singhal was an RSS propagandist who was given the resposnsibility of VHP. Singhal graduated in metallurgical engineering from Banaras Hindu University in 1950. The slogan, 'Chandan hai is desh ki maati, tapobhoomi har gram hai, har bala devi ki Pratima, bachcha bachcha Ram hai', was sung in this very dharmsansad, which means that every daughter of the country is personification of a goddess and every son of the land is personification of Ram. This song was sung by Ashok Singhal himself. Few people would know that he sang well. Dr Karan Singh was also among the speakers at this dharmsansad. Karan Singh was Kashmir's former Maharaja's son and had served as a cabinet minister in Indira Gandhi's cabinet. That time he was an MP. Karan Singh pressed upon connecting personal life and politics with the principles of Hindu religion in his speech. He also expressed regret over Hindu religious places in the country being ignored. He said that they cannot even light a lamp at Ram Janmabhoomi. He said that this was shameful. At that time people took Karan Singh's voice at the dharmsansad as Congress's soft stand on Hindutva. Later this very stand got the lock opened at Ayodhya.

A proposal was passed in this very dharmsansad that three most holy places of Hindus be returned to the Hindu society. Among these three places were Ayodhya's Ram Janmabhoomi, Mathura's Krishna Janmabhoomi and Kashi Vishwanath temple. At that time there was no proposal for these religious places with VHP. It was for the first time that freedom of these temples was demanded by a platform and Ayodhya was on top of the dharmsansad's priority list. The dharmsansad formed 'Ram Janmabhoomi Mukti Yagya Samiti' for this. It was decided that the first meet of the 'Yagya committee' will take place on 18 July 1984 in Ayodhya. Gorakhpeeth's chief mahant Avaidyanath was selected as the committee's president with common consent on the meet on 18

July. Gorakhpeeth has been majorly ruled by the Nagpanthi Kanfata community. It was Mahant Avaidyanath's guru, Mahant Digvijay Nath, who was making arrangements for placing the statues on the night of 23 December and 24 December 1949. (At present, the chief of this panth is UP's CM Yogi Adityanath). Former minister of the Congress party, Dau Dayal Khanna, was made the committee's general secretary who was here to take revenge for his insult from Indira Gandhi. Ayodhya's Maniram Das Chhawani's mahant, Nritya Gopal Das, and Digamber Akhada's mahant, Ramchandra Paramhans, were made the vice president. VHP's Onkar Bhave and Mahesh Narayan Singh became the committee's secretary. Along with this, 35 religious gurus were made part of a board of guardians. To promote the whole idea of freeing Ram Janmabhoomi, a chariot was started from Bihar's Sitamadhi in September 1984. This is the same district which Hindus believe to be Sita's birthplace. So the journey of this chariot from one birthplace to the other heated up the situation even more. It was decided that on 7 October, saints from all over the country will gather on the banks of River Saryu in Ayodhya, will pledge to free Ram Janmabhoomi and march towards Lucknow. The chariot or the rally reached Lucknow on 14 October 1984. This changed into a big gathering. Around this time, Mukti Yagya committee's vice president Paramhans Ramchandra announced that he will immolate himself if Ram Janmabhoomi's lock was not opened by 1986 Ramnavmi. Paramhans was fighting this case since 1950. He was the chief of Ayodhya's Digamber Akhada. This akhada belonged to the Ramanand sect. Paramhans was stubborn by nature and he could even give up his life for the Ram temple. On 7 October 1984, around fifty thousand people pledged to get Ram Janmabhoomi freed. From here started the 'Ram Janki Rath Yatra' that went around the whole country. In this yatra, Ram-Sita were placed in an iron box. There were about one lakh people at the Lucknow gathering. This was the biggest rally in Lucknow till then. After the day long gathering, Mukti Yagya committee's president Avaidyanath met CM Narayan Dutt Tiwari. He gave him the letter requesting to hand over all three religious places to Hindus. To promote this demand and expand the movement in society, Sangh called for poori-sabzi from households belonging to all castes; specially Dalits. This poori sabzi became the meal of people attending the gathering. This strategy by VHP was to take this movement to Dalits and other smaller castes. These castes did not participate in any movement till now. Starting from Lucknow, the rath yatra had to reach Delhi on 31 October via Chitrakoot. Lakhs of people would welcome the yatra from the Red Fort. During this time people from small villages started becoming part of the movement and coming to see the rath or chariot. This movement had started growing bigger and was reaching far away areas as well. By then Ashok Singhal had become the new face of Hindutva.

A sad incident happened when this rath yatra was about to reach Delhi. Prime Minister Indira Gandhi was assassinated. She was shot dead by her own bodyguards. Ram-Janki chariot was stopped near Sahibabad. There were anti Sikh riots throughout the country. The army was sent to many cities. Indian politics took a sudden turn. Rajiv Gandhi became the prime minister after Indira Gandhi's death. Rajiv Gandhi, who had stayed away from politics, was a pilot with the Indian Airlines before this. He had married Sonia Maino from Italy. Till then, he had no idea about religion or politics. He entered politics after the death of his brother and became the Prime Minister after his mother's death although he was mainly interested in modernization of India through technological progress. Unaware of the Indian society norms and communities, very soon Rajiv Gandhi found himself in between the Hindu Muslim tensions. No matter what decisions he made, he would sink deeper in it. Then a historical decision came that shocked the nation. It changed the political scenario in the country. The society got divided into groups. The question was, 'will there be different law for Hindus and Muslims?'. A debate started on this. In 1985, SC ordered that alimony be given to a divorced Muslim woman Shah Bano. Muslim fundamentalists opposed SC's decision. Protests started in the name of Islam in the country. Pressure was put on Rajiv Gandhi to make a law to reverse the SC's decision. Rajiv Gandhi was not good at taking decisions. He was unaware of the country's issues. First he supported the court's decision and later backtracked under pressure from the fundamentalists. The Rajiv Gandhi government had to face a lot of embarrassment because of this.

In the name of appeasing Muslims, the country got divided in different communities. 'Ek desh-do kanoon' or 'one country-different laws' became the basis of Hindu Muslim tensions. Shah Bano was from Indore. She was a helpless mother of five children, who was thrown out of the house by her husband Mohammed Ahmad Khan. She had approached court to demand alimony for the sake of her five children. Indore's judicial magistrate fixed ₹25 per month as her monthly allowance. Shah Bano went to the High Court against this order. The High Court increased the allowance to ₹ 179.20 per month. Mohammed Ahmad Khan considered this decision against Shariyat. He went to the Supreme Court. As this was related to Personal Law Board, Muslim Personal Law Board became a party in the case. According to Shariyat a divorced woman is eligible for alimony only during iddat or the period a woman must observe after the death of her husband or after a divorce, during which she may not marry another man. Its purpose is to ensure that the male parent of any offspring produced after the cessation of a nikah is known. Usually this is a period of three months. After this, the responsibility of the husband is over.

Chief Justice Yashwant Vishnu Chandrachud, Rangnath Mishra. O. Chinappa Reddy and E.S. Venkatchalayya's bench in SC declared the allowance as Shah Bano's right. SC said that any provision against helplessness is the same for all Indians. Fundamentalists opposed this decision. They protested in the name of religion proclaiming Islam to be in danger. They screamed that this was interfering with their religion. A minister in the Rajiv Gandhi government, Arif Mohammed Khan made a historical 70 minutes long speech in the parliament in favour of the decision. Khan says that he had done this on the instructions of the prime minister. He says that when he made the speech in favour of the decision in the Lok Sabha, Rajiv Gandhi wrote a letter to him, congratulating him for the great speech. Khan tells that, that day whatever he had said was the voice of his inner conscience and that he wanted to pull the society out of its bad state. But later Rajiv Gandhi gave into the pressures of some Muslims. Then Rajiv Gandhi asked Arif Mohammed Khan, 'Are you a social worker? The Muslims want to live in the same state. So let them. They vote for us. You have to keep this in mind.' To appease the Muslims, Rajiv Gandhi changed the law for Muslim women. He had great support in the parliament. He had 416 MPs in the Lok Sabha. And so he passed a new law in the parliament and reversed the SC's order. Now there were two different laws for women's rights in the country on the basis of religion. There was a sharp reaction to this from the Hindu society. The government was questioned and Rajiv Gandhi had no answers.

This issue was used by BJP through RSS and VHP. In the Shah Bano case, government had announced an amendment in the constitution by making a separate law for Muslim women. Now it was time to appease the Hindus. Hopeless, Rajiv Gandhi saw a new ray of hope in Ayodhya. Ayodhya was a sensitive case. Every activity in the case was reported by the Intelligence Bureau. Every year the petition to unlock the Janmabhoomi was filed in the Faizabad court. A copy of the same always came to Delhi through the Intelligence Bureau. The minister for internal security in the Rajiv Gandhi government was Arun Nehru. He was also Rajiv's maternal cousin. He knew this matter. He presented an idea to Rajiv Gandhi and Rajiv Gandhi liked the idea. (On the basis of his conversation with Arun Nehru) He believed that this would shift the focus of Hindus from the Shah Bano case to Ayodhya.

Prime Minister Rajiv Gandhi told Maulana Ali Miyan Nadvi, the then president of Muslim Personal Law Board, that they would eventually amend Muslim women law but would have to be sensitive to the sentiments of the other side. 'It's a long-standing demand of Hindus that Ram's birthplace should be unlocked. I will have to consider their demand as well.' This meant that the Prime Minister was making a quiet package-deal with the Personal Law Board. Maulana didn't say anything and remained quiet. Rajiv Gandhi considered his silence as their consent. Later Board members asked Maulana Nadvi, when news about this was published in an Urdu newspaper. Maulana said that Rajiv Gandhi had not asked him but he had heard of it. This mystery was unfolded by the secretary of the board, Maulana Abdul Karim Parikh, in an Urdu weekly. The then cabinet colleague Arif Mohammed Khan also agrees to this event. He says, 'A settlement was made between the Muslim leadership at that time and Rajiv Gandhi, under which a law was to be enacted in the Shah Bano case for Muslims and unlocking in Ayodhya for the Hindus.' Arif Mohammed Khan says that that was the reason Ali Miyan was never against the temple movement. On the contrary he was critical of the movement by the Babri Action Committee. To wash off the loss by Shah Bano case and to thwart BJPs plans, Congress was now engaged in the unlocking at Ayodhya. Rajiv Gandhi was made to understand that if doors of the Ram Janmabhoomi temple are opened, then, negative Hindu sentiments due to Shah Bano issue will become favourable again. It was a take off for the plan. On the other hand, countrywide marches called Ram rath yatras had been started by VHP. Demand for opening doors of the birthplace had become stronger. These rath yatras were attracting crowds all over the country.

Seven chariots called, Ram-Janaki-Rath were dispatched in different directions on 23 October 1985. Gathering of large crowds in these marches made the government cautious. Second dharmsansad was organized on 31 October 1985. There it was decided that if the locks of Ram Lalla temple were not opened by 8 March 1986 then from 9 March 1986 onwards the 'opening of lock' movement will turn into 'breaking of lock'. All the Ram-Janki-Rath were to return to Ayodhya by 8 March 1986 so that a firm decision about unlocking could be taken by 9 March 1986.

The communal atmosphere was deteriorating in the country, due to the announcement of overturning the Supreme Court verdict on Shah Bano issue. The majority was extremely agitated. Even Congress party MPs were not in favor of this. Arif Mohammed Khan's 'stand' even forced the progressive Muslims to think. But after promising the Muslim Personal Law Board, Rajiv Gandhi had reached a point where it was difficult for him to turn back. The only way now was to quickly do something for the Hindus so that the Shah Bano issue could be taken off the nation's mind.

This was the last week of November 1985. Rajiv Gandhi called for a meeting with Ali Miyan Nadvi, Minnatul Rehmani (Secretary of Board), Jia-ur-Rehman Ansari (Central Minister) and some other people. This was to discuss the bill that was to overturn the decision of the Supreme Court. Other people present in the meeting were law minister Ashok

Singh, another minister Arun Nehru and Arun Singh.

The meeting went on for more than three hours. Every section of the bill was discussed for half an hour each. When the board gave its consent on the matter of the bill then the Prime Minister also gave his approval. There was an agreement on the bill. The meeting was over. Rajiv Gandhi assured everyone that the bill would be presented on the first day of the budget session.

As soon as the meeting was over, Makhanlal Fotedar informed Arif Mohammed Khan. He said, 'You should reach the Rajaji Marg residence of law minister Ashok Sen. Content of the bill has been finalized. You should also have a look at it and make suggestions if you have.' Arif tells that he immediately reached Ashok Sen's house. He was shocked after reading the bill. Section three of the bill was negating all demands made by the Muslim Personal Law Board. Section three stated that 'a "fair" and appropriate amount of compensation shall only be decided within the period of "Iddat"'. Ashok Sen told Arif Mohammed Khan to not reveal this point anywhere outside. Now that all parties had agreed, it may brew a fresh controversy. Perhaps Muslim leaders had made this mistake because of their limited knowledge of the English language.

Everything had been decided. The bill was to be presented. To indicate what was to follow, Zia-Ur-Rehman Ansari called a Momin Conference at Siri Fort Auditorium of Delhi. Zia-Ur-Rehman came from Unnav region of UP and in the cabinet his position was opposite to Arif Mohammed Khan. In this very Momin Conference Rajiv Gandhi announced a Parliament session had been called from 5 February 1986, proclaiming that 'We will overturn Supreme Court verdict on the very first day of the parliament session'. The very next day, his speech received sharp reactions from across the country. On 18 January IB and RAW chiefs paid a visit to Rajiv Gandhi. Both informed him that the situation was not normal in the country. Tension was rising, and riots could happen. If the situation remained the same, then things could get out of control.

At that point in time Arun Nehru and Arun Singh were the closest to Rajiv Gandhi. Rajiv Gandhi called both of them the next day, IB and RAW chiefs were called back again in front of them. Arun Nehru had just become State Home Minister. He held charge for internal security. IB used to report to him. Before him, Arif Mohammed Khan was the State Home Minister. Then internal security was called, Police division. In front of both the ministers, the chiefs of secret services again mentioned the precarious situation prevailing in the country. Arun Nehru asked, what the way out was. The officers replied that they needed to somehow stop Hindu reaction against the bill.

After both top officers left, Arun Nehru said, 'To have the door opened at Ram Janmabhoomi, VHP is organizing Rath-Yatras across the country. It has announced that if the door is not opened at a specific date the "unlocking movement" will turn into "lock-breaking" movement.'

Rajiv Gandhi asked in dismay, 'So can it be unlocked?'

Arun Nehru said, 'I don't see any issue in it because there is no link between the core case and the lock. It has been placed for administrative purposes. The District Magistrate said that for administrative reasons there should be a lock, so it was put there. If the Magistrate says that lock is not needed, then it will be opened.'

Arun Nehru says that Rajiv Gandhi at once said, 'talk to Vir Bahadur. Tell him to get it done.' Vir Bahadur Singh was the Chief Minister of Uttar Pradesh. Arun Nehru immediately spoke to Vir Bahadur Singh. He told him how and what was to be done. But didn't say when it was to be done. Arun Nehru wanted that Rajiv Gandhi should himself tell Vir Bahadur Singh. In a little while, Arun Nehru called up Vir Bahadur Singh and handed the phone to Rajiv Gandhi. Rajiv Gandhi spoke in front of everyone. Vir Bahadur immediately took the responsibility for the task. Vir Bahadur Singh sent a message to VHP through Mahant Avaidyanath that they should admit a petition in the court to have the lock removed at the Ram Janmabhoomi. Being from Gorakhpur, Vir Bahadur Singh was close to Mahant Avaidyanath.

Arif Mohammed Khan says that it was not a difficult thing from an administrative point of view. Every year such petitions were filed in Faizabad. The judge issued a notice to the district administration. The district administration used to give an affidavit that doing so would not be feasible, it could lead to riots. Then the petition got cancelled. When Vir Bahadur Singh didn't receive a positive response from VHP, he had the petition filed through a lawyer with Congress background, his name was Umesh Chand Pandey. The very next day the judge issued a notice and DM/ SSP both appeared in the court. Both said that they didn't have any objection. If the door was opened, they would handle it. They would not allow a law and order problem to arise. When the judge asked if both had asked the state government of their 'stand', then both said, 'This does not concern the court. We are at the spot. This is within our jurisdiction. We can decide.' The court officer informed that the Honourable Judge needed some more time. But I told him that a *Doordarshan* team had come from Lucknow. This convinced the Honourable Judge that the state government was fully aware of this issue. He had no basis to dismiss the petition. The Judge ordered. The door was immediately unlocked.

The lock was opened on 1 February 1986. Muslims reacted sharply The Muslim women bill was to come to Parliament on 5 February. Arif Mohammed Khan says, 'I met the Prime Minister on 3 February. Expressed my concern. I said it's a very sensitive matter. This can lead to a big crisis. Muslim Women bill will get sidelined. Muslims will come out on the streets.' The reply of the Prime Minister to Arif Mohammed Khan was shocking. Prime Minister said, 'I had informed Muslim leaders about opening of the lock. They will not oppose.' Arif was in disbelief. Who had Rajiv ji spoken to or made a deal with? No one knew anything. But Rajiv Gandhi was convinced. On that very day a statement by the Muslim Personal Law board president, Ali Miyan, got published in a Lucknow publication, *Kaumi Awaz*. In this statement he had asked Muslims not to pay too much importance to the opening of the lock. He said that there were many other mosques that were occupied by the adversaries. So this was not an important matter. A matter that had Babri Masjid Rabta committee and Babri Masjid Action committee constituted in Delhi and Lucknow, Ali Miyan taking it so lightly, was evidence enough that some agreement had been reached between him and Rajiv Gandhi.

Arif Mohammed Khan affirms this. He says that was why Muslim Personal Law board didn't show any opposition during the time of Rajiv Gandhi. However, the Muslim Personal Law board did become aggressive after Rajiv Gandhi's demise because now the man who had made the promise was no more. It can be said that Ali Miyan not only criticized the conduct of Babri Action Committee on the movement, but also wrote in his autobiography unsparingly that actions of these people greatly harmed Muslims. On page 130 of the fourth chapter of his autobiography Ali Miyan writes, 'I have witnessed as many as twenty thinkers that the way Babri mosque movement was run, invoked Hindu revivalism in the hearts of majority. A task at which even the tallest Hindu religious authorities and evangelist had failed. From Islamic perspective this was not only naivety and ignorance but a mass suicide. It's so, if your actions lead the neighbouring community undergo a historical and hostile religious revival which is against any mosque, Madarsa and Islamic lifestyle.' He further writes, 'Their ignorance and lack of understanding will not let this matter resolve.'

These words indicate that Ali Miyan was not in agreement with Babri Action Committee movement. He didn't want this movement to go on.

On the issue of unlocking, a Faizabad lawyer M.A. Siddiqui sought help of the High Court because the district judge had refused a review petition. Challenging the order of opening of the lock, Mohammed Hashim appealed with the Lucknow bench on 3 February 1986. A tailor by profession Mohammed Hashim Ansari was part of this conflict since 1949. He had a tailoring shop in Ayodhya. Hashim told the High Court that he had read namaz for the last time in 1935. Hashim is no more now but he was a kind man. He was quite popular among the saint community.

There was no animosity between Hashim who had been fighting the court case against Ram Janmabhoomi for a long time and the sadhus-saints of Faizabad. He truly represented the Ganga-Jamuna culture. On the court dates of Ram Janmabhoomi-Babri mosque case, he and Paramhans Ramchandra Das often shared an 'Ekka' to go to Faizabad District Court. On Hashim's petition, High Court ordered to maintain status quo. Meaning the doors remained unlocked. Six days after the opening of the lock, on 6 February 1986, Babri Action Committee came into existence. At a gathering in Lucknow, this action committee was formed under the leadership of Maulana Muzaffar Hussain Kichauchvi. Mohammed Azam Khan of Rampur and Zafaryab Jilani of Lucknow became its conveners. Known for his controversial statements, Azam Khan later became minister in the Samajwadi Party government.

The All India Muslim Majhlis-E-Mushawarat took up this issue at the national level. A day of condolence was observed across the country on 14 February 1986 against the opening of the lock. Rajiv Gandhi met the leader of Majhlis-E-Mushawarat. A central action committee was formed under an ex-IFS officer Syed Shahabuddin. Under the leadership of Syed Shahabuddin all the Muslim MPs registered their protest to Rajiv Gandhi. After the opening of lock all 41 Muslim MPs wrote a letter to Prime Minister Rajiv Gandhi on 3 March 1986. They demanded immediate intervention of the Prime Minister. It stated that whatever happened in Ayodhya should be cancelled and that the Babri mosque should be handed over to the Muslim community. The letter said—

'We Muslim MPs request for taking adequate measures to fulfil our following demands–

- Your immediate intervention and quick action to hand over Babri mosque to the Muslim community.
- A writ petition should be placed at High Court by the UP Government against the order of Faizabad District judge's order passed on 1 February 1986.
- The district judge has said in his order passed on 1 February 1986 that officials are free to take measures to maintain law and order, so, status quo should be maintained on the issue of Babri mosque as it existed on 31 January 1986.
- All the cases related to this matter should be resolved within six months.
- A team consisting of MPs of all political party representatives should be sent to Babri mosque and facility to take photos and mapping should be provided to the same team.
- State Mediums should be instructed to not promote the said premises as Ram Janmabhoomi.'

On 3 March 1986, the MPs who signed this letter were—Lok Sabha MP Kazi Jalil Abbasi, Akbar Jahan Begum, Sarfaraz Ahmed, Abida Ahmed, Akhtar Hassan, Abdul Hannan Ansari, Ibrahim Suleman Sait,

Gulam Mehmood Banatwala, Bashir T Hussain Dalwai, Abdul Rashid Kabuli, Aslam Sher Khan, Mohammed Ayub Khan, Mehfooz Ali Khan, Zulfikar Ali Khan, Syed Shahabuddin, Sultan Salaudding Owaisi, Fakir Mohammed ESM, Ahmed Patel, Aziz Quraishi, Salahuddin, PM Syed, Hafiz Mohammed Siddique, Saifuddin Soz, Tariq Anwar, Gulam Yajdani, Jain-Ul-Bashar and Rajya Sabha MP Syed Hashim Raza Abidi, Hamanullah Ansari, Asrar-Ul-Haq, FM Khan, Mohammed Hashim Kidwai, Bibi Abdullah Koya, Asad Madni, Gulam Rasool Matt, Mirza Irshad Beg, Rafiq Alam, Gulam Mohiuddin Shal, Shamim Ahmed Siddique and Rao Wali Ullah.

Protests erupted thought the country. Witnessing the flare-up, VHP again jumped into the battle. On 19, 20 and 21 April 'Ram Janmabhoomi Mahotsav' was organized. It was Ram Navmi on 21 April. Lakhs of people congregated there without making any call for the gathering. Babri Action Committee also organized Muslim Conference on 20 April in Faizabad. Fears of a clash arose. Seeing increasing tension, government banned the Muslim Rally. A procession marched from Taat Shah Mosque in Faizabad. Police used force to stop the rally. On the other hand, six Ram-Janaki raths were doing rounds in different parts of the country. This was also fuelling communal tension at various places. Government banned these raths on 11 June 1986. VHP postponed rath-yatras after the ban. This averted direct conflict, but the power struggle continued from both sides.

Witnessing the worsening atmosphere, government used its huge majority and introduced the Muslim Women bill. After passing it in Parliament in May 1986, the Supreme Court order was overturned. This made the hardliners happy, but they were still annoyed on the issue of Babri mosque. On 23 and 24 December, Shahabuddin merged all the committees active on the Babri mosque issue and made a unified 'Babri Masjid Coordination Committee'. Shahabuddin was its convener. This committee announced the boycott of 1987 Republic Day. This act was denounced throughout the country. Even those leaders, who were Babri supporters, criticized it. Upon seeing the protest from all quarters, coordination committee backtracked on its 'boycott' on 24 January 1987, but it announced Bharat Band on 1 February 1987, a big rally on Boat-Club on 30 March 1987 and announced a march to Ayodhya.

During this time two major developments happened across the country. First, Congress became nervous because of the nationwide Muslim protests and started searching for a moderate route on the Ayodhya issue. Prime Minister Rajiv Gandhi constituted a 'group of ministers' in his cabinet to find solution to the Ayodhya issue. PV Narasimha Rao was made its president. Although it's another matter that the very same Narasimha Rao brought this very matter to a logical conclusion on 6 December. Anyhow, there was some movement in the Rajiv Gandhi government regarding Ayodhya. On 8 May 1987, Home Minister Buta Singh asked the UP Chief Minister that he should send a timebound and structured plan to the Central government. The Central government was now engaged in finding a solution to this issue. On the other hand, opening of the lock had been a setback to the VHP, because the Ram Janmabhoomi movement appeared to be slipping from their hands. To regain control of the leadership, VHP hardened its stance.

Now they made a fresh demand of temple construction at the disputed site in the month of June. Congress's efforts to separate VHP from this movement gained momentum. Chief Minister Vir Bahadur Singh was put to this task, so that temple construction could be done through the government appointed trustees. A plan was given to Rajiv Gandhi in which the three domes of the mosque were to remain in their place and the temple was to be on the pillars at the same spot. Three domes would have remained underneath. Rajiv Gandhi tasked Buta Singh, who was Home Minister at the time to explore possibilities of the temple.

But Rajiv Gandhi remained engaged in finding another non-BJP means of temple construction. Chief Minister of UP, Vir Bahadur Singh hailed from Gorakhpur. He had a local and cast centric bonding with Gorakh-peeth chief Mahant Avaidyanath. Mahant ji was the leader of temple movement. Devendra Bahadur Rai was security officer for Vir Bahadur Singh, who later became the SSP of Faizabad. The structure got demolished on 6 December 1992 while he was the SSP of Faizabad. Later D.B. Rai resigned and was elected as Member of Parliament from BJP. D.B. Rai tells, 'One day Vir Bahadur Singh called me and asked, can you drive. I said—yes. He asked me to send my car, driver, security, secretary all on leave. "I have to go somewhere. I will go with you in your car." That night quietly Vir Bahadur Singh went to a retired income tax officer, Mohan Singh's Lucknow home. Mohan Singh took us to a room, there president of Ram Janmabhoomi Mukti Yagya Samiti's president Mahant Avaidyanath was already sitting. Mohan Singh left after escorting us to the room. Now there were only three of us. Vir Bahadur Singh started—"Rajiv ji wants, like Somnath a magnificent temple to be constructed at Ayodhya. But the Central government will construct it. There are only three conditions to it. First—Central government will pay for the expenses of temple construction. Second—BJP will have nothing to do with temple construction. And Third—disputed structure will not be demolished. A roof will be put over pillars from all sides. And a grand temple will be constructed on its roof. The structure will remain as it is. The plan is that the disputed structure is already weak. Without repair it will fall by itself in some days. After which only Ram Janmabhoomi temple will remain there." Avaidyanath laughed at this proposal of Vir Bahadur Singh and said, "How will BJP and VHP gain from this? Congress will get its political benefit." Then the conversation ended at a point where it was agreed that Avaidyanath ji will speak with other leaders of VHP and then inform about his views. But Avaidyanath ji never spoke on this matter again and this opportunity was missed in accessing gains and losses.'

These events are a proof that Rajiv Gandhi was making behind the scenes efforts to somehow have the temple constructed. The reason was that constant dharmsansads, saint gatherings, rath-yatras etcetera were flaring up the communal tensions in the country. Religious tensions were already on the rise in the country and politically it was quite harmful for him.

Chapter 6

THE BENEVOLENT APPEARS

This was the night between 22 and 23 December 1949. It was a long, dark and chilly night. The night between 22 and 23 December was the longest night. Nothing was visible in the thick fog. The air was still. Gods were resting in the temples in the narrow lanes of Ayodhya. Sadhus were sleeping in maths or monasteries. There was a spine-chilling silence in this town of twenty thousand inhabitants. It was a pitch-black night. Just before midnight, five prominent people gathered on the banks of the river Saryu. Saryu was flowing steadily. This place was also filled with godliness. Signs of Ram were present here as well. This was the place where lord Ram had entered Saryu to end his life. That's why there is a temple of Swargdwar or gateway to heaven here. In Hindu religion, Saryu is considered one of the sacred rivers.

Saryu originates from the sacred Mansarovar. It's called Karnali at its origin. When it reaches northern India through Tibet and Nepal, it becomes Saryu. After it reaches Basti, its name changes to Ghaghra, that merges with Ganga when it crosses Balia.

The five people gathered on the banks of Saryu were Mahant Digvijay Nath of Gau Raksha Peeth, a non-Hindi speaking saint of Devaria, Baba Raghav Das, Baba Abhiram Das of Nirmohi Akhada and Ramchandra Paramhans of Digambar Akhada.

In this secret operation, Hanuman Prasad Poddar 'Bhaiji', the founder of Gita Press of Gorakhpur, was also present for overseeing the arrangements. Some people say that Sangh Pracharak, Nanaji Deshmukh was also present in this group, a group that is credited for 'the appearance of God'. Paramhans Ramchandra Das also said it, although clandestinely. But whenever Nanaji was asked about it, he neither agreed nor denied it. Whenever asked, he evaded the question.

Among these men, Mahant Digvijay Nath was a revolutionary sadhu. He was the Mahant or the head priest of Nathpanth's top body, Gau Raksha Peeth. (The same position that Yogi Aditya Nath holds today). Avaidyanath was the teacher of Aditya Nath and Digvijay Nath was the teacher to Avaidyanath. Digvijay Nath had been imprisoned for the Chauri-Chaura incident during the freedom struggle. He was the state head of Hindu Mahasabha at that time. Digvijay Nath hailed from the same family in which Bappa Rawal and Maharana Pratap were born. He was named 'Rana Nanhu Singh' in his childhood. Full of political acumen, Mahant Digvijay Nath was a tall person with broad shoulders. He had the eloquence for conversation and was also an excellent lawn tennis player. In a conspiracy, his paternal uncle gave him up for adoption at Gorakh Nath temple and handed him over to Yogi Phool Nath of the Nath clan. For usurping the property, the uncle spread the rumor that the nephew was lost at a fair. After schooling, he studied further at Saint Andrews College at Gorakhpur. Due to his love for lawn tennis he was close to the Collector of Gonda, K.K.K. Nayar and Maharaja of Balrampur, Pateshwari Prasad Singh. Often these three got together in Gonda for lawn tennis. A recital of Ramcharitra Manas was done at the Ram Janmabhoomi's platform from 14 to 22 December 1949. One of the organizers of this 'Navahan recital' was Digvijay Nath, although the actual organizers of the recital were 'Ramayana Maha Sabha', a cultural organization. This 'Navahan Paath' got over on 22 December. That was the reason why some devotees were still present in the *pandal*.

The second person, Saint Baba Raghav Das was a 'Chittapawan Brahmin' from Pune. After the entire family of Raghavendra Sheshappa Pachachurkar perished in a plague in 1891, Raghavendra (childhood name) travelled to Allahabad, Banaras and reached Gazipur. At Gazipur he met a famous saint called Mauni Baba. After getting ordination from Mauni Baba, he reached Barhaj (Devaria) to Yogiraj Anant Mahaprabhu. His guru died within a year. It was then that he became Baba Raghav Das from Raghavendra and took over the Ashram. He joined the freedom movement. Because of his aggression, Hindutva centric overview and Satyagraha, he soon became popular. He joined Congress in 1920 and the legislative assembly by-election was held in 1948. Pandit Govind

Vallabh Pant had to get back at Acharya Narendra Dev. Baba Raghav Das was the political sadhu of Congress. Congress fielded this sadhu against Acharya Narendra Dev. By then, this sadhu had already raised the issue of liberating Rama's birthplace. In this by-election, Govind Vallabh Pant also aggressively canvassed in favour of the Ram Janmabhoomi. This was because Acharya Narendra Dev had support of the Muslims of Ayodhya and Faizabad. By now Congress had built the Somnath temple at Junagarh. Congress was now close to Hindu nationalism. Govind Vallabh Pant did an aggressive political campaign among the Hindus of Ayodhya and declared Acharya Narendra Dev anti-temple. Acharya Narendra Dev lost elections to Baba Raghav Das. This was the first test of the issue of 'Ram Janmabhoomi' in Indian politics.

When Chandreshwar Tiwari, son of Bhageran Tiwari, came to Ayodhya in 1930, he was Ayurvedacharya. When he met Paramhansa Ram Kinkar Das at Digambar Akhada Chhawani, he received a new name, 'Ram Chandra Das' and a new task, that of liberating the Ram Janmabhoomi or Lord Rama's birthplace. He was involved with this movement since 1934. He was also the city-president of Hindu Mahasabha. In 1975, he became the mahant or the head priest of Digambar Akhada and in 1989, the president of the Ram Janmabhoomi Nyas. He was well versed in Sanskrit. He had a good command over the Vedas and Indian scriptures. He was a blunt, aggressive and strong willed sadhu, known for his stubbornness. He announced in 1985 that if the doors were not opened, he would self-immolate. Digambar Akhada was a prominent Akhada of the Ramananda Sect. The Kar sevaks, who were fired upon in 1990, were being led by Paramhans Ramchandra Das. I had great affection for Paramhans Ramchandra Das and was quite close to him. A simple and innate Ramchandra Das often used to tell me stories of the Ram Janmabhoomi struggle.

On that night the fourth member who reached there was Hanuman Prasad Poddar, the founder of the Gita Press. Influenced by the 'Bang-Bhung' movement, he took a vow for 'Swadeshi' at the mere age of thirteen years. In 1914, he became active with Hindu Mahasabha after he met Mahamana Malviya. Affectionately people called him 'Bhaiji'. 'Bhaiji' got involved with the Ram Janmabhoomi movement. His first act towards it was to publish the Ram Janmabhoomi edition in *Kalyan* magazine. But later, he also started looking after the saints who were involved in the movement. The responsibility of arranging idols, prayers, prasad and clothes was upon Bhaiji.

Six feet tall and stubborn, sadhu Abhiram Das was counted among the warrior sadhus. A Maithil Brahman from Darbhanga, Abhiram Das came from a poor family. He was uneducated. He could barely write his name. Abhiram Das used muscle to earn a name for himself and not his brain. He exercised for hours at the akhada and wrestled till the age of 45 years. He was a tall and strong naga ascetic, wih a firm posture. He carried a five-feet-long staff that had a steel cover at one end. Abhiram Das was a Naga ascetic of the Ramananda Clan for fifteen years. No one had ever heard him holding a religious spiritual debate. But he was active in the akhada. He knew all the moves. He was famously known to have a *siddhi* or blessing from lord Hanuman.

He was known in Ayodhya as the redeemer of Ram Janmabhoomi. He died on 3 December 1981 and when his Vimaana (a sadhu's funeral bier is called Vimaana) was carried, instead of Ram-Ram chants, slogans of, 'Ram Janmabhoomi ke Uddharakamarrahein' meaning, long live the redeemer of Ram Janmabhoomi, echoed in the surroundings. In the later days Abhiram Das had started calling himself the Mahant of Ram Janmabhoomi temple. He was a sadhu of Nirvani Ani Akhada of Hanuman Garhi. Abhiram Das saw lots of dreams in his sleep. Often in his dream, he saw Ram Lalla or the child Ram, who asked him to free his birthplace. Abhiram Das maintained this opinion that he must free Janmabhoomi. For this, once he met the City Magistrate, Gurudutt Singh. Gurudutt Singh's son Guru Basant Singh said that his father said to Abhiram Das that you have seen this dream now, but I have been dreaming of it for many years now. After this, Abhiram Das 'managed' many officers of similar ideology at the local level and made them part of his strategy.

All these people now take a 'Saryu-dip' in the freezing river and wear new clothes. There are about 30 to 40 other ascetics with them. 'Bhaiji' is carrying an ashta-dhatu (eight metal alloy) idol of lord Rama, that he had had from his childhood days. The idol is worshipped there itself. Then it is placed in a bamboo basket and covered with a cloth. Baba Abhiram Das is carrying it over his head. Ramchandra Das is holding a copper-pot filled with river water and this group now moves towards Hanuman Garhi, singing bhajans. Between Rama's birthplace and Hanuman Garhi, there is a secluded patch. Then there was no math, temple or house close by.

There were some people just before the Ram Chabootra or platform, outside Ram janmsthan or Ram's birthplace. They were performing akhand-keertan. Sadhus were carrying a lantern. About two dozen policemen (PAC) were sleeping in the tent and two of them were on alternate sentry duty. A 'Navahan' recital of Ramcharitmanas had been going on for the last nine days. Today was the day of Yagya-Hawan. That is why there were so many policemen on duty today; otherwise there were only three to four policemen daily. When the group of sadhus reached the Ram Chabootra, Constable Sher Singh was on guard duty. Sher Singh knew Baba Abhiram Das. They had an equation of exchanging cannabis and opium. Abhiram Das wanted to climb over the wall with the idols. Sher Singh understood the situation. Without uttering a word, in an emotional state, he opened the lock and let seven to eight sadhus inside the sanctum-sanctorum. The rest of the saints were watching the events unfold while sitting on the Ram Chabootra.

The first thing that these sadhus did was to beat up the muezzin of the mosque, Mohammed Ismail, a short, stocky and dark man, and entered the sanctum-sanctorum. Paramhans told later that the muezzin was wearing a long kurta and lungi on that day. First, he charged at Abhiram Das because he was the one carrying the idol. Abhiram Das broke away from him and then followed a fist fight. When the muezzin felt that he couldn't win the fight, he ran through the darkness. He kept running without thinking where he was going and why he was running. After running for two hours Ismail reached Ghosiyana (Pahadganj) of Faizabad. This was a village of Ghosi Muslims. Muslims of this area were the first to get the news of Babri mosque being desecrated. Ismail didn't go back ever again. He was one of the witnesses of the event. He had seen this significant event in the history of Independent India. Muezzin's job at a mosque is to call for the Azan. No namaz was read at the mosque, so no Azan was done either, but Ismail took care of the building.

In the light of the lantern, the floor of the sanctum-sanctorum was washed with water from the Saryu river. Then a wooden throne was kept there and a smaller silver throne was kept over it. The idol was placed after putting a cloth over it. A lamp and incense sticks were lit. The idol was placed amid chants. Prayers started. Sher Singh's duty was till twelve at night. But Sher Singh extended his stay for an hour, until the entire task was done. At one o'clock he woke up his fellow constable Abdul Barkat, a Muslim man, and sent him for duty. In the glittering light when Sepoy Barkat saw the idol, his blood froze. He was stunned! To him, accepting the miraculous story of Ram Lalla's appearance was a better option than explaining his one hour delay for the duty. Sepoy Barkat told as a witness in the FIR that at around midnight there was a divine light around the middle dome. When the light dimmed a little, he could not believe what he saw next. Idol of child Ram was present there along with his three brothers. This statement of Abdul Barkat suited the group that had brought the idol, because his statement was proof of a miracle.

Inside and outside the building, red mud was used to write Sita-Ram and Jai Shri Ram. There were three domes in the four-hundred-year-old building. The space under the three domes was enough for namaz by ninety people. Verses of Quran were written on the inner walls. Imam's seat was under the central dome, under which was written, 'a place for angels to descend'. There were two courts in the premises. One was immediately after the three domes that had the Ram chabootra and second outside its peripheral wall. By now sadhus and saints had gathered in both the courts. Most of them were from Nirmohi and Nirvani Akhada.

There has been a rich and valorous tradition of akhadas among Hindus. In the eighth and ninth century, at the time of fading Buddhism when Shankaracharya established Vedic Dharma, these akhadas were constituted for safeguarding the religion. Adi Shankar founded four maths in the four corners of India. Badrik ashram in north, Dwarka in west, Puri in east and Shringeri in south. They were named as Jyotish

Peeth, Sharda Peeth, Govardhan Peeth and Shrengeri Peeth. Protecting maths and safeguarding Hindu religion from increasing threats from Islam was the reason for the constitution of akhadas where monks were taught skills of fighting, along with scriptures. There were two sects at the Akhadas–Shaiv and Vaishnav. Those who worshipped Shiva and Acharya Shankar were the Shaivas and those who worshipped Vishnu and followed Ramananda were called Vaishnav. Ramananda was a Vaishnav guru born centuries after Shankaracharya. Shaiva sect had six main akhadas and Vaishnavas had seven. The Hindu religion relied upon these thirteen akhadas. The monks of Shaiva Akhadas were called 'Naga' and monks from the Vaishnava Akhadas were known as 'Vairagis'. Nagas and Vairagis were always ready to pick a fight. Nagas didn't wear clothes and Vairagis wore white clothes. The head of each akhada was the 'Shrimahant' and their spiritual guru was called 'Maha Mandelashwar'. There are four sects among Vaishnavas—Ramanuji, Ramanandi, Nimbark and Madhav Chaitanya. There has been a domination of Ramanandi sect in Ayodhya and that's why Ramanandi monks have always fought against all the attacks on Ram Janmabhoomi. Nirvani Akhada was one among the three military organizations that killed and got killed for the protection of religion. It had two sections—Nirmohi and Digambari Akhada. Its centre is at Ayodhya. Virvani Akhada has its centre at Hanuman Garhi. Earlier it was Hanuman Teela or Hanuman temple. 18th century onwards, Mughal rulers dominated northern India. Navab Safdarjung (1739-54) of Awadh gave seven beegha land at Hanuman Teela to Baba Abhayram Das. Asif-Ud-Daula, the great-grandson of Safdarjung gave money to have a fort-like temple built. Later, Navabs of Awadh donated lands to have the Garhi or the fortress extended. Baba Ramdas became the first Shrimahant or the inheritor. And it became the centre for Naga Sadhus of Nirvani Akhada.

The Mahants of the Akhadas cannot induct new monks. A monk is ordained by the Mahant of the maths. New entrant is called 'yatri' meaning the traveler, or 'chhota' meaning the young one. For the next three years he is called as 'bangaidaar' or the follower. His job is to help in the prayer rituals. After that for three years he helps in the kitchen in cooking and serving food. Then he is called 'hudadanga'.

Further, he serves as 'muratiya' for three more years. So after a difficult twelve-year-long phase he is called a Naga or Vairagi. Mostly there are Ramanandi Vairagi sadhus in Ayodhya who fought against the Islamic invaders.

Around four o'clock in the morning, the ceremony of founding the idols at the Ram Janmabhoomi was complete. The news reached the tent outside that God has appeared. By half past four, suddenly bells of the temple started ringing. Sadhus blew the conch and people present there began to sing out loud—

भए प्रगट कृपाला दीनदयाला कौसल्या हितकारी।
हरषित महतारी मुनि मन हारी अद्भुत रूप विचारी।।
लोचन अभिरामा तनु घनस्यामा निज आयुध भुज चारी ।
भूषन बनमाला नयन बिसाला सोभासिंधु खरारी।।

Bhaye pragat kripala deen dayala kausalya hitkari
Harshit mahtari muniman hari adbhut roop vichari
Lochan abhirama tanu ghanshyama nij aayudh bhujchaari
Bhushan banmala nayan bisala sobha sindhu kharari

This prayer was written by Goswami Tulsidas on Ram's birth. He wrote it almost at the same time when Babri mosque was made the temple place. When PAC personnel heard this chorus, they woke up from their slumber and challenged the sadhus. They fired few rounds in the air but by then, court around the birthplace was packed with sadhus. There was no space inside and this dissuaded the police to enter.

By now, the news of the idol's appearance had spread. While prayers of the 'appeared idols' were going on, two kilometres away, preparation for the second phase were on at the printing press at Shringar Haat area of Ayodhya. Gopal Singh, minister of Hindu Mahasabha in Ayodhya was busy getting as many pamphlets printed by morning as possible. The matter being printed in the pamphlets was the appearance of Ram Lalla in the Babri mosque. Devotees were requested to reach there and pay a visit. The owner of this press was Brahma Dev Shastri and the press was called Narayan Press. Bramha Dev Shastri was a good friend of Gopal Singh Visharad. He published a Hindi newspaper *Virakt*. Ayodhya police station was one kilometre away from the Ram Janmabhoomi, where the incident took place. By morning, station in-charge, Ramdev Dubey reached the spot and was briefed by constable number 7, Mata Prasad, of the whole incident. The station in-charge quickly registered an FIR. Here is the FIR for you—

First Information Report Dated 23 December 1949
   Station In-charge report dated 23 December, under section 147/295/448 Indian penal Code which has been registered by Pandit Shri Ram Dubey, Senior Sub Inspector, Station In-charge Ayodhya, Faizabad.
   Against

1. *Abhay Ramdas*
2. *Ram Shukl Das*
3. *Sudarshan Das resident Ayodhya, Faizabad and fifty-sixty other persons, Name & Address, unknown, Police Station, Ayodhya.*

As per the verbal communication by Constable No. 7, Mata Prasad, at around 9 in the morning when I reached Janmabhoomi, I got to know that a group of fifty-sixty people have opened the lock, scribed on walls and stairs of Babri mosque, have placed the idol of lord Rama. They were asked not to do it by constable number 70, Hansraj, but they didn't listen. PAC personnel were then sought for help. But by then people had entered the mosque. Senior officials inspected the spot of the incident and were ready for action. Later there was a mob of five-six thousand people. The mob attempted to enter the mosque, shouting slogans, singing bhajans. But because of adequate arrangements nothing happened. Perpetrators of the crime (accused) Abhay Ramdas, Ramshukl Das, Sudarshan Das and fifty-sixty other people, whose name and addresses are unknown, have used force and created riots and by placing the idol, desecrated the mosque (turned it impure). The officials on duty have witnessed the same. The matter has been viewed and found correct.
   Sig./ SO Ramdev Dubey
   I, head Moharir, attest that the said report has been registered according to the statement made by the Sub Inspector.
   Sig./ Head Moharir

By morning, the news of the appearance of the idols had spread everywhere. The child Ram's idols were only seen in Ayodhya. This time the idol that was 'made to appear' was brought by Bhaiji (Hanuman Prasad Poddar).

The temple was destroyed by Mir Baqi. This temple's Ram Lalla idol now reached Orchha Palace. It is considered that Ram Lalla rules this city of Madhya Pradesh and not the state government. How Ram Lalla reached Orchha is no less interesting. Orchha is about 20 kilometres from Jhansi. Here there is a temple of King Rama. There is a legend that Rama stops at Ayodhya every night and reaches Orchha in his child-state early in the morning. Rama who fulfilled his responsibility in every relationship like that of Shabri, Kevat, Nishad Raj, Sugriva, Vibhishan and Kaikei, also fulfils his responsibility with the queen of Orchha. The reason for Rama coming over to Orchha was the devotion the Queen of Orchha had for him. Orchha King Madhukar was a devotee of Radha-Krishna. But his queen Kamlapati Ganesh Kunwari was a devotee of Rama. One day the King made a light-hearted comment that if your Rama is greater than Krishna, then why don't you bring him to Orchha? When it came down to showing 'power of devotion', the queen decided to bring Rama to Orchha. From Orchha to Ayodhya, she walked for many miles. She made a hut close to river Saryu and started to pray. There is a story that she sought blessings from Tulsidas as well. This further strengthened the queen's resolution. Even after months of prayers when there was no result and she did not see Rama, she jumped into the river. Seeing the extent of her devotion, Rama appeared in the river. When the queen told him her wish, Rama placed a condition that he will be the one to rule where ever he goes. Orchha will have the rule of Rama and the monarchy will have to go. In 1631 on the day of Ramnavmi, the queen gave away Orchha to King Ram. After this, it has been the same tradition. There are idols of Sita, Lakshman and Hanuman along with Rama in the Orchha temple. There is a procession of Ram-Baraat in December. The policemen of Madhya Pradesh salute Raja Ram at the dawn and dusk.

On the other side, by afternoon of the next day, news of Ram Lalla's appearance, had reached the far-flung villages of Faizabad. The way propaganda machinery was activated, it appeared that it was planned well in advance. This is a less known fact that one day prior to the appearance of idols, chief of RSS, Madhav Sadashiv Golvalkar 'Guruji' was in Ayodhya. After this, he went a hundred kilometres away to Jaunpur where he stayed for three days to participate in a volunteer training programme. Guruji had an eye on these events as well, although those who made the idol appear were all associated with Hindu Mahasabha. But the activeness of Sangh can be figured by Guruji's presence there.

As the sun showed up in a foggy sky on 23 December, panic in the administration got worse, because by afternoon, about five thousand people had gathered in the disputed area. Prayers and singing of devotional songs had started. Although not in Ayodhya, the news of communal tension between Hindus and Muslims had started to trickle down from Faizabad. Looking at the level of tension, Faizabad city Magistrate Gurudutt Singh (I will explain his role later) and the local administration imposed section 144 and 145 and took the building under its control.

Local administration appointed Priya Dutt, the president of Faizabad municipal board as the 'receiver' and handed over the disputed premises to her. Receiver put a lock on the iron bar main gate of the sanctum sanctorum. Four priests and one purser were allowed to pray and offer food to the deity. This happened quickly so that no orders of maintaining status quo are passed and situation remains 'as is'. There was no order to put a lock but the premises was locked. Under section 145, the Magistrate of Faizabad ordered, 'I city magistrate Faizabad-Ayodhya, am fully satisfied with the information received from the police and other trusted sources that there has been a dispute between Hindus and Muslims over Ram Janmabhoomi and Babri mosque area, Ramkot's one section, over the worshipping. This area where it is suspected that peace will be disturbed comes under my jurisdiction. I impose section 145 of CRPC and appoint Priya Dutt, the president of Faizabad-Ayodhya Municipal Corporation's board as the 'receiver' of this place, who will take care of this section after the dispute that emerged on 23 December 1949.' The receiver took over on 5 January, 1950. According to the order of additional city magistrate, the receiver also handed over a plan of upkeep of the premises.

To maintain pressure of the crowd and keep the administration from acting, Abhiram Das and his disciples went to local schools and told that Ram has appeared at the Ram Janmabhoomi. This was done so that people reached there in large numbers. For this, Abhiram Das and Mahant Ramchandra Paramhans had prepared in advance. They had constituted a cultural organization by the name of 'Akhil Bharatiya Ramayana Mahasabha' to enable gathering of people when needed. Ramchandra Paramhans was its General secretary, Gopal Singh Visharad was its joint secretary and Abhiram Das was the secretary (organization). Ramayana Mahasabha had associated Naga sadhus of Hanuman Garhi and it often organized nine-day recital of Manas at the Ram Chabootra, close to the disputed structure. This helped in keeping people active for the temple cause and gave them a reason to gather around it. The nine day long Navahan recital had ended on the day the idols were placed. An announcement was made through loudspeakers that lord Ram has made an appearance and all Hindus should pay him a visit. Guru Basant Singh, son of City Magistrate Gurudutt Singh says that his father had deployed many cyclists and they were bringing him minute-by-minute information in Faizabad. When City Magistrate Gurudutt Singh and collector K.K.K. Nayar got information of the idols being installed and the mosque being full of sadhus, they reached Ayodhya in a car. FIR of the incident was lodged at nine in the morning. It took the District Magistrate one and a half hours to send a two-line radiogram to the Chief Minister and Chief Secretary. District administration was wasting time and the crowd was constantly growing to witness the miracle. Chief Secretary of the combined state, Bhagwan Sahai and IG Police, B.N. Lahiri called up from Faizabad that idols and publicity material should be removed from the mosque. At 3 p.m., the DIG reached the spot straight from Lucknow. He handed over a written message from the Chief Secretary Bhagwan Sahai to the collector. The message was—

Dear Mr Nayar,

Our policy is to maintain status quo. Changes can be made with an agreement between both communities, but situation cannot be allowed to be altered with force or deception.

To implement this policy, if necessary (minimum required) force can be used.

If possible, avoid the regretful decision of firing as much as possible, so that it does not create other issues. This objection does not imply on making large scale arrests.

To keep the situation under control on the ground, it is left to your discretion.

Mr K.K.K. Nayar
District Collector, Faizabad
23.12.49

Bhagwan Sahai
Chief Secretary, Uttar Pradesh
Administration

To bring attention to the issue, some Muslim leaders and Ulema from Deoband of Uttar Pradesh sent a telegram to the Prime Minister Jawaharlal Nehru. Nehru directed the Chief Minister of UP, Govind Vallabh Pant and Home Minister of the state, Lal Bahadur Shastri to have the idols removed from the mosque. Messages from the centre were arriving constantly at Lucknow and they were being redirected to Faizabad to have the idols removed immediately. On 24 and 25 December, a high-level meeting took place for the entire day. It was decided in this meeting that the idols will be taken out of the sanctum sanctorum and placed outside on the Ram Chabootra. But the City Magistrate of Faizabad and K.K.K. Nayar were adamant that merely an announcement of removing the idols will result in bloodshed and they will not be able to implement it. Chief Secretary called the commissioner of Faizabad to Lucknow and reprimanded him for not removing the idols in the morning itself when there were only few people at the spot. He also questioned why the people responsible for placing the idols had not been arrested yet.

In response to this, the District Collector K.K.K. Nayar wrote a four-page letter to the Chief Secretary and told him that if the desired actions were taken, they could lead to the serious consequences. There could be widespread communal riots and bloodshed. Nayar writes—

Deputy Commissioner Building
Faizabad

Shri Bhagwan Sahai, ICS
Chief Secretary of the Uttar Pradesh Government
Lucknow

26 December 1949

Dear Bhagwan Sahai,

I was informed by the Commissioner after I returned from Lucknow that during your conversation with him you had asked him—

1. Why the district officers were not careful enough to stop the idols being taken inside the mosque?
2. Why was the idol not removed from there?

The DIG said that it was again questioned as to why the idol was not removed on the 23rd morning itself, when there were very few people present there. Perhaps the answer can only be sought by stating facts.

The idol was placed in the night between 22nd and 23rd. There was no intelligence warning. I received the latest CID report on matters in Ayodhya on the 22nd. Neither in this report nor in any of the previous reports was there any indication of a plan for hidden or forceful placement of idol in the mosque. We had not received input from any government or private source of such a plan. Only a rumour was there that on the full moon night, during the Navahan recital, there can be an attempt of entry in the mosque. But no such attempt was made.

In this regard, those Muslims who met me and often meet other senior officials, also never suspected of any plan to forcefully or secretly place Ram Lalla idol in the mosque.

Their complaint was always about the destruction in the open area outside the temple. In fact, this act is as surprising to them as it is for others. This has been accepted by a delegation which included Rehmat Hussain lawyer, Himayatullah Kidwai lawyer, Anees-ur-Rehman and many others. One representative Anees-ur-Rehman said that on the 21st evening, a teacher from Maharaj High School of Ayodhya had announced that Hindus should place idols in the mosque and stop Muslims from Namaz. (23rd was a Friday). There was no mention of the said speech in the CID report. When I asked Anees-ur-Rehman why he did not bring my attention to this matter then itself, he said that he didn't think it to be important, because there was a CID official present there. I feel that Anees-ur-Rehman was himself not convinced that there is any chance of such a thing happening, or else he would have gone to the local officials and informed them about it.

I would also like to tell that the leader of the people responsible for this incident, Abhiram Das is neither a Mahant nor a leader. His name has never come forth in this regard. The speeches given by Baba Raghav Das and other leaders did not support violence, so there was no need of acting against them. And hence, there is no question of arresting the leaders or taking any action against them. Anyway, I believe arrest could not have stopped this undesirable event, because those determined sadhus have a wide wave of sympathy of the masses on this matter. The arrests could have worsened the situation in some other way.

To enter the mosque, one must cross the temple premises, and that can be used anytime. Besides there are always people in the temple premises, while the mosque remains empty except for the Friday prayer.

To stop Hindus from entering the mosque forcibly or secretly, police force would have to be deployed on a permanent basis and this would have cost thousands of rupees on a monthly basis. Although as per the local historical records of the last 36 years, there have been many riots and many lives have been lost. Yet I don't think deploying a permanent police post at the mosque would have been a wise decision.

With due respect I wish to know that to stop such unfortunate incidents, can the government think of deploying permanent police posts at this religious site or similar other sites like Banaras, Mathura etcetera. And if the government does not decide to do so, will the district collectors will be held responsible for any unfortunate incident in future, no matter how much of a surprising and unsuspecting incident that is.

Why is the idol not being removed and why was it not removed on the 23rd morning? These questions seem very simple. It is possible to remove the idol if police force is available. Because of less resistance, it is also possible to remove it at night. But in my opinion without carefully thinking of the consequences, removing the idol would have been an administrative shortsighted and dictatorial step. Now with the available police force, the disturbed situation can be dealt with. But it was not possible with the limited resources available on 23rd. I still have my doubt that in the areas far away from the headquarters if we will be able to do anything in case communal riots erupt. A hasty decision to remove the idol could have lead to a bigger problem for the government and being loyal to the government, I could not have acted without having clear directions form the government.

I still can't imagine how to have the idol removed from there. If this is to be done according to the religious rituals, then I will not get an appropriate Hindu priest, who is ready to put his life and salvation at stake. If this is to be accomplished somehow or by any means, then the government may have to face protests from all the sections of Hindus. I should be told clearly if the government is ready to face such a situation.

The crisis that we face today should not result in a bigger crisis is our priority. Keeping this in mind, I have taken every step in a very careful and prudent manner.

In the end I would have to say that while we continue to discuss smaller steps that are to be taken locally about the manner in which this crisis has arisen, we are ignoring the real larger issue which has resulted in many riots and loss of hundreds of lives in Ayodhya. This problem will have to be faced. Although being careful will change the shape and time of the crisis, but in the absence of a real solution this will rise again. It can't be avoided for long and even after independence people are not ready to listen to the orders of local officials or leave an old obsolete movement.

    I am sure that my candidness will not be misunderstood. It was necessary for me to remove misconceptions. Those district officials who had no support from the local people have tried their best to maintain peace, administrative prestige and to protect the policy of the government. They definitely deserve more credit than this.

Yours
KKK Nayar, ICS
District Collector

Before the government could respond to this blunt reply, the very next day Nayar shot another letter to the Chief Secretary. He expressed his inability to remove the idols. He almost warned the Chief Secretary that even after his contrary advise, if the government wanted to remove the idol, he should be removed from his position first.

Upayukt Bhawan   27 December 1949
Faizabad

Dear Bhagwan Sahai,

This letter is about the Ayodhya issue and in continuation of my letter DCS 301/C.

    Commissioner returned from Lucknow and he told me and Police Superintendent about the plan to secretly remove the idol from the mosque and bring it outside at the Janmabhoomi temple. Yesterday evening this plan was discussed between Commissioner, DIG, SP and me and in the evening IG, DIG (PAC) and I discussed it.

    I am not in agreement with the plan of removing the idol and do not wish to initiate it, because it will be a big threat to the peace of the district. This can create a grave situation, which can be unprecedented in the history of this dispute. The situation in the district is bad and it's said that in the event of clash between police and officials, it will not be possible to immediately or easily confiscate firearms from the licensed firearm holders. In my view, all Hindus demand that the idol be left as it is and they are ready to kill or be killed to protect it. The depth of emotions, determination and vows taken to support the movement should not be ignored. When the storm rises, we will be able to contain the riots within the limits of the city, but we will have to use guns. This will result in loss of many lives, not only in the shootout but also due to the explosive situation that will arise because of it. Today this rumour is circling that it's being considered to remove the idol. It is told that in retaliation Hindus are planning to attack Muslim habitats and have the intention to burn and loot. If this happens, it will create a storm in which it will be difficult to save Muslim lives to an extent that it will not be possible to safeguard my own officers and their property. I could not find a single person even among the Congress people who is a Hindu and in support of removal of the idol.

Looking at the outpouring of public emotions, any step of this nature will be like showing a lit matchstick to gunpowder. It is impossible to logically and rationally analyse the consequences of this act.

Not only will I not get any Hindu priest, but I will not get a single Hindu, who will agree to remove the idol even with any kind of lure. Kripal Singh and I have tried hopelessly to find such a person who would do this for us when needed, but we have failed. None from the district will do this, because that will put his life and property in danger from the entire Hindu community. We had suggested that the Commissioner and DIG help us by getting a person from outside. Someone who can accomplish this, but they have not agreed on finding a suitable person for the task. I doubt that the government will be able to find a suitable person where we have failed. If we spoke to a suitable priest and that priest refuses, which is likely, then there is a possibility of our plan becoming public. If somehow and through someone, the idols are removed from there, then the storm of resentment and anger will spread even beyond the district borders. This will not only malign the officers of the district but also the government.

I sincerely request that the government should listen to me and understand that using force in the current situation can lead to catastrophic results.

The police superintendent agrees with me on this matter. It is our well thought opinion that we must not even think of using force because this can lead to violence and pillage.

Now the question is what should be done under the circumstances? Placing an idol in a mosque is defiantly illegal. This has not only put the local authorities in difficulty but the government as well. We will have to think of a way of handling the situation, without paying a heavy price and without making sacrifices. I have a solution and the government can think over it.

I propose that the mosque be taken under possession and the entry of Hindus and Muslims should be banned, except priests. Priests can perform rituals and prayers. This prayer can continue inside the sanctum sanctorum. This priest or priests will be appointed by the order of the Magistrate. Rest of the matter should be handed over to the civil court. Muslims should not be given possession until the civil court decides in their favour.

This formula can be criticized for the reason that because of this, the forceful and deceitful possession will continue. This will not resume the previous status immediately. But this has many benefits and can be considered.

If the civil court decides in favour of Hindus, bloodshed and pan country riots can be avoided.

Some sort of agreement can be reached while the matter is subjudice in the civil court (I want an agreement to be reached). Some Muslims agree to this idea that they be provided with another mosque of the same cost at another location and then they will give up this mosque. They can be actuated for it. But if the situation leads to riots, those Muslims will not agree for a solution like this. This may lead to riots in future.

Even if agreement is not reached and in the end, the civil court rules in favour of Muslims, the situation will not be worse than the situation right now. By then, the situation would have cooled down a little.

Although the government will be accused of not immediately restoring the pre-existing situation. But it will have a legal and valid argument that the matter of public rights is in a civil court and the property is acquired by the magistrate. The entry of Hindus and Muslims is banned and the matter of restoring the status is also under consideration by the magistrate. An order by the government cannot legally influence or change it, until a decision is made. In my opinion, any provisional order by the government given to me or to any other magistrate who acquires the property, for restoring the pre-existing status, will be illegal. Because the legal process is on, its decision will be taken by the associated magistrate with due jurisprudence. The government cannot give an illegal directive to rectify an illegal situation, to appease, even on a valid complaint in which the matter is sub judice.

I would also like to say that restoring the previous status is an ideal situation, but this cannot be praised and promoted. I have been at that place for a long time and handled the situation with almost no help. Today slogans are being shouted, 'Nayar stop injustice, Nayar open gates of the God'. I am facing this criticism without any complaint. But surely, I have no reason to be soft towards those who are accusing me everyday and those who have put me and the entire administration in this exceptionally difficult situation. Even after this I will advise to restore peace. I firmly believe that a solution should be found without paying the heavy price of life and property.

The police commissioner and I do not agree with the removal of the idol. Nor do we wish to initiate it. The alternate solution which I am placing before the government has scope of successfully maintaining peace and order. If this solution is not acceptable and government decides to face the consequences of removing the idols, it is only right that after losing confidence of the government and to implement an impractical solution which is not right or needed, neither judicious nor justified from legal perspective, I will not be asked to implement it.

If the government decides to remove the idols at any cost, then I would request that I be relieved from my duty and my charge be given to an officer who sees goodness in this solution, which I fail to see. As far as I am concerned, my conscience does not allow me to do this, because I am aware of the problem that it will cause to a lot of people.

Yours
KKK Nayar, ICS

Letters from Nayar placed the government under pressure. A nervous Chief Secretary, Bhagwan Sahai called up Nayar to tell him that he has received his letter and that he should do what he deems fit at the location, but should keep in mind that there is no force used against anyone. But yes, the Chief Secretary maintained his 'stand' that the government disagrees with the current situation. In the meanwhile, Prime Minister Jawaharlal Nehru was constantly expressing his worry on the matter. He asked the Home Minister Sardar Patel to talk to the Chief Minister, Pant, of UP.

When District Commissioner K.K.K. Nayar was not ready to listen to the government, Prime Minister Jawaharlal Nehru sent a cable to Chief Minister Govind Vallabh Pant.

New Delhi   26 December 1949

I am disturbed with the events of Ayodhya. I sincerely hope that you will give your personal attention to this matter. Objectionable examples are being set, which may have devastating results.

Yours
Jawaharlal

Prime Minister wrote to the Governor general C Rajgopalachari as well—

Copy, C Rajgopalachari
New Delhi, 7 January 1950

Dear Rajaji,

Last night I have written a letter to Pant ji and sent it through a person going to Lucknow after which, Pant ji called me up. He said that he is very worried and personally attending the matter. He wants to take action, but he wants that some known Hindu leaders should inform the people of Ayodhya of the right situation. I have informed the Chief Minister about the letter that you sent me in the morning.

Vallabh Bhai is going to Lucknow at the request of Pant ji. This is regarding the Lok Sabha elections.

Yours
Jawaharlal

The correspondence between centre and state continued. But during this period, nothing significant happened in Ayodhya except for one thing. A local, Mohammed Hashim Ansari, filed a petition in a local court for having the idol removed. But the court referring to the injunction asked to maintain 'status quo'. Now a civil dispute started. Two cases were filed in the civil court by Hindu Mahasabha Minister Gopal Singh Visharad (Visharad was his degree) and Paramhans Ramchandra Das, which were filed after 1950 as number 2 and 25. It was demanded in these petitions that the state and Muslims should be prohibited from removing idols from the disputed structure. Entry of Muslims should be banned and the court to also ensure that rituals and prayers are not interrupted. On the request of Gopal Singh Visharad, the civil judge ordered on 16 January 1950 that—

'Notice to be issued, as prayed, for issuance of provisionary orders. The opposing parties are also to be informed that unilateral temporary prohibitory orders have been issued.'

Petitions were again filed for clarification/amendment of the interim order. Upon this the court again issued an order on 19 January 1950, 'as petitioned by the parties, removal of idols in question and the obstruction of prayers that are performed, is being temporarily prohibited. Accordingly, the order stands amended as on 16 January 1950.'

After hearing arguments of both sides, court validated the previous provisional prohibitory order through a fresh order on 3 March 1951. After this, on 26 April 1955, High Court also issued affirmation of the temporary prohibitory order.

Gopal Singh Visharad was a lawyer by profession. He was the lawyer for Hindu Mahasabha, Faizabad in the Janmabhoomi case. After he passed away, the case was handled by his son Rajendra Singh. Rajendra

Singh recalls that on the day the idols appeared, Mahant Abhiram Das came over to his school and announced that idols have appeared and asked the children to go with him to see the miracle.

One more case was filed by Anees-Ur-Rehman who lived close to the disputed structure. His version was that the idols had been placed in the premises. He was being stopped from entering the premises. His rights should be maintained. Anees-Ur-Rehman made tin boxes near the place. He lived close to the Ram Janmabhoomi. He was a police informer. For months now he had been sending letters to the police about updates like who came there, construction of Hawan-Kund, sadhus increasing in numbers etc. He did this until 1950. Later he sold his shop and went to Pakistan. This is as Hashim Ansari related it to me.

In the meanwhile, Prime Minister Jawaharlal Nehru wrote another letter to Pant ji to know the current situation in Ayodhya.

Copy, Govind Vallabh Pant,

New Delhi, 15 February, 1950

Dear Pant ji,

I will be happy if you updated me on the situation in Ayodhya. As you know, I give great importance of its impact on the entire country and especially on Kashmir. When you came over last time, I had suggested that if you feel the need, I will go to Ayodhya myself. If you still feel that it should be done, then I will try to make time for it. Although I am too tied up.

Yours
Jawaharlal Nehru

There was no consensus on the Ayodhya issue between Prime Minister Jawahalal Nehru and leaders of Uttar Pradesh Congress. Uttar Pradesh was a battle ground for many power centres within Congress. The Chief Minister at that time, Govind Vallabh Pant was close to Home Minister Sardar Patel. His efforts to remain in power gave him a reason to align with Hindus. Baba Raghav Das was an example. Pant was interested in having Narendra Dev lose assembly elections. As Naredra Dev was a challenge for him while he was in Congress and now even after joining the Socialist Party, he was not letting him be. Nehru was with Narendra Dev. Faizabad became a ring. Pant aligned with pro Hindutva people through Baba Raghav Das. What was Prime Minister Jawaharlal Nehru thinking about the Uttar Pradesh government and some leaders of Congress and what his state of mind was, is revealed in a letter written to the assistant of Mahatma Gandhi, K.G. Mashruwala.

Copy
KG Mashruwala
New Delhi   5 March, 1950

Dear Kishorilal Bhai,

I thank you for your letter written on 5 March. I am replying in short. Tomorrow morning I am leaving for Calcutta.

I fully agree that the Indian press is also not free from the charges. But there was a time when things were better. Since then situation has deteriorated. The press in Pakistan is in an even worse situation. Still the West Bengal government has had some success in restricting the excesses of the press. The atmosphere in Calcutta is so volatile that it's very difficult to have any kind of control. The kind of posters that have been put up openly, will provoke violence.

There is no doubt that the treatment of Hindus in East Bengal is extremely bad. Muslims are also living in the shadow of fear. They have also lost few lives. People coming from Eastern Bengal to Western Bengal are much more than those Muslims who are going from Western Bengal and Eastern Assam.

You have mentioned the mosque of Ayodhya. This incident has happened two to three months ago which has deeply disturbed me. Uttar Pradesh government has shown courage but what has happened is no less. The officials of Faizabad have either played a mischief or they have not taken any steps to stop the developing situation. There is no truth that Baba Raghav Das has instigated the situation, but it is the true that once the incident took place, he gave his approval for it. In UP, many people from Congress including Govind Vallabh Pant have condemned the incident at a different time, but failed to act fearing widespread riots. I have been worried about these things and I kept asking Pant ji for his attention to the matter.

I am convinced that if our behaviour remained right then it will be easier to maintain relations with Pakistan. Today many Congress leaders have become communal in their views towards Pakistan, effect of which is visible in their behaviour towards Muslims in India. I am unable to understand what needs to be done to maintain order in the country. When people are excited, even talks of maintaining good relations teases them. Bapu may have been able to do it, but we are too small to do it.

I fear that under these circumstances, people in Calcutta will follow the peaceful protest march of Bapu.

Yours
Jawaharlal Nehru

Nehru wanted to come to Ayodhya, but Pant ji kept avoiding it. In this matter he remained in close contact with Home Minister Patel. Prime Minister Nehru asked Home Minister Patel to talk to Chief Minister Govind Vallabh Pant. Patel first went to Lucknow, held talks, understood the situation, gave necessary directives and then wrote this letter.

New Delhi   9 January, 1950

Dear Pant ji,

Prime Minister has already sent a telegram on the developing events in Ayodhya. I also spoke to you about it in Lucknow. I feel that this controversy has arisen at a wrong time for the entire country and your state. These big communal issues can only be sorted with talks between different sects. As far as Muslims are concerned, they are busy in establishing their new trustworthiness. We can say this logically that they have just overcome the shock and its aftermath. In such a situation it does not seem possible that their loyalties will have a dramatic shift. In your own state, communal issues have always been difficult. I feel even after all this, communal harmony has increased since 1946, which is a big achievement. We have our own issues in Uttar Pradesh. These are organizational and administrative, which has resulted in the formation of many camps. If we let any one camp benefit from the situation, it will be very unfortunate. Keeping all this in mind, I feel that this matter should be solved in a friendly manner with people from both religious communities. I feel, emotions have an important role in whatever took place. In such a time, such matters can only be solved with peace, when we have the agreement of the Muslim community. There is no question of solving these matters by force. In such a situation all legal sides and powers must maintain peace in all circumstances. So, peaceful and conciliatory methods should be the only options. No support is to be given to any unilateral or aggressive step. I agree to a large extent, that it should not be allowed to become a burning issue and the ongoing issues should be solved peacefully. No fact should obstruct friendly talks. I hope that you will succeed in your efforts in this direction.

Yours
Vallabhbhai Patel
Respected Pundit Govind Vallabh Pant
Chief United Province, Lucknow

Sardar Patel not only praised the steps taken by Chief Minister Pant, but also held groupism in his party responsible for this problem. Chief Minister Govind Vallabh Pant replied to the letter of Sardar Patel.

Lucknow
13 January, 1950

Dear Sardar Sahab,

I am short of words to thank you for the trouble you took to come down to Lucknow on my request which was without any prior information. I was avoiding troubling you considering your tedious Bombay tour, but some things worried me. Whenever I am troubled, I look towards you. In the moments of tension and depression you give me strength like a light. Whenever I recall the events here that took place in your presence, I feel ashamed. This will give you an idea of a constant anguish rising inside me. Despite this, we are discharging our duties in the best way we can.

Selection committee has selected its party and following candidates. Should I have faith that a final selection will be made today. I have been told that this list has been received in a positive manner.

I wish to thank you for your letter regarding the Ayodhya matter. That will be a big help to us here. Efforts to solve the issue peacefully are underway and should succeed. However, a lot is still temporary, mentioning which can be dangerous.

Thanks

Yours
Govind Vallabh Pant
Respected Sardar Vallabhbhai Patel
Deputy Prime Minister
Government of India
New Delhi

Dissatisfied with the action taken so far in Ayodhya, Prime Minister Jawaharlal Nehru again wrote to Chief Minister Pant. This letter reflects his disappointment and dejection on the events of Ayodhya.

Copy
Govind Vallabh Pant
New Delhi   17 April, 1950

Dear Pant ji,

Events in Uttar Pradesh have anguished me deeply. Perhaps this is the climax of things I have been thinking for long.

I have been thinking that the communal situation in the entire Uttar Pradesh is getting worse. The land of Uttar Pradesh is becoming foreign for me. I am not at ease there. I have been associated with Uttar Pradesh Congress Committee for 35 years, but now I feel surprised at its ways of functioning. This is not the way of functioning of Congress that I know of, but this is that which I have opposed throughout my life.

I found that the minds and hearts of people who were pillars of Congress party are now filled with communalism, which is unknowingly crippling them. Whatever took place regarding the mosque and temple was wrong, but the most regrettable part was that some of our own people were involved in it. It all happened with their approval.

I feel that for some reason or for mere political benefit, we have become victim to this disease, which is spreading throughout India, even in our province. Sometimes I feel I should leave everything aside and concentrate only on this. Perhaps I will do it someday. If I did that it will be a crusade with all the strength I have in me.

The reports that reach me on smaller events reveal the true picture. If any Muslim is roaming alone, he is provoked for a fight and told to leave for Pakistan or slapped. His beard is pulled. In the lanes, Muslim women are a target of obscene comments and scoffed – Go to Pakistan.

Yours
Jawaharlal

Nehru appears helpless in his letters. He wants to be seen secular but does not want to become unpopular among the majority. As a Prime Minister, he was running a country that had a huge Hindu majority. The nation had become independent. The fire of communal violence was everywhere. The anger of partition was in everyone. The majority then had become Hindu. There was an ongoing power struggle in Congress. In such a situation, Nehru could only remain secular to a certain extent. He was very sensitive about his popularity. He was not ready to compromise his popularity for any higher principle. That's why Nehru was acting within the limits of an average Hindu's tolerance.

Nehru, Sardar Patel, Govind Vallabh Pant, Gurudutt Singh and K.K.K. Nayar, all were under immense pressure of the Hindu sentiment.

Later Gurudutt and Nayar were under considerable influence of Hindu Mahasabha. The story of Ayodhya begins with Abhiram Das. He wanted to place the idols where Lord Ram was born. He had made it the mission of his life. Two disciples of Abhiram Das are still there Satyendra Das and Dharam Das. Satyendra Das is the priest of the current Ram Janmabhoomi temple in the tent. He gets a pay and Dharam Das is the Mahant of the Sankat Mochan temple of Ayodhya. Both recall that Abhiram Das often saw a dream in which Lord Ram expected him to free his birthplace. Abhiram Das met the City Magistrate Gurudutt Singh regarding this.

Gurudutt Singh's son, Guru Basant Singh, said in one of the interviews that his father told Abhiram Das, 'Since I have been posted in Faizabad, it is my wish too.' Gurudutt Singh was a graduate from Allahabad University and had come through civil services of the united province. Six feet tall with a thick moustache and of firm resolute, Singh never wore a hat. He always wore a turban. Once when an English officer asked him why he did not wear a hat, he immediately replied, 'Why don't you wear a turban?'

It was decided in the meetings between Abhiram Das and Gurudutt Singh when the idol will be placed in the disputed structure. But when and how it would be done was discussed in the later meetings. During this time K.K.K. Nayar became the collector of Faizabad. Nayar was from Alleppey in Kerala and joined civil services in 1930. Before Faizabad, he was stationed as District Magistrate in Gonda. Gonda was the adjoining district of Faizabad across Saryu. At Gonda, he came in contact with the King of Balrampur, Pateshwari Prasad Singh, and later with the Hindu Mahasabha. A deep emotion developed in him for Ram Janmabhoomi. An alumnus of Madras University, Nayar knew Hindi, Udru, and English along with French, German and Spanish.

The idea to free Ram Janmabhoomi in Ayodhya first occurred to these three friends, King of Balrampur, Pateshwari Prasad Singh, Mahant Digvijay Nath and K.K.K. Nayar. The basis of their friendship was their religion. They were united with the common thread of being Hindus and their love for tennis. K.K.K. Nayar was Gonda's District Magistrate. Later from 1 June 1949 he became the District Magistrate of Faizabad.

These three people with similar ideology often got together at Balrampur. Maharaja Pateshwari Prasad, who was born on 1 June 1914, was brought up under the supervision of a British officer, Colonel Hansen. He studied at Mayo College in Ajmer. There he acquired his skills at horse-riding and lawn tennis. Even after having led an English lifestyle, Pateshwari Prasad Singh remained engaged in spreading the Hindu life philosophy. He was also associated with Hindu Mahasabha. In 1947 K.K.K. Nayar became the District Magistrate of Gonda. He became a good friend of the Maharaja while he was posted there. Maharaja organized a big Yagya ceremony in 1947. Swami Karpatri, a religious Hindu leader also came for it. Karpatri was the guru of the Maharaja. Maharaja had deep respect for him.

Karpatri was a Siddha Dandi ascetic. He was an 'Udbhat' scholar. He had written many books. His book *Ramrajya and Marxwaad* was well-known. Karpatri had been bestowed with the title of 'Dharma Samraat'. He had been the president of the committee that appoints Shankaracharyas. Karpatri was an impressive orator. In 1940, he had founded Dharma Sangha in Banaras, an organization for safeguarding traditional Hindus. He started publishing a daily newspaper, *Sanmarga* from Banaras in 1940. Later it published from Calcutta as well. For placing religion appropriately in politics, he also founded a political party by the name of 'Ram Rajya Parishad'. Pateshwari Prasad Singh helped him in this endeavour. Four members of this party had reached the Parliament. In 1951, 24 members of Ram Rajya Parishad were elected in Rajasthan Vidhan Sabha. Karpatri was an ascetic political leader.

Harnarayan Ojha, born at Pratapgarh in Uttar Pradesh, left home at the age of eight. He performed strict ascetic practice in a straw hut on the banks of Ganga in Banaras. After renouncing worldly life, he accepted only as much alms as fit his palms. This was the reason he got the name 'Kar-Patri' or 'palm-bowl'. After becoming a proper monk, he picked up a staff of resolution to establish Dharma in politics. In 1966, Karpatri was leading a procession at the Parliament in protest of cow killing. The police fired at the protest procession in which dozens of sadhus died.

Karpatri lived at the Kedar Ghat of Banaras. He was a monk who liked to read and write. That's why he was associated with other learned people in the city. I often went to his place with my father. During one of the conversations, he once told us about the struggle of the entire history of Ram Janmabhoomi movement. According to Karpatri, the Ram Janmabhoomi freedom movement had its roots in that yagya.

Mahant Digvijay Nath also reached there just a day before the final day of the yagya. Collector of Gonda, K.K.K. Nayar was also present there. This was the place where it was first discussed that the Hindu holy places that were occupied by foreign invaders should be freed by Ram Rajya Parishad. Digvijay Nath was of the view that this issue is already on the agenda of Hindu Mahasabha. All four were quite close in their opinion. This idea that Ram Janmabhoomi be freed was between Karpatri and Nayar. The next day, while leaving district headquarters of Gonda, Karpatri promised Nayar that he will seriously consider the proposal and give his views. The very next day after reaching the yagya in Balrampur, Nayar straightaway went to Karpatri and Mahant Digvijay Nath. Both welcomed Nayar. The three of them again discussed ways of handling Ayodhya. When Nayar was asked about the plan, Mahant Digvijay Nath placed the entire plan to regain Kashi Vishwanath temple of Varanasi, Shri Krishna Janmabhoomi in Mathura and Ram Janmabhoomi in Ayodhya. After this, Nayar promised Digvijay Nath that he is ready to renounce everything, even his post, to achieve this goal. With this background, it was a coincidence that a few days later Nayar was appointed as the collector of Faizabad.

Now, Nayar, Gurudutt Singh and Abhiram Das joined the plan. They didn't even inform the state government of the idol being placed, until a mob of fifteen to twenty thousand people started singing bhajans or devotional songs. Later when they were pressurized to have the idols removed, they offered to be removed from their positions, but didn't agree to remove the idols. Guru Basant Singh, son of Gurudutt Singh says that his father had told him that both had decided to resign if the government remained adamant on their decision of removing the idols.

K.K.K. Nayar took retirement after being posted out of Faizabad in 1952 and became a Member of Parliament in the fourth Lok Sabha through Jansangh from Bahraich, UP. His wife Shakuntala Nayar also got elected three times though Bharatiya Jansangh in Lok Sabha, from Kaisarganj in UP. She also remained member of Uttar Pradesh legislative assembly. Even Nayar's driver became a Jan Sangh MLA from a nearby seat. Gurudutt also first became chief of Faizabad Jansangh, and later he was elected MLA of Jansangh from Faizabad city.

Whatever took place in Ayodhya was also because UP had not come out of the shock of partition. The Magistrate had the courage to do what he did because of the communal environment that prevailed in the country. They took advantage of a heightened emotional state in an immature democracy and ensured the placement of idols there. If the country was not divided, this would not have happened. And If at all something like this would happen the government would have removed the idols. But the government didn't have the courage then.

This was the time when the nation was going through the tragedy of partition. The harmony between Hindus and Muslims was bloodstained. The divide of suspicion and enmity between the two was at its worst. The nation was burning in the fire of counter-violence and revenge. People were divided. In such a time, the foundation for the biggest dispute of free India was being laid in Ayodhya. All parties tried to benefit from this dispute including sadhus-ascetics, mullah-maulvis and even the state and Central government. What took place on the night of 22-23 December 1949, at the disputed premises in Ayodhya, burnt the nation not once, but many times and it continues to burn. To understand the secrets that lie in the heart of Ayodhya, it is necessary to understand the significance of this date.

Chapter 7

AYODHYA BENEATH THE LAND

The Ayodhya conflict is ancient. Many battles have been fought over it. Many movements led. The basic question behind all of this was one—did a Ram Mandir exist at the same place before the Babri mosque was built? Has the Babri mosque been built after demolishing the Ram Janmabhoomi temple? This one question intriguing generations for two hundred years was also in front of the Allahabad High Court now. It was hoped that a solution could be found by conducting an excavation on the land. So, the court decided to explore this option in an attempt to reach a conclusion.

History books cannot encapsulate a country's cultural heritage. Every country has its own historical uniqueness. There are archaeological evidence and historical values. Besides historical and archaeological facts, there is no psychological or cultural commitment. Perhaps this is why history and archaeology became the centre of the Ayodhya conflict. This conflict's biggest question was whether the Babri mosque was built after demolishing a temple.

Since the Babri Masjid Action Committee was formed in 1986 as a reaction to the court's decision to unlock Ram Janmabhoomi, the committee and its leader Syed Shahabuddin had declared many times that if it was proved that there was a temple before Babri Masjid was built and the current mosque was built after its demolition, they will not consider it a mosque according to Shariyat. They said that the Muslim leaders would themselves go and demolish it. To challenge this, both sides started collecting historical and archaeological evidence. At that time Chandra Shekhar was the prime minister and six rounds of meetings took place between both sides. In the sixth meet, when experts for the Babri side did not turn up even after four hours of waiting, it ended inconclusively. Before this both sides had even done a give and take of evidence on the subject. Prof. R.S. Sharma, Prof. Athar Ali, Prof. Surajbhan, Prof. D.N. Jha and Javed Habib presented evidence from the Babri committee's side and Prof. B.P. Sinha, Dr Swaraj Prakash Gupta, Prof. Harsh Narayan, Prof. K.M. Lal, Prof. Devendra Swaroop and Baldev Raj Grover presented evidence from VHP's side.

Now history and archaeology had become the Ayodhya conflict's central points. Historical evidence were being investigated by all sides. After demolition, in January 1993 India's president asked the SC through 'presidential reference' if there was a Hindu temple or a Hindu religious place before the Babri structure was built. The Supreme Court felt that the government wants to use it to their advantage and hence, after a long hearing it refused to give its opinion on the matter and returned the reference done according to constitution's Article 143 (A).

Allahabad High Court found the answer to this question in its decision given on 30 September 2010 on the conflict. Allahabad HC accepted the report by Archaeological Survey Of India which said that evidence of existence of a Hindu temple in the tenth century was found under the mosque during an excavation. A bench of three judges based their decision on this report by ASI. ASI had mentioned in its 574 page report that it submitted to the HC that carved stones, stone pillars, broken statues of gods and goddesses, things used in a temple, amber, octagonal shaped figurine used to hang on pillars made of black stones were found during excavation at the disputed site. It also mentioned finding the base of 50 pillars which were evidence of presence of a huge Hindu structure there. It said that these pointed out to the presence of a temple before the mosque there. These archaeological evidence completely resembled the specifications of temples built in North India. We will talk about this decision in detail later. First let's see how seriously the Indian government took it.

The Indian government published a white paper on the Ayodhya demolition in February 1993. In para 2/3 of the white paper, it was revealed that during the talk held between the two parties to reach an amicable solution to the conflict, the question that came up was whether there was a temple that was razed by Babur where the mosque stood then. The Indian government's white paper also said that the Muslim leaders insisted that if it was proved that there was a temple there earlier, they would hand over the conflicted land to Hindus willingly.

Tackling these very questions, the Lucknow bench of the Allahabad HC also saw a way out through the archaeological evidence. It asked ASI the same question. ASI or Archaeological Survey of India is India's top archaeological research and investigation agency which was formed by the British in 1861. HC told ASI to get the GPR study of the area where Babri stands before excavating it. GPR study means 'ground penetrating radar'. This technique helps in establishing the structure and composition of land without digging it which helps in finding if there are evidence inside it that can tell if there was a structure ever on that land before the mosque was built. In this method, antennae of high capabilities send electromagnetic waves inside the land. These waves encounter different structures inside the land while the speed of these is being recorded in a computer. This helps prepare a map of the structures inside the land. In Ayodhya, an Indo-Canadian firm 'Tojo International' conducted the GPR study on HC's order at the disputed site from 30 December 2002 to 17 January 2003. The study's report was submitted in the HC through ASI on February 17.

This report had shocking revelations. From the surface of the land to half a metre deep and further to about five and a half metres deep, evidence of three different kinds of construction from three different eras were found. Things like ancient pillars, walls, platforms, floors of stone and the foundation of an ancient building were found. This survey was the first to hint at the presence of another structure underneath the land which could only be confirmed with the help of excavation.

Looking at the results of this survey, Allahabad HC told ASI to excavate the disputed site on 5 March 2003 and collect evidence. HC handed over copies of the order to both parties with the instruction that media must not get a hint about it. On 5 March 2003 HC gave ASI an order to start excavation at the disputed site in a week's time and to submit its report to the court within a month. The court asked ASI to find out what is beneath the structure. The court also asked ASI to keep the 10 feet area around Ram Lalla free from excavation and to ensure that the excavation process does not impact worship at the temple. It ordered excavation to happen inside covers. The media was to be kept outside. What was found during the excavation was also not to reach the media on a daily basis. Each relic found to be listed with its picture. Stratigraphy to be done by a scientific method. High Court also ordered that the group involved in the excavation to include both Hindu and Muslim archaeologists to make the whole process transparent. Both parties were also permitted to keep lawyers and supervisors during the excavation.

On high court's order, ASI started the excavation on 12 March under the leadership of ASI's superintendent archaeologist V.R. Mani along with his 14-member team. Other members in the team were Shubhra Pramanik, P.K. Trivedi, A.R. Siddiqui, P. Venkatesh, S.S. Rao, G.S. Khwaja, T.S. Ravishankar, C.V. Patil, A.A. Hashmi, Vishnukant, A.C. Prakash and Zulfikar Ali. The HC bench that gave the order of excavation included Justice Sudheer Narayan, Justice S.R. Alam and Justice Bhanwar Singh.

The relics found in the initial digging made the Babri supporters anxious. The result was that the camp supporting Babri mosque issued a statement calling the excavation unfair. Their argument was that this cannot be the basis of demolishing a religious monument. If evidence are found that there existed another community's religious structure at some point in history, it will give legal recognition to a wrong principle and set a wrong precedent. They demanded it to be stopped. The ones who issued statements included Prof. Irfan Habib, K.M. Srimali, Suraj Bhan and advocate Rajiv Dhawan. People who signed this petition also raised a question on the objectivity of ASI. They also questioned the capabilities of ASI to carry out such a difficult and scientific procedure. Although at the time when Chandra Shekhar was the prime minister and later when P.V. Narasimha Rao became the PM, the same wise men turned historians for the Babri mosque and gave theories and evidence to prove that there was already a mosque there. These wise men were also part of the dialogue between both parties. They would give evidence in favour of the mosque in each meeting. But when they found archaeological evidence going against them, they ran away from the situation saying that if Babri is demolished, it may start a whole new series of demolishing historical monuments, that too lawfully. In a way they were admitting their drawback because till now, none of the Babri supporters had ever accepted the possibility of another community's structure under the Babri mosque. This was, in a way, the first time they accepted such a possibility. Up till now, this camp had been asserting with full force that the Babri mosque was built on an empty land. But changed circumstances had forced them to change their stand and strategy.

On the HC's order, ASI got the excavation done at the Ram Janmabhoomi between 12 March 2003 and 7 August 2003. After it was complete, ASI submitted its report in the court on 22 September 2003. ASI's team lead and superintendent archaeologist Dr B.R. Mani told the court the working process of methodology followed by ASI. The whole process was recorded and videographed. This excavation was completed in the presence of legal supervisors, lawyers and representatives from related parties. To ensure transparency, all the excavated pieces were sealed in the presence of both parties. These were then transferred to the strong room provided by Faizabad's commissioner the very same day. The strong room was sealed after opening it every day.

Due to security and other formalities, there was some delay in the excavation work. Monsoons made the situation worse. The whole area had to be covered with multicoloured waterproof sheets. This caused dampness and darkness in many trenches. Monkeys also started jumping on these sheets. Thousands of monkeys were there in Ayodhya's Hanuman Garhi and Ram Jamnbhoomi area. To deter the monkeys, these sheets were supported with bamboo sticks. This created a situation of utter darkness and started causing issues in photography. Lights had to be placed in the trenches at levels that were many metres deep. Grills and pillars all around made it difficult to even walk in the area.

ASI dug at a total of ninety points. The whole area was divided into fifty parts. This included the eastern, southern, western and northern areas along with the platform. Excavation happened in all these areas and directions in a systematic order so as to get a hint about the nature and cultural background of the structures. ASI confirmed that there was another structure present under the structure that existed. The relics proved that there used to be a Hindu temple in the eleventh century. A petroglyph and Lord Shiva's statue was also found in the excavation.

The first thing ASI said was that there is a 'cultural mount' in the conflicted area and the one kilometre area around it. This meant that any work on the land brought changes in the layers and that leads to an increased level of the land. This is called a 'cultural mount' or a 'cultural deposit'. Such cultural mounts were found till about 10.8 metres deep in the land. This also meant that there were human activities going on there for thousands of years. To reach a conclusion, ASI divided it into nine segments. The first was from 1300-300 BC. Second was Shung dynasty from 200-100 BC. Third was Kushan dynasty from the first to the third century. Fourth was Guptkaal from the fourth to the sixth century. Fifth was after the Guptkaal ended from the seventh to the tenth century. Sixth was Poorv Madhya kaal from the 11th to 12th century. Seventh was Sultanat or Madhya kaal from 12th to 16th century. Eighth was Mughal kaal in the 17th century and ninth was Uttar Mughal kaal.

During excavation in Ayodhya few relics were found in the northern ground whose existence appeared to be about thirteen years older than Jesus. These were called 'northern black polish wear' in the language of archaeology which meant earthenware polished black or decorative items. Some evidence were found during the excavation which included earthenware, broken scales, pieces of glass, flat round things, broken animal statue and an iron knife. But no evidence was found that suggested the existence of a structure. They would have probably been destroyed by the increasing human activities with time. Although archaeologists suggested that if they went away from there and excavated near the river, evidence of such a structure could also be found.

The second era was that of the Shung dynasty. Here, for the first time, structural relics of bricks and stones were found. There are historical evidence that Shung dynasty's rule came into Ayodhya in 192 BC. The kings of the Shung dynasty won Ayodhya with the help of Greek soldiers. While excavating, a statue of a goddess made of terracotta was found under the conflicted land. Some other terracotta statues were also found during the excavation. A grinding mill made of stone was also found. Some statues along with garlands were also found.

The Kushan period from the first to the third century was rich with respect to earthenware. From here a big kiln was found along with statues of animals and humans. They also found pieces of bangles, portions of a broken water tank made of terracotta, hair pins and a copper rod. A floor made of huge bricks was also discovered which belonged to this very period. Between the fourth and the sixth century, it was the rule of Gupt rulers. There weren't many changes seen in the construction or architectural activities during this period. The relics found from this time period included terracotta statues and a copper coin. The front of the coin had the picture of the king whereas the back had a picture of Garud along with the hero of the legends, Srichand Gupt. After this, it was time for Uttar Gupt Rajput period between seventh and tenth century. From this period, they found a square shaped brick temple, which also had a door in the east direction. This structure was in a shabby condition. Despite this, a drainage line could be seen in its northern wall to help drain the water. This was a specific feature of the temples of that era. During the excavation, a huge structure from the early eleventh and twelfth century were also found which was 50 metres long from north to south. Here there was a thick floor made from broken bricks. This was next to a big and broad wall in the North-South direction. It seemed that this structure existed for a very short while because only four out of the base of 50 pillars found in excavation had reached this level. They also found a broken red stone inscripted with some letters. Archaeologists said it was from the 11th century. In the relics of this structure was found the construction of a huge structure, that had three phases—A, B and C. In phase A, a huge wall was constructed (wall no. 16). This was 50 metres long and was going in the North-South direction. At one place, construction of a new style was also found. A floor made of lime, mud and bricks was also found. A shelf like structure was made on this. This floor was surrounded by thin walls. In phase B, this surrounded area was filled with mud. Pieces of bricks were laid on these. On top of this, a floor made of lime, pieces of loose rock and bricks was laid. A foundation was also there to hold pillars and structures strongly in place. This was part of phase C. A 4 to 5 centimetres floor was laid on top of this. There were square shaped nets made of pebbles and sandstone to lend support to the pillars. The floor around most of the pillars' base was found broken. The base of the pillars was also in a bad state. Around 50 such bases of pillars were found whose foundation was made of pieces of bricks.

The excavation revealed that there were 17 lines of pillars from north to south direction. Every line had 5 pillars. There were only 12 pillar bases in the total 50 pillar bases found during excavation that could be seen completely. 35 could be seen partially whereas 3 could be seen only in pieces. The central pieces of these bases could not be found. The reason of this was that the temporary Ram Lalla temple was standing there and that area could not be dug. This huge structure was different from the residential structure. This was also an evidence that its construction was done with the aim of public use. The Babri Masjid was built in the sixteenth century on this very huge structure. Babri mosque's main room's centre stood on the lower structure's wall number 16's central point. Its central point had a square shaped crater in the east direction whose western fragment gave the hint of a floor made of big bricks. This construction gave the sense of a place where an important object was kept. There was possibly an image of a Garud here.

During excavating the multiple layers, bones of animals were also found from different time periods. But in the northern and southern parts of the trenches, skeletons were also found. These skeletons were from the Northern Mughal era. Various structures from the Shung and Gupt era were found. Their nature or utility could not be figured. From the Gupt era till the Uttar Mughal era, symbols of residences at different levels started disappearing. According to experts, the area below the disputed site was a public place till the time the structure was built in the Mughal era. This was a limited space where people lived around it. The black polished earthenware, found in a big number at this place, confirmed that Ram and Ayodhya's story was older than Krishna and Hastinapur.

ASI's report also has some specific symbols that are found in north Indian temples. These symbols were:

1. The archaeological remains of a huge temple top under the disputed structure.
2. Sequential statues dating back to tenth century till the time of the construction of the disputed structure.
3. Structures made of stones and decorative bricks.
4. Broken statues of a divine couple.
5. Motif of a lotus.
6. A square shaped temple whose water flow was towards the north.
7. 50 pillar bases next to the huge structure.

Simply put, ASI had established in their report that the Babri mosque was not built on plain land. The relics found at this place belonged to an ancient religious structure. Babri mosque's northern room's wall number 5 stood directly on temple's western wall (wall number 16). The bricks used to fill the base for wall number 5, had been collected from the demolished temple. Mosque's southern base wall (wall number 6) directly stood on the old temple's two pillars' base. Wall number 6 was directly connected with wall number 16. This area had a two-centimetre thick layer of lime over it. This was the main wall and proved that the shelves made in wall number 16 were closed after the temple demolition and before the mosque was built. These shelves were made to place statues of gods and goddesses. Babri mosque's wall number 7 stood on three pillar bases of an old temple. This was right in front of the south-facing room. These facts also proved that the Babri mosque was built over an existing structure.

They also found a 10.8 metre thick layered structure during excavation. The nature of these in all 9 time periods was the same. This hinted that this place was never touched. Also, this was never used for residential purpose. Four floors were also found at this place. Floor number 3, which was found under floor number 2, was established through carbon dating to be of a time period between 900 AD and 1030 AD. Floor number 2, with which 50 pillar bases were connected, was clearly the floor of the temple. Floor one was on top of floor 2 which was the mosque's floor.

The relics found in the excavation are mostly from the same time periods that have been used in the construction of the Babri mosque. This made it evident to ASI that a temple did exist there on that land. These relics included sanctum santorum, semi pavilion, broad pavilion, a pushkarni in the north east, broad walls and remains of the previously demolished temples. ASI said in its report to the the HC that their report could need some changes. The reason for this was that many people who worked to very tight deadlines were involved in preparing the report. The court agreed to let ASI make any changes that it felt were right. ASI also gave the outline of an optional timeline in which no changes were made till the fifth timeline. Some changes were made in the later nomenclature. But no changes were made in the time periods related to the century. ASI also drew attention to the fact that there was so much debris at that place that it was difficult to identify the layers accurately. It became evident after this excavation that the Ram platform was constructed in five different phases. The main reason behind this wasn't clear. This could also be a pond of water. But during its last phase, it looked like a small stage although while looking at the 22-metres-long corner from east to west side and 14-metres-long corner from north to south, it appeared to be a huge construction.

The base of this structure was at least 2.67 metres deep. This was made of seven layers. Every layer had blocks of concrete that were joined with a lime mixture. There was a tank-like construction on top of this structure. The initial look of Ram's platform resembled the account given by Catholic missionary Joseph Tiefenthaler. A traveller from Austria, Joseph had been at this place from 1766 to 1771. He had described it as a square box. This was five feet above the ground and covered with lime and stones. People would take three rounds of it and would bow kneeling during worship. During the excavation, ASI found many such things that confirmed the structure under the mosque to be a non-Muslim structure. These included many statues, pillars, statue of lord Shiva, jewellery and statue of a divine couple along with some other things.

Bones of animals were also found in the excavation. Historians supporting Babri accused ASI of ignoring remains of animals that were found in every layer. According to them, ASI did not even keep a record of the bones of animals found at these places. According to historian Jaya Menon, she was present at the site of excavation and she did not protest against the bones being thrown away. People who were digging did not collect the bones. They, in fact, threw them away. Prof. Irfan Habib accused ASI of ignoring this evidence that refuted the existence of a temple there. He said that the bones of animals had cuts that proved that these animals were eaten there. He argued that these bones went against the idea of the existence of a temple there.

HC thought over this point. According to HC, the bones found were of animals from different time periods. These bones were in the materials brought from nearing areas to even out the land from time to time. It was natural to have bones of dead animals in soil brought from populated areas. Examining these would only give information of their origin. This would not make a difference to the relics found during excavation, the different layers or their nature. The court also said that it was not true that bones of animals in such a huge number can be found only at a mosque or an Idgah-like Muslim religious place. Islam is very clear that a religious place cannot be used for residential or eating purpose. The existence of animal remains could be of relevance if some other similar objects were found that hinted at a residential place or a township.

ASI's report also had brief comments on three parts of the inscriptions found during the excavation. Among these, one was found in Nagri and the other in Arabic. One of the Arabic inscriptions was of the 16th century Naskh style. An 'ayat' from Quran was inscribed on it. The other Arabic inscription was also in the initial style of the 16th century. This had 'Allah' inscribed on it. According to ASI the five letter phrase inscribed in Nagri belonged to the 11th century.

This excavation by ASI only confirmed the Hindu beliefs and claims. Besides these, records of revenue and Waqf papers, accounts of foreign travellers and British rulers, and verdicts given in earlier cases related to Hindu gods and goddesses only weakened the Babri claims. ASI submitted its 574 pages report along with pictures in the court on 22 September 2003. This report established the existence of a Hindu temple in the 11th century under the demolished mosque. On the basis of these evidence, all three judges of the HC agreed that the centre of the disputed site was Ram Janmabhoomi. The important thing was that all three judges agreed on the question of the sanctum sanctorum.

When the structure was razed on 6 December 1992, some of the big bricks collected from the domes had 1930 and 1924 inscribed on them. It was obvious that those bricks must have been of the same years, which meant that the current structure would also be of that period. After demolition, details of these bricks along with their picture were published in newspapers. Before this, in June 1992 when the Kalyan Singh government aquired the 2.77 acre land and started levelling the land for the temple construction, evidence of the existence of a temple emerged. On 12 June 1992 some stone blocks hit the bulldozer while levelling the land. Some archaeologist noticed that these were part of the top of a temple! This had things like amber, door pillars, five broken statues, gyanlata etc. A team of archaeologists arrived in Ayodhya to study these. This team included ASI's former Director General, Dr Yagya Dutt Sharma, former director K.N. Shrivastav, V.R. Grover, Prof. Swaraj Prakash Gupta, Shardendra Mukherjee and Dr Devendra Swaroop. When these people looked a little deeper, they also found the floor of the temple made of big bricks. Later the Babri committee rejected these evidence saying that these were brought from elsewhere and placed there. When ASI submitted its report in the court report and HC made it the basis of its judgement, Babri experts said that the point of contention wasn't this at all. They argued that the court wasn't supposed to find out if there ever existed a temple on that land or not. Instead the court was to figure who is the rightful owner of the land.

On 6 December, when Babri was demolished, big evidence that confirmed the existence of a temple was discovered. Along with ruins of an ancient temple, a five feet long and two and a half feet broad inscription was also found. This inscription of 20 lines had 30 shloks inscribed on it. This inscription on a red stone was scripted in Nagri and the language was Sanskrit. Most parts of the engraved inscription were in verses. To read and understand these inscriptions, epigraphists specializing in that time period were called. These included Indian government's former archaeologist, K.B. Ramesh, Nagpur University's Professor Ajay Mitra Shastri and Kashi Hindu University's Professor T.P. Verma. Prof. Verma was an expert in reading 'gahadwalkaleen' writings. All three scholars reached the conclusion that the inscription was of the 12th century during the rule of Gahadwal King Govind Chandra (1114-1154). The inscription says that 'this temple's top is like a golden Lotus. It is dedicated to lord Vishnuhari who killed the ten headed Ravan.' It also mentioned Ayodhya and Janmabhoomi.

The translation of the the 20 lines in the inscription are:

'The one who was the wisest in this world and was the son of the cloud, his nephew Naychandra gained dominion and control over Saket Mandal with the prasad offered by the best king, King Govind Chandra and got this beautiful temple of Shree Vishnuhari built. The amazing temple that could never be built by earlier kings was done by him. Who is this other pious man who killed Hiranyakashipu, stopped Balasur in the battle, cut Baliraj's Bahu into pieces, witnessed Bhuvikram and killed the enemy?'

HC took this inscription into consideration. But the other party totally rejected it. This inscription plays a pivotal role in resolving this long-standing bitter conflict. Allahabad HC's decision gives answers to all these questions. This decision cleared both the picture and fate of the disputed site to quite an extent. This historic decision by Allahabad HC's Lucknow bench declared Ayodhya's conflicted land as 'Ram Janmabhoomi'.

This historic decision was given on 30 September 2010 by a bench of judges that included Justice Sudheer Agarwal, Justice S.U. Khan and Justice D.V. Sharma. This case of 1989 was heard by 18 judges. Some of them retired and some even got transferred. Not only judges, even lawyers changed. In fact, a third generation of lawyers was fighting the case by now. HC said in its order to divide the 2.77 acres of land into three equal parts. The place where Ram Lalla's statue is placed was handed over to Ram Lalla. This can be called the first part. The second part that included Ram's platform and Sita rasoi was given to Nirmohi Akhada whereas the third part was handed over to the Central Sunni Waqf Board. Bench of all three judges of the HC made ASI report the basis of their decision. The court also gave, as the basis of its decision, the religious belief that Ayodhya is Ram's birthplace. All three judges said that the claims by the Sunni Central Waqf Board on behalf of Muslims were beyond legal timelines and hence dismissed these. Two judges of the bench, Justice S.U. Khan and Justice Sudheer Agarwal considered defendant Sunni Waqf Board entitled to one third share with majority in the case of Gopal Singh Visharad. All three judges also agreed that statues of lord Ram were placed inside the conflicted mosque on 22/23 December 1949.

The mosque was built by Babur or on his order. The court order clearly said that this place was lord Ram's birthplace. The court also mentioned in its verdict that huge relics of a temple were found during the excavation carried out by ASI and the mosque was built on the ruins of the temple. But the judges had a difference of opinion on whether the temple was broken while constructing the mosque. The decision also said that for convenience, the 70 acres land acquired by the government must also be included while dividing the land. An interesting fact was that one of the judges hearing the case, Dharamveer Verma, was retiring the next day i.e., 1 October. If they did not give the verdict on 30 September, the whole proceeding would have to be done all over again after his retirement. The special bench of HC hearing the case of ownership rights of Ayodhya's conflicted land had changed 13 times in 21 years. These changes in the bench were due to retirement of judges, their promotions or transfers.

One big important factor about this decision was that Ram Lalla was to remain where he was placed initially. Hindus consider this as Ram's birthplace. HC put a stay of three months on its own decision. Status quo was to be maintained during this time. All parties were given this time to go through the verdict and appeal in the Supreme Court if they wished to. The verdict's main point was also that the basis of declaring the disputed site as Ram's birthplace was faith.

Justice D.V. Sharma did not agree to the formula of division of the land. According to him, Hindus have had special rights with respect to worship on the outer boundary around the disputed site. He said that they had been worshipping inside as well in a similar way and so they had a right on the entire land. In his 'decent note', Justice Sharma clearly wrote that the disputed site is lord Ram's birthplace. According to Justice Agarwal, the central dome of the disputed site was Ram's birthplace. This is what Hindus believed. It was their faith. Justice Khan also did not completely deny this. Although he said prior to 1949, Hindus started considering the area exactly under the central dome as lord Ram's birthplace. He was also of the same opinion that the area under the central dome should be given to Hindus.

Justice Agarwal and Justice Sharma agreed that the mosque was built after demolishing a Hindu temple. But Justice Khan did not agree to this. According to him, the mosque was built on the ruins of a temple, that these temple remains were way older and had been there already, and that is why some of it was even used in the mosque's construction. Justice Agarwal and Justice Khan were in agreement on the point that till 1992, the structure that existed there was a mosque only. But Justice Sharma didn't agree to this. According to him the disputed structure was built against the principles of Islam and hence cannot be considered a mosque.

Main points of Justice S.U. Khan's decision were:

1. The disputed structure was constructed by Babur or on his instructions.
2. There is no direct evidence that proves that the disputed site is related to Babur or to the person who got it built or on whose orders it was built.
3. No temple was demolished to construct the mosque.
4. The mosque was built on the ruins of a temple. But these remains were lying on that land already for a long period of time. This was the reason why some of it was even used in the construction of the mosque.
5. Hindus have considered that Lord Ram's birthplace is an area in the big area of the disputed site and the disputed structure is a small part of it. Although this kind of faith was not related to a specific small area inside the big area.
6. Much before 1855, the Ram platform and Sita Rasoi had come into existence and Hindus were worshipping them. This was

a very strange and unprecedented situation that there were religious areas of worship for Hindus inside a mosque. Namaz and regular worship coexisted and were conducted inside the same mosque.
7. Ownership lay with both Hindus and Muslims for the disputed site.
8. Statues were placed under the mosque's central dome for the first time in the early morning of 23 December 1949.
9. In light of this, both parties are declared the joint 'title holder' of the disputed site. The area under the central dome, where the temporary temple is established, is allocated to Hindus.

Main points of Justice Dharamveer Sharma's decision:

1. Disputed site is lord Ram's birthplace. This is seen as a divine place and is worshipped as Ram's birthplace. Ram is worshipped here in his young form.
2. The disputed structure was built by Babur. The year is not confirmed. But this was done against the principles of Islam and so it cannot have the character of a mosque.
3. This disputed structure was built in place of the old structure after demolishing it. ASI proved that this structure was a huge Hindu religious place of worship.
4. The statues were placed in the disputed structure's middle dome on 22/33 December 1949 at midnight.
5. The case of Sunni Central Waqf Board versus Gopal Singh Visharad and others; Nirmohi Akhada plus others versus Shri Jamuna Prasad Singh and others was 'time barred', which meant it was out of the legal timeline.
6. It had been established that the land in the case was Ramchandra's birthplace. Here Hindus were generally allowed to worship 'charan-paduka', Sita rasoi and other statues. It was also established that Hindus had been visiting this disputed site as the place of Ram's birth.

Main points from Justice Sudheer Agarwal's judgement were:

1. According to the faith and belief of Hindus, the area under the central dome was Ram's birthplace.
2. The disputed site was always considered a mosque and Muslims have been visiting it for namaz. Although it is not proved that it was built during the rule of Babur in 1528.
3. In the absence of any concrete evidence, it is difficult to tell when the disputed structure was built. But it is clear to quite an extent that its construction happened before Joseph Tiefenthaler travelled through the area of Awadh (1766-1771).
4. The disputed structure was built after demolishing a non-Islamic structure (Hindu temple).
5. Statues were placed in the central dome on the night of 22-23 December 1949.

This decision paved way for the construction of the temple. But both parties were dissatisfied because they hadn't demanded division of the disputed site. Most people were of the opinion that this wasn't a legal decision but a 'formula to reach a compromise'. All parties appealed against the court's decision. Supreme Court put a stay to the HC's order and started the hearing again. Ram Lalla, still inside the tall, yellow steel enclosure, sat waiting for the court's order.

Chapter 8

STRUGGLE

Ayodhya is the truth of India. The truth of India's history, its present and its future! But the irony is that neither do we wish to know the truth, nor do we really know it. Looking at it from any point, you will find that Ayodhya carries all dimensions of India's heritage—culture, traditions, political history, religion and profanity. But we did not try to understand or change any of this. Instead, at every time and stage, governments used it to their benefit. Ayodhya was always cheated. Nobody tried to understand the truth of Ayodhya. At least this is what Ayodhya's history of struggle tells us.

Ayodhya means invincible. We know the meaning of 'yuddh' (battle). Yodhya means the one that you can fight. A human being fights the one against whom there is a chance of winning. Hence Ayodhya means the one that you cannot conquer or simply invincible. But if we look at Ayodhya's struggle, every attacker first tried to conquer Ayodhya. That inscribed slavery, dependency and injustice in our psychology.

It is written in *Atharva* veda that Ayodhya was created by the Gods and was like heaven. According to Valmiki *Ramayana*, the city of Ayodhya was settled by Manu. History books say that Ayodhya was the capital of Kaushal district. At that time there were 16 major districts in India and Kaushal was one of the bigger and more prosperous districts. Ayodhya was its capital. It is considered to be the time period, 500-600 years before Christ. Paniki is another ancient scripture. That also mentions Ayodhya. Kalidas's *Raghuvansham* is Ram's story. So naturally Ayodhya is mentioned there as well. But the fact is that Ram was revered in the era of Kalidas as well and Ayodhya was established as a pious city. *Ramayana*'s exact time period is not established, so I will not mention it. Even then the question always raised was whether there was a Ram temple in Ayodhya. Centuries have gone by in a struggle to get an answer to this pointless question. No government had the strength to find the truth. You will easily find what Mughals did to Ayodhya in history textbooks. But what happened with Ayodhya after the Mughals left is interesting.

Mughals were thrown out of Delhi. Englishmen or the British came to power. Ayodhya was constantly anxious. Ayodhya began to explore its identity all over again. The British were with Ram in their opinion. British officials, not once but many times, mentioned Ram in their reports. The British travellers also saw Ram in Ayodhya's identity. Despite all this, Ayodhya remained entangled in long legal battles. The legal cases starting from the times of the British created a pile of evidence. These evidence are a reflection of Ayodhya. Allahabad HC's decision also has a mention of it. To know Ayodhya's truth, it is crucial to identify these evidence.

Between the year 1608 and 1611, British traveller William Finch came to Ayodhya. Finch lived in London and worked for the East India Company. He was travelling to different districts of India looking for local produce that could become a source of potential business. After reaching India, Finch wrote, 'The grand bhawan dedicated to lord Ram is in ruins now. Hindu priests worship Ram and conduct prayers on remains of the structure even now. Devotees from all over the country come here to offer prayers. It's called Ramkot.' The meaning is clear. Hindus were praying on an elevated platform even after demolition of the Ram temple and construction of Babri Masjid on its remains. This is when the Babri mosque had already come into existence. The grand structure that Finch talks about was actually a tall mound that was called Ramkot.

The book *Sahifa-E-Chahal Naseh Bahadur Shahi* was written by Bahadur Alamgir's daughter and Aurangzeb's granddaughter in the latter part of the 17th century. The author of *Hadeeka-E-Shaheda*, a book printed from Lucknow in 1856, Mirza Jaan had cited the book written in Persian in which Aurangzeb's granddaughter in 1707 wrote about Ayodhya—'Keeping the success of Islam in mind, Muslim rulers must not show any leniency towards Hindu idol worshippers. They must be treated as slaves and charged a tax. Besides this, at Mathura, Krishna's birthplace, Ayodhya, Sita Rasoi and Hanuman Garhi, temples were razed to build mosques. These must be used for namaz and specially Friday's namaz. There should be more strictness and Hindus must not be allowed to worship and conduct prayers publicly. Also, it must be ensured that the sound of temple bells don't reach Muslims.'

A lot of documented evidence like these tell us that Ayodhya has been considered as Ram's birthplace for hundreds and thousands of years. Ayodhya's identity remained Ram's capital even after the Babri mosque was built. In 1735, a document with the signature of Faizabad's Kazi on it was found which said, 'There was a horrible fight over claim on the mosque among Muslims. The mosque that was built by the emperor of Delhi. At that time this mosque was under the ownership of Awadh's first nawab, Burhan-Ul-Mulk Saadat Ali Khan (1707-1736). On the issue of Ayodhya and Kashi, Mughal emperors even tried to strike a bargain with Hindus. There are evidence of this as well. In 1765, at the time of attacks from Afghans, Nawab Shuja-Ud-Daula asked for help from Maratha king Raghoba. A message was sent to King Raghoba that if Marathas offer their support to the Mughals, the holy cities of Hindus, Ayodhya and Kashi, will be returned to them. But this could not be done because at that time, Marathas were trying to conquer Punjab and so this deal could not be sealed. Ayodhya and Kashi could not be freed from the rule of Mughals.'

Muslim Personal Law Board gives the same logic over and over, that the era when Babri mosque was built was the time when legendary poet Tulsidas was alive. Their argument was why a Ram bhakt, like Tulsidas had never mentioned the demolition of Ram temple anywhere in his literature? How was it possible? The Allahabad HC got the answer to this question in a testimony during a hearing. Tulsidas has given a detailed account of Ram Mandir's demolition and construction of the Babri Masjid. He has also mentioned when Mir Baqi created a ruckus in Ayodhya. The kind of torture he inflicted on Hindus and built the Babri mosque after demolishing Ram temple. This detailed account has been narrated in Tulsidas's composition, 'Tulsi Doha Shatak'. Jagadguru Rambhadracharya, credited with the knowledge of many languages, presented his testimony in the Allahabad HC. He was the top scholar at Rambhakti shakha. He lives in Chitrakoot and is visually impaired by birth. He cited Tulsidas's Doha Shatak in front of the court. Rambhadracharya also presented the context by Goswami Tulsidas in front of the court that elaborated the atrocities inflicted by Babur's commander Mir Baqi and demolishing of temples to construct mosques there.

> Mantra upanishad brahmanu bahu puraan itihaas.
> Jawan jaraaye rosh bhari kari tulsi parihaas.
> Seekha sutr se heen kari, bal te hindu log.
> Bhamri bhagaye desh te, tulsi kathin kujoog.
> Babar babarr aaeke, kar leenhe karwaal.
> Hane pachaer pachaer janal, tulsi kaal kraal.
> Sanbat sar vasu baan bhar nabh, greesham shatru anumaani.
> Tulsi awadhi jad bhawan, anrath kiye ankhaani.
> Ram janam mandir mahi mandirahi, tori maseet banay.
> Jabhi bahot hindun hate, tulsi kinhi haaye.
> Dalayo meer baaki awadh, mandir ram samaj.
> Tulsi rowat hridye ati, trahi trahi raghuraj.
> Ram janam madir jahan, lasat awadh ke beech.
> Tulsi rachi masit tahan, meer baaki khal neech.
> Ramayan dhari ghant jahan shruti puran upkhaan.
> Tulsi jawan ajaan tahan, karaan ajaan.

Tulsidas has written above that Mir Baqi demolished the Ram mandir, constructed a mosque in its place, plundered and killed many Hindus. It seems as if this is an eyewitness account of what happened in front of him. At that time, there was neither the Babri Action Committee nor the Ram Janmabhoomi Trust. Tulsidas must have written what he saw. Some Hindu left wing critics question the authenticity of Tulsidas's Doha Shatak. Left wing critic Namvar Singh has been my guru. He told me that the authenticity of this scripture Doha Shatak is doubtful. But HC took it into consideration and that is the reason why I am mentioning it.

There is one more piece of evidence that tells us about Ayodhya's truth. Babri Masjid's inner wall had an inscription. There was no controversy over this. This inscription, written in Persian in 1528, clearly said that the Babri mosque was built by Mir Baqi on Babur's instruction. This inscription is of the year 1528, the year when Babri Masjid was built. It was inscripted—

> 'With the order of emperor Babur,
> the edifice of whose justice is so high
> that it unites the earth and sky,
> powerful Mir Baqi is the one
> this building of angels is built by.'

After this Abul Fazal who wrote the biography of Akbar has mentioned the importance of Ayodhya for Hindus in *Ain-i-Akbari* in 1598. Abul Fazal wrote, 'Ayodhya, that is usually known by the name of Awadh, that is spread almost 80 miles in the east and around 40 miles in the north, is considered as a holy land. This is among the biggest cities of Awadh and is believed to be one of the oldest cities. This was the home of lord Ramchandra in *Treta* yug who is considered the ideal king and known for his religious devotion. Looking at the faith and devotion for Ram in Hindus, Akbar had also released coins that had Ram and Sita engraved on it.' In the year 1695-96, Aurangzeb's minister Sujan Rai Bhandari wrote— Ayodhya is Shri Ram's capital and the most holy city of Hindus. But that also did not have the mention of Babri Masjid.

Similarly, Austrian missionary Joseph Tiefenthaler also wrote about Ayodhya between 1766 and 1771. Joesph's writings were in German. Later it was translated in French, then English and later into Hindi. Joseph also knew Hindi and Sanskrit. The mention of this account is also there in Allahabad HC's decision. Jospeh Tiefenthaler wrote— 'Awadh that most Hindus know by the name of Ayodhya, is identified as one of India's most ancient cities. Now the city does not have a huge population. The city had a magnificent temple on the edge of the river, which was razed and a mosque was built in its place. Aurangzeb wanted to promote Mohammed's religion. He wanted to convert Hindus to Islam. So he demolished the religious places of Hindus. He demolished the temple in Ayodhya and instead made a mosque with two platforms there. There was a famous spot here, Sita Rasoi or Sita's kitchen. This was also called the platform of Sita, Ram's wife. Ram's platform was also here. Aurangzeb demolished that and built a mosque with three domes. Although a lot of people also say that this mosque was built by Babur. Fourteen pillars of black stone were also added to the mosque. These are the same pillars that hint at the existence of Ram's platform. Aurangzeb or Babur, whoever was responsible for the demolition of this temple, had done it only to demean Hindus. But Hindus continued to pray at both places. One that is called Ram's birthplace and the other, Ram's platform. On the 24th day of Chaitra (month), Hindus gather here in big numbers from different parts of the country and celebrate Lord Ram's birthday.' Joseph's account created confusion whether the Babri mosque was built by Babur or Aurangzeb. Although Joseph cleared this confusion later by writing that a lot of people say that Babri Masjid was built by Babur. This traveller priest visited 22 states of India.

Ram Janmabhoomi was taken over and a mosque was built there. This has been verified in Awadh's gazetteer of 1877. P. Carnegie has written in the gazetteer, 'When Muslims tried to conquer Hanuman Garhi, they had to pay a heavy price for it. They were successful in conquering Ram Janmabhoomi in their third attempt. Around 75 Muslim were killed in the battle at the gate of the Babri mosque and 11 Hindus lost their lives. Till this point, Hindus prayed here. But to avoid regular clashes, the British divided it with an iron railing. Muslims could read namaz inside it and Hindus made a platform outside the railing where Hindus worshipped.'

A Muslim, Mirza Jaan, who took part in the jihad in 1855 wrote in 1856—'Mughal emperors demolished temples in Kashi and built mosques out of the debris of these temples. The same thing happened in Ayodhya. Ayodhya is known to be Ram's father's capital. This is the most holy city for Hindus for worship. Here temples were demolished and using its stones and broken walls, mosques were built. The huge temple was razed and later the same spot was turned into the mosque's ahata. Emperor Babur did one very good thing. In 1526, he demolished a temple and made a magnificent mosque there. But the problem is that this mosque is still known as Sita's rasoi mosque!'

In 1856, the rule of nawabs ended in Awadh. The English conquered it. Two years after this, on 30 November 1858, Babri mosque's muezzin appealed in court where Babri Masjid was written as the birthplace mosque. In this appeal, it was mentioned that 'Janmsthan masjid' or birthplace mosque has been desolate for hundreds of years. 'Hindus have occupied it. There are prayers being conducted there regularly. Hindus must be stopped from conducting prayers.' The meaning was clear. At that time also, namaz could not be held at the Babri mosque and Hindus were constantly worshipping there.

Till the time VHP and BJP started the Ayodhya campaign, it was known that Babri Masjid was built in place of Ram Mandir. But after the Ayodhya campaign, left wing historians called it a lie spread by the English—a lie that, according to them, was spread to divide Hindus and Muslims. Their argument was that Ayodhya has always had a very prominent character outlining religion and culture. This is true as well. In all of India's religious scriptures, Ayodhya has always been on top. Buddhists believe that Gautam Buddha lived here for many years and practiced austerity. Their religious scripture *Saket* mentions this. Jains believe that their first tirthankara Rishabhdev (Adinath) and the other four tirthankars were born in Ayodhya. In Fahiyan's journey's account, there is a mention of five Jain temples in Ayodhya. Jains' 22 tirthankars out of 24 were Ikshwakuvanshiya. The capital of Ikshwakuvanshiyas was Ayodhya again. But no evidence of a struggle in Ayodhya among Hindus, Jains and Buddhists is found. British officers and organizations always pressed on proving it a Hindu city. It started with Montgomery Martin. The British government had given him the task of collecting East India's historic and geographical facts. Montgomery was a British historian and statistician born in Ireland.

He wrote history of the Indian empire in five segments in 1838 in which he declared Ayodhya as a Hindu city and nearby Faizabad a Muslim city. Patrick Carnegie, who was the first British commissioner of Faizabad, took this theory forward. Carnegie wrote the gazetteer of Awadh. In this, masjid was referred to as 'masjid-mandir' for the first time. According to him, Awadh's nawab's chair was transferred from Ayodhya to Faizabad in 1740. After this Ayodhya started developing as a Hindu city. W.C. Benett also prepared the gazette of Awadh. He commented about Ayodhya in 1877. Benett said, 'Whether this happened because of the atrocities by Aurangzeb and the growth of a nationalist feeling thereby or because of the success of Marathas or because of the popular translated version of *Ramayana*, the fact is that Ayodhya once again became famous as a holy city in the eyes of public.' The gazettes that came later verified Benett's facts. For example, Barabanki gazetteer (1902) and Faizabad gazetteer (1905). Both these gazettes were written by H.R. Neville. Neville was a British official who was also a historian. He repeated the same facts in his writings.

Martin was the first person who mentioned the mythological story of Vikramaditya. He also gave a description of the demolition of the temple by Babur or Aurangzeb. His descriptions were based on details collected by Francis Buchanan. He also mentioned pillars made of black stones inside the mosque and said that these were taken from a Hindu building. ASI (Archaeological Survey of India) considered these as the strongest evidence in favour of the temple. Later Edward Thornton confirmed these facts in his gazetteer in 1858. Thornton was Gorakhpur's DM in 1838. After this, Sir H.M. Elliot wrote that King Vikramaditya came to Ayodhya. He got temples constructed at 360 places. These temples were considered holy for their connection with Ram. Most British historians of the 19th century said that all these 360 temples were later demolished by Muslims. After Auranzeb's death, Hindus built temples again on the remains of the demolished temples. Carnegie writes as an example—'This is a proven fact that Ayodhya had three important Hindu temples at the time when Muslims won. These included Janmsthan temple, Swargdwar temple and Treta's Thakur temple. First time, Babur got a mosque built which still has its name inscribed on it. Aurangzeb did the same thing to the second temple whereas a mosque was built on the third by him or his successor. All this was done on the basis of the famous principle of Islam according to which Islam is imposed on all those conquered.'

Peter Carnegie writes that Janmabhoomi refers to the place where Ram was born. Swargdwar referred to the door through which he entered swarg or heaven and Treta's Thakur was the place he had made the great sacrifice. Neville repeated Carnegie's account and added—'Demolition of temples, profanity and sacrilege in the city created a divide and a lot of bitterness between Hindus and Muslims.'

A leading archaeologist of the nineteenth century, Alexander Cunningham was an officer in the British army who had also conducted excavations at Sarnath (Varanasi) and Sanchi later. He has written in his report of 1862-63—'Ram's birthplace or his birthplace temple was in the heart of the city'. Later Cunningham became ASI's first director. In 1819, John Leden translated the account of Zahir-ud-Din Muhammad Babur in English. Leden lived in Scotland and was a historian. He wrote that on 28 March 1528, Babur camped near Ayodhya. William Erskine claimed to have obtained a document in 1826. This document verified that Babur stayed in Ayodhya for a fortnight and was part of the construction activities in Ayodhya. Erskine was a member of the British parliament. He had obtained this document when he was in the army. In 1922, Annette S. Beveridge translated *Babur Nama* in English. She verified that Babur camped 72 miles north of Ayodhya on 28 March 1526. Babri supporters accuse the British writers of not maintaining an objective stand while remembering these events that unfolded in Ayodhya. They only focused on calling Babri Masjid Janmsthan or birthplace.

These accusations by historians supporting Babri are false because the interest of British writers was not mainly in Ayodhya's Hindu past. Alexander Cunningham had not gone to Ayodhya looking for Hindu-Muslim struggles. He had gone to look for those Buddhist monuments and places that have been mentioned by Chinese travelers Fahyan and Huay Nasang whereas Carnegie argued that the pillars of the mosque resembled Buddhist pillars, although he accepted the local belief that Babur built a mosque in place of a Janmsthan mandir or a birthplace temple. But this can hardly be taken as an evidence of the involvement of British historians.

There are claims and counter-claims regarding Ram's birth as well. According to computer calculations, Shri Ram was born on the afternoon of 10 January 3114 BC. According to the Indian calendar, this is the ninth day of the month of Chaitra in the Shukla paksh. This is the time and date when Ramnavmi is celebrated all over India. It is said in Valmiki *Ramayana*'s Ayodhya kandserg 4 shlok (16-17-18-19) that

Dashrath wanted to make Shri Ram the king of Ayodhya. Sun, Mangal and Rahu had surrounded his stars. In such circumstances either the king dies or he becomes a victim of conspiracies. Dashrath's zodiac sign was Pisces and his stars were revti. The condition of his stars on 5 January 5089 BC was something like this. This was the day when Shri Ram left Ayodhya for a 14-year exile. That time he was 25 years old. His age is told through many shloks in Valmiki *Ramayana*. When Ravan died, the day was 4 December 5076 BC Ram had completed 14 years of exile on 2 January 5075 BC. Shri Ram returns to Ayodhya when he is 39 years old.

English traveller William Finch travelled through India from 1608 to 1611. Finch has mentioned the faith of Hindus regarding Ram's birthplace. Finch, who reached India 80 years after Babur, verifies an active presence of Hindus on the land. The interesting thing is also that he did not mention Muslims reading namaz there at all. This fact raises the question if the mosque was left unattended just after it was built. All these facts were evidence of how holy this place was to Ram bhakts or his followers. Walter Hamilton has also mentioned the crowd of pilgrims in his gazette of 1828. These took shelter near the area. The ancient city of Awadh and remains or relics of Ram's capital can still be seen here. Hamilton also said that *dharmbhikshus* take rounds of temples and statues. They bathe in the holy waters and organize traditional festivals.

Awadh's nawab Wajid Ali Shah has also verified these facts. In 1822, one of Faizabad's court's local daroga or sub-inspector Hafizullah also said that the mosque built by Babur stands on Ram's birthplace. On 12 August 1855 Awadh's last nawab Wajid Ali Shah (1847-1856) sent a letter to British citizen, Major James Autrum. This included five documents that verify the long-term disputes between Hindus and Muslims. These documents were—

1. Awadh's daroga, Mohammed Nihaluddin's report, who was appointed by the king to investigate and find out if there is a mosque in Hanuman Garhi or not.
2. Faizabad's sub-inspector, Hafizullah's document that he had submitted in the court.

3. Faizabad's Imam's document.
4. A copy of Faizabad's kazi's stamped document of 1735.
5. The sealed statement of 40 local residents of Faizabad on the tensions between Hindus and Muslims.

This mosque was built by one of the former sultans of Delhi. But later Hindus declared that they have no intentions of interfering with the mosque. They said that the wall that was erected to separate the mosque from the worship area of Hindus was demolished during the rule of the current king. Hindus slaughtered a pig inside the mosque and its head flew off. They also demolished the mazar of Shaheed Khuja Huti which was near the mosque. Nawab had an issue with the fact that not only were the priests and hermits big in number, but they also had the support of Raja Man Singh and Raja Kishan Dutt along with other landlords.

According to scholars that support Babri, during the great revolt of 1857 priests of Hanuman Garhi gave shelter to British officials and helped them and their families escape to Gonda. After the rebellion settled, British officials rewarded all those who had helped them. This resulted in amplification of Ayodhya's king, Raja Man Singh's estate. Priests also received some rent-free land and they were also provoked to establish their claim on the Babri mosque. During this time, the issue of Janmabhoomi and Babri Masjid rose again.

According to the local administration, the communal situation in Ayodhya was sensitive since 1855 and a bloody war between Hindus and Muslims was possible at any point. That is why administration recommended that the settlement on the issue be reviewed again and separated the areas of worship of both communities. According to the new arrangement by the local administration, Hindu mahants were permitted to create a stage or a platform in front of the mosque so that Ram's birthplace could be marked. A reticular wall was erected between the mosque and the platform. Hindus were not permitted to enter the inner premises and Muslims were not allowed to enter from the eastern gate. They could only enter the Babri mosque through the north gate.

However, in this whole point of view, the writings of Joseph Tiefenthaler were ignored, who had travelled to Awadh a century before the rebellion. He had mentioned prayers and worship by Hindus on the platform, which is clearly a construction way older than 1857.

Proof of medieval history also reinforces the devotion of people towards Shri Ram in Ayodhya. In the twelfth century Qutubuddin Aibak made Bakhtiyar Khilji governor of the area. Qutubuddin took over the governance of Delhi in 1206. He died in 1210 and his son Aramshah took over control. But his brother-in-law, Iltutmish, dismissed him from the ruling position within a year. After this Nasiruddin Mohammad Shah became the Governor in 1325. Kamruddin Karan and Farhat Khan were appointed by Muhammad Tughlaq as governor of this area. Mughals gave a great deal of attention to Ayodhya. Many scholars also have to say that Babur himself went to the Ram Janmabhoomi along with the army in 1538. The Mughal Sultanate took control over Awadh. Akbar, Sultan of the Mughals, divided his entire kingdom into twelve provinces. Among them, Awadh was the most important. It was very challenging for the Sultan sitting in Delhi to handle all of this. The condition of Mughals was very weak from the time of Mohammed Shah till 1722, when the new governor Saadat Khan took charge. He had come to India in 1705 AD and had become close to Mughal emperor Mohammed Shah. He was appointed as the governor of Awadh in 1722. During this period, there were eight governors in a time period of around 139 years. There were five districts in Awadh and these were Khalilabad, Gorakhpur, Bahraich, Faizabad and Lucknow.

The boundary of Awadh extended from the Himalayas in the north, Bihar in the east and Allahabad province's Manikpur in the south. This province was 230-mile-wide and spread over an area of 1,0171,080 bigha land. The local king and landlords had spread mismanagement and there was unrest in the area. Saadat Khan overcame them. He built his palace near Ayodhya and settled a new city, Faizabad. This city became the new government's capital. Nawab Wajid Ali Shah built paved roads between Lucknow-Kanpur-Lucknow and Faizabad so that Hindu devotees could easily go to the Ganga River and visit the Ram Janmabhoomi.

It is a fact that the nawabs of Awadh adopted the strategy of Emperor Akbar. The strategy of being tolerant towards other religions and thereby strengthened the rule. The founder of Awadh Royal House, Nawab Sadar Khan had employed Hindus in big numbers in his army. This is how he attained his goal. Kora's Durjan Singh Chaudhry remained in his service for a long time. Deewan Atmaram was from Punjab and was a devotee of Ram. He would often visit the Ram Janmabhoomi. He had such close relations with Nawab Saadat Khan that the Nawab went to Ram Janmabhoomi with him on the occasion of Ramnavami.

During the rule of these nawabs, namaz was never offered at the Babri structure. Nawab Shuja-ud-Daula's son Asaf-ud-Daula changed his capital from Faizabad to Lucknow in 1775. He believed in Allah and offered namaz regularly. He had asked a maula to offer namaz on his behalf. During his administration also, he gave Hindus the same kind of respect that was given to them by the previous nawab. Asaf-ud-Daula's Hindu deewan (minister), Maharaj Tikait Rai remained on top positions. His palace was as big as King Naval Rai's. Maharaj Tikait Rai also settled down towns like Tikait Nagar and Tikaitganj. He got the Ram Janmabhoomi temple whitewashed in Ayodhya. Asaf-ud-Daula was the only nawab who had got the writing done on the Babri structure that said 'this place was safe for worship of Gods for Hindus.'

Now begins the process of litigation in Ayodhya

After 1857, multiple evidence kept proving the claims of Hindus on the land. These evidence also proved that there were special preparations made for Hindu festivals there. The first available evidence of the Ram Jamnbhoomi conflict is the report of Awadh's sub-inspector Sheetal Dubey that was filed on 28 December 1858. This has a mention of Punjab resident Nihang Sikh Fakir Khalsa's worship in the middle of masjid-janmsthan. Nihang had organized a prayer service (puja and havan) for Guru Govind Singh and had also established an emblem of God inside the campus of the mosque. According to the report there were twenty-five Sikhs who attended this religious flag hoisting ceremony there.

After two days, khatibandmuazzin of the Babri mosque, Mohammed Asgar gave a complaint letter to the British officials in this matter (case no. 884, Mohalla Kot Ramchandra, Ayodhya). His complaint letter is the oldest personal document of this case that throws light on the situation of that time. According to this complaint, a Nihang Sikh from Punjab and a government servant had made a mud platform near Mehrab and Imam's platform. They also placed a religious pictue on it. They ignited fire there to light up the place and worship. Ram was written with coal all over the mosque. Mohammed Asgar also said that the birthplace was lying deserted in the outer area of the Babri Masjid (the courtyard inside the four walls of the mosque), where Hindus had been praying for years. He said that due to a conspiracy by station officer Shivghulam, hermits built a platform in one night. By the time this could be stopped, the deputy commissioner suspended the station offier and fined the hermits. But by now the platform's height was already one yard. Mohammed Asgar asked city kotwal to visit the place and demolish the new construction. He requested him to remove Hindus from there. He also asked the idols and statues to be removed from there and writings on the walls to be washed off.

The authenticity of this document and the identity of its writer are beyond doubt. Allahabad HC accepted these documents as irrefutable proof in its order. The court said that Hindus can conduct prayers and worship inside the mosque, in the Ram chabootra or platform and Sita Rasoi. This would have been impossible if the whole campus was owned by Muslims.

Justice S.U. Khan noticed the acceptance of Muslims from the middle of the 19th century. He noticed that the Hindus used the outer part of Ram Chabootra. Justice Khan also took cognizance of the fact that the dispute at this place was recognized in 1885 and this is noted in the records of various government officials since 1885.

On 30 November 1858, an order was passed that Fakir Singh should be ousted from there, which was informed by station in-charge Sheetal Dubey, Sheetal Dubey also informed Fakir Singh about this. In his report of 1 December 1858, the station in-charge Sheetal Dubey again said that Fakir Singh kept insisting that every place belongs to the Nirankar or the almighty and justice should be done with him. Despite repeated reminders, he did not vacate the place. After this, many orders were issued in this regard, this stated that if Fakir Singh does not leave this place, then he should be arrested. Finally, on 10 December 1858, the station in-charge reported that the flag has been removed from the 'birthplace mosque' and Fakir Singh has been removed. But in that report, there was no mention of namaz being read in the Babri Masjid or that of the restoration of it. The next available record is an application for the Babri Masjid, filed in the court of Deputy Commissioner by mosque in-charge Mir Raajib Ali (Mir Raajib Ali vs Askoli Singh). This is a plea for removal of the platform built inside Babri Masjid. Mir Raajib Ali said that about thirty days ago, the defendant Nihang made a small platform in the graveyard next to the Babri Masjid, which he was extending constantly. Also, about six months ago, Mahant Hari Das of Hanuman Garhi forcefully tried to construct his house.

In this regard, the matter was registered and the Mahanta had to pay personal bond to not interfere. The commissioner found that a flag was hurled at the grounds of the mosque to create tension and terror, the flag was removed.

Mir Raajib Ali also protested that when the muezzin give call for prayer, the opposing party starts blowing conch shells. This had never happened before. He wanted that 'the newly built platform, which was never there, should be demolished. Also, the other party should be asked for an affidavit that they will never illegally interfere in the mosque property and not blow conch shell during prayer calls'. On 12 March 1861, Mir Raajib Ali, Mohammad Asgar and Muhammad Afzal again filed the same complaint as they already had on 5 November 1860 that the platform that was built at the birthplace near the Babri Masjid and which was not removed despite the orders, should be removed. Meanwhile, a second complaint was filed on behalf of Mutwalli Muhammad Afzal of the Babri mosque. It was stated in it that a month ago, 'Vairagiyan janmasthan Ram' had illegally constructed a small room within the mosque premises in just few hours. His intention was to keep idols inside the room. The Vairagi could slowly extend the construction which he was habitual of. Due to this construction a lot of riots had happened among the locals. Muhammad Afzal was demanding that the room be demolished, and the mosque should be saved from the anger of the Vairagis.

Asgar miyan appeared to be a seasoned litigant. Every month he put in one application. In one of his petitions, a claim was filed over twenty-one tamarind trees. The petition emphasized that the post of 'Khatib' and 'Muezzin' of Babri Masjid of Awadh is ancestral and twenty-one tamarind trees had been in possession of their ancestors since ancient times, so the tamarind trees should be given to the defendant and the other party should be evicted from the graveyard.

Meanwhile, in its judgment of 22 August 1871, the court found that the ownership of Mohammad Asgar is well established over the birthplace and the tamarind trees in front of the mosque Babur Shah's gate. But the ownership of the land was not established. The court said—The graveyard and porch are on a common ground in front of the 'mosque birthplace', so this land cannot be private property. In the case of Mohammed Asgar versus Mahant Baldev Das, the court ordered removal of 'Charan Paduka' on 7 November 1873, which was allegedly made in the disputed premises. Mohammad Asgar appealed to the court to implement the order of 7 November 1873. He said that on one hand, 'Charan Paduka' was not removed and on the other hand, Mahant Baldev Das had built a stove in the same premises, which was never there. He claimed that every part of the place inside the boundary of the mosque belonged to the mosque and that it should be handed over to the Mutwalli of the mosque and not to the Hindus.

For this reason, local officials allowed the plaintiffs to construct a new door towards the north side of the mosque wall. According to the order of the court, idols could not be removed. Baldev Das continued various activities on the wall and whenever he was stopped, he became aggressive and ready to fight. The Allahabad High Court took cognizance of the fact that the complaint was a proof of a stove existing in the Babri Masjid campus in the year 1877.

In April 1877, Mohammad Asgar submitted another application that the local officers had opened the door between the wall which separates the temple and the mosque, which was not appropriate. On

14 May 1877, Commissioner Faizabad demanded a report from the Deputy Commissioner. The Deputy Commissioner said, 'The opening of this door was necessary to give the visitors a different path to the birthplace during the festivity/ fair. There was only one way to go open. The crowd was large, and lives were in danger. I had spotted the place myself for another opening. This petition is only an attempt to offend the Hindus, so that they rely on the mosque for the sake of opening or closing the other door. There can be no interest of the Muslims in this.' The commissioner rejected the appeal because the door was opened by the Deputy Commissioner in the interst of the public.

Justice S.U. Khan noticed this fact as well, that in the beginning, there was only one door in the East wall. But in 1877 the British authorities opened the second door to the north. It was handed over to the control and authority of the Hindus despite serious objections by the Muslims. The requirement for the second door was due to the huge number of Hindu devotees, who assemble at the platform for worship twice every year. The need to control the crowd was felt. Now this had become an issue of dispute between Hindus and Muslims. Eventually a weak agreement was drawn that a European official will identify another passage to avoid any doubt of prejudice towards either Hindus or Muslims.

Mohammad Asgar now filed a complaint against Mahant Raghubar Das of the birthplace and claimed rent for the period 1881-82. It was for the use of the platform near the gate of the mosque. It was said in the petition that—'The courtyard in front of the birthplace-mosque and platform is the property of the plaintiff, where Kartik Mela and Ram Navmi are organized since ancient times. On the other days, flower and sweet shops are there. Contract for this was for 35 rupees per day. The plaintiffs and the defendants had agreed to divide this amount on a 50-50 basis. But before the 1881 Kartik-Snan and Ram Navmi, with wrong motives the defendants divided 30 rupees as against the contract of dividing 35 rupees. This was done for both festivals/fairs. No approval was sought from the plaintiff either.' Mohammad Asgar requested that the order be passed to give this amount along with a fine.

On 18th June 1883, this lawsuit was also dismissed by the trial court. Faizabad Sub-Judge Hari Kishan said that Mohammad Asgar claimed the rent for the platform and the table, accepting the fact that both were in possession of Raghubar Das. He failed to maintain the rent claim. He presented a witness Ganga Prasad Kanoongo, who testified in favor of him, but the judge did not believe it.

The Allahabad High Court found that this application does not prove that the prayers were continuously being read by Muslims. On some occasions like Ram Navmi in Ayodhya, outsiders could use land to open shops. Mutwalli shared this rent with the priests of Nirmohi Akhada, who managed the other places of worship in the square and the outer premises. But Mohammad Asgar was not someone to accept things easily; he filed another petition as a Mutwalli and Khadib of the Babri Masjid. In this complaint he said that he had the right to have the mosque wall painted. But Raghubar Das was preventing him from doing so. Raghubar Das's right is limited to the platform and 'Sita-Rasoi.' He said that the wall and gate were part of the mosque alone. He had the right of cleaning them.

On this issue, Assistant Commissioner Faizabad passed an order on 22 January 1884 and said, 'Raghubar Das is prohibited from doing repairs etc. in the inner and outer part of the courtyard, and Mohammad Asgar is advised that he should not lock the outer door of the mosque. The outer door will be left open. It is very necessary to show absolute impartiality and the status quo should be maintained.' Allahabad High Court found that this order clears the intentions of the officers to remove obstacles for the entry of people in the disputed campus.

Now it was Raghubar Das's turn. He appealed to the Assistant Commissioner on 27 June 1884, which said that despite the prohibition, Muslims were painting those areas which had never been in their possession. This fact would be made clear upon inspection.

Now comes the real case, in which after small fights, the permission to build a temple was sought for the first time. Mahant Raghubar Das filed a claim on 29 January 1885, asking for permission to build a temple on 21 feet by 17 feet platform-birthplace or the Chabootra-janmsthan, which was in possession of Raghubar Das. The petition stated that there was no building on top of the platform and due to this he and others endure a lot of trouble because of the heat, cold and rains in different weather. Therefore, if a temple could be built to cover the platform, then no harm would come to anyone. If the temple was constructed, then it would be a relief for himself and would also benefit many other fakirs and pilgrims.

In his petition, Raghubar Das said that the Deputy Commissioner Faizabad had stopped the construction of the temple in 1883 due to the objections of some Muslims. After this he also requested the local administration, but on receiving no response from them, he gave notice to the Secretary Local Government office. But there was no reply from there as well, that is why he had to file the case.

A map was also attached with the complaint. Faizabad's Deputy Judge (Sub Judge) directed the court commissioner, Gopal Sahay Amin to prepare a map of the entire Babri Masjid Campus. This map was like the maps submitted by Raghubar Das. It showed that the inner courtyard and built area was with the Muslims and the outer courtyard, which had Sita Rasoi or Sita's kitchen and Ram Chabootra, was under the possession of the Hindus.

The Allahabad High Court came to the conclusion that the Sita Rasoi was made before 1884, the High Court said, 'It is beyond comprehension that Mir Baqi or someone else had allowed the Hindu symbols to remain within the mosque while constructing the mosque on the disputed premises, so that the Hindu would continue to worship within the premises. We put this question to Mr Jilani (lawyer of Babri side) and he clearly stated that no Muslim will allow the idol worship within the limits of the mosque.'

The Allahabad High Court believed that when the mosque was built for the first time, the existence of any Hindu construction could not be allowed inside the premises. It seems that the mosque was abandoned right after its construction, so the local Hindus used it to create a symbolic structure to worship. They considered it to be the birthplace of Lord Ram. In this manner the altar came into existence at the mosque's courtyard and priest Tiefenthaler also noticed it.

In response to Mahant Raghubar Das, Mohammad Asgar filed a written statement on 22 December 1885. In it, he said that Babur built the mosque and engraved 'Allah' at the entrance and approved 'forgiveness' or exemption for the mosque's expenses. Therefore no one else can claim the right to build there unless the king or any of his successors give him permission to do so or grant any part of land to him. Therefore, plaintiff Mahant Raghubar Das cannot be the owner of the land. Raghubar Das had not presented any documentary evidence of the ownership of the property. In such a situation, he had no right to construct a temple over it.

Mohammed Asgar stressed, 'If the plaintiff understands that he or Hindus have right over this property then it's not correct. It is apparent that Muslims on occasion, organize different functions at imambaras, mosques, domes and other monuments. On some occasions, Hindus also offer 'Nazr and Niyaz' or offerings. They don't stop their entry into Muslim buildings. Similarly, Muslims also enter religious buildings of the Hindus.

Therefore, by going into a building to make offerings does not make the person an owner of the building. It is also clear that from the construction of the mosque to the year 1856 there was no platform at this place. It was built in 1857 and the order of digging up the platform was passed by the Muslims. The civil court cannot ignore these facts.'

Justice S.U. Khan said that Mohammad Asgar did not deny the truth of the map presented by Raghubar Das. After the inspection of this place, Faizabad's Sub Judge Pandit Harikishan passed the verdict on 24 December 1885 in this case. He wrote, 'Inspecting this place makes it clear that the 'charan' or the footmarks are engraved on the platform, which is being worshiped. There is a statue of Thakurji installed on top of that platform. The platform is in the possession of the plaintiff, and all the offerings are kept by the plaintiff.

This fact has also been acknowledged by the defendant Mohammad Asgar. The plaintiff's witnesses also confirm the ownership of the plaintiff that a circumference of a concrete wall has been set up to maintain the rights of Hindus and Muslims. The defendant's witnesses argue that they are unaware of the ownership of the plaintiff. There is a wall between the mosque and the platform, which is clearly visible in Amin's modified map. It is also clear that there are different walls between the mosque and the platform. This fact is supported by the peripheral wall that the government constructed before the recent controversy. Earlier both Hindus and Muslims used this place for worshipping and namaz. In the year 1855, after a feud between the Hindus and the Muslims, a boundary wall was raised to prevent future conflicts, so that Muslims could read namaz inside the wall and Hindus could pray outside the wall. Therefore, the land outside Chabootra and boundary wall belongs to Hindus and plaintiff.'

According to the Sub-judge—

'The permission to build a temple has been sought at a place where there is a single corridor for usage both by the temple and the mosque. The place where Hindus worship is in their possession from ancient times, on which no question can be raised on their proprietary rights. Around it is the wall of the mosque, and the word 'Allah' is inscribed on it. If the temple is built at such a place, then there will be the sound of the temple bell and the conch, when both Hindus and Muslims pass through the same path. If Hindus are allowed to construct a temple, then one day a criminal case will start, and thousands of people will be killed.'

An appeal against this decision reached the District Judge. Faizabad District Judge Col. F.E.A. Chamier heard the case of Mahant Raghubar Das. After examining the spot, he wrote in his judgment on 18/26 March 1886—'It is very unfortunate that a mosque has been built on the land which Hindus have considered to be particularly holy. But since this incident is 356 years old, it is now too late to provide relief in this matter. At most, the status quo of both parties can be upheld. Its entry is from the door, on which Allah is engraved. Right after this there is a cemented platform on the left, which is the right of Hindus. There is a tent over a small wooden structure.' Chamier dismissed the lawsuit, because there was no basis of the plaintiff's right.

Acting Judicial Commissioner W. Young also ruled in this matter on 1 November 1886. He found that the Hindus wanted to build a new temple at this platform in Ayodhya. This place was in the area around the mosque. 'This mosque was built 350 years ago as a result of Babur's fundamentalist and atrocities. Babur deliberately chose this place as his sacred place according to Hindu mythology.' He also pointed out that within the parameter of the mosque, Hindus had very limited rights to reach certain places. They have been constantly trying to extend these rights for many years now and trying to construct structures at both the places. These places were Sita Rasoi and Ram Janmabhoomi. This judge was also against any kind of change in the status quo.

In the year 1889, A. Fuhrer wrote in an ASI report—'In Ayodhya Babur's mosque was built by Mir Baqi at exactly the same spot where there was Ramji's birthplace.' Similarly, William C. Venette wrote in the Gazetteer of 1872 in Oudh, 'Ram existed or not, in which period did Ram live, if Shriram was fictional or a real miraculous man, all this is not as important, as is the fact that Shriram is an ideal of Hindus, founder of an ideal ruling-system. A hero to a very large segment of society. Ram's life is an inspiration to the people. Therefore, even today the enthusiasm and devotion of people makes Shriram's birthplace the holiest place for the Hindus. Even today, large mass of devotees, throng at Ram's birthplace.'

This story is of the legal battles regarding every little matter of the Ayodhya dispute. Now begins the string of riots on this controversy, riots erupted in Ayodhya and Faizabad on 20 and 21 November 1912 because of the cow slaughter on Bakrid. The letter written by Faizabad Commissioner to the Chief Secretary of the United Provinces on 5 December 1912, mentioned a confidential report of the DM Faizabad on the riots. According to municipal rules, the slaughter and sale of cow meat in Ayodhya was prohibited.

This report said that a large number of pilgrims come to Ayodhya for three most important bathing festivals, on 18 November for the parikrama or orbital of Devostani Ekadashi and on 23 and 24 November, for Kartik Purnima. During this time there may be riots due to the animal sacrifices. In a letter written on 25 January 1913 to the Home Secretary of the Government of India, Chief Secretary of the United Provinces, R. Bern, said—

'An eternal reason for differences is the existence of the mosque at this traditional place of Ram's birthplace. It was built by Babur in 1528, who destroyed an ancient temple and used its material to construct a new structure. Before the merger of Awadh in 1856, there had been many occasions when the bitterness between Hindus and Muslims turned into bloodshed. However, there was no major disturbance till the recent incidents after Gadar. This is because the Muslims of Ayodhya are no longer able to show their authority over numerous Hindu temples and organizations that control religious establishments.'

According to the report of the Home Department, in the year 1911, from the total population of 12,575 of Ayodhya, the total number of Hindus was 10,927. Muslims were 1,623. According to Burns, since 1906 relation between Hindu-Muslim was stressful because of the desire of Muslims to open a slaughterhouse in Ayodhya. In 1911, Hindus informed the officiating deputy commissioner that Muslims are contemplating animal sacrifices on the Bakrid. They found that perhaps a quiet sacrifice was done in the year 1910. Although there was no credible evidence that there had been a cow slaughter in Ayodhya before that.

To reach a compromise, he convened a meeting of Hindus and Muslims and allowed cow sacrifice near a Sikh temple outside the city. However, a riot broke out and the army had to be called in.

Witnessing this brewing controversy, the Lieutenant Governor visited Ayodhya on 18 July 1915, so that a mutually acceptable formula of cow-slaughter issue could be found. But he failed to find any solution. Once again riots erupted in Ayodhya on 27 March 1934 on Bakrid. The next day, Faizabad commissioner sent the details of the reasons for rioting to the Chief Secretary of the United Provinces. He told that the reason for the riots was the cow-sacrifice in nearby Shahjahanpur. There was no official record of cow's sacrifice in Shahjahanpur. This time the permission of cow-sacrifice at Jalpa Nala was given to the Muslims of Shahjahanpur. Immediately after the sacrifice, mob of Hindus demolished the slaughterhouse and set it on fire. Most of the people in the crowd were the villagers of Ayodhya.

In the meantime, a large crowd of Bairagis in Ayodhya attacked the Babri Masjid, which was secluded and slightly away from the main road. This news reached the Deputy Collector after some time. He reached the spot with five policemen. That was the total force he had. They saw that at least 200 Bairagis are trying to demolish the mosque. The deputy collector said in his report, 'The Bairags have caused a lot of damage to the mosque. The entrance is almost entirely demolished. The contents of the inside have been burnt.

The metal on three main domes was removed and at least one dome was badly damaged.' The issue got escalated and tensions in Faizabad increased.

C.V. Chintamai raised the issue in Vidhan Parishad. He raised it in the legislative council. In response, member of the Home Department (Home Member) Jagdish Prasad said that Hindus had opposed the new trend of sacrificing the cow in Shahjahanpur as an act that was never done before. They moved towards the Babri Masjid and began to demolish the wall. Babri Masjid was separated from Sita Rasoi and birthplace through only one wall and it was felt that the mosque wall was attacked from the premises of these places, so that this act cannot be caught. By the time District Magistrate and other magistrates reached, the mob had entered the mosque; they had demolished the peripheral wall and had started making a hole in the dome.

In the wire sent to the Home Department of Delhi on 29 March 1934, on behalf of Chief Secretary Lucknow, it was confirmed that the mosque was badly damaged. In one of the statements given in the Legislative Council, Sir Henry Hague also confirmed that two small mosques in Ayodhya and a large mosque named Babri were attacked.

On 16 April 1934, the Chief Secretary of the United Provincial Government, H. Bomford, informed the Chief Secretary M.G. Helet that orders have been given to deploy a punitive police force in Ayodhya. It will be at the expense of the Hindu residents of Ayodhya. Also, losses will be assessed for claims of compensation. This information of compensation of losses comforted Muslim society.

Damage compensation of ₹85,000 to Muslims created a lot of anger among the Hindus. Several representations were given to the government in this regard. In a statement issued by some lawyers, landlords and municipal commissioners, it was said that Muslims failed to provide any evidence of the prevalence of cow sacrifice in Shahjahanpur in the past. Also, the District Magistrate was informed that Ram Navmi snan or bath, in which lakhs of pilgrims arrive in Ayodhya, will be on 24

March and it should have been considered while taking a decision on the issue of cow sacrifice. Then how was the permission for sacrifice of cow in the Jalpa Nala given on 25 March? After this vandalism, in an order on 12 May 1934, Muslims were allowed to start the cleaning and repair of the mosque from 14 May 1934 onwards. Despite the completion of the repair work on 25 February 1935, the contractor complained that the British officials did not pay the wages.

Mutwalli Kalab Hussain of the Babri Masjid wrote a letter to the secretary Sunni Waqf Board, of his knowledge that the mat used at the time of namaz was available only for daily use. The rest of the mats were kept separately with Imam Maulvi Abdul Gaffar. The muezzin used to bring those mats only on Friday. They were returned after the namaz. The reason was that most of the mats had been stolen from the mosque. In the letter, it was written that this mosque is built at a place where riots occur frequently and every year there is danger to the peace. By this incident, the Allahabad High Court concluded that only Friday prayers were held at Babri Masjid and the outer premises were not in control of the Muslims.

The City Magistrate of Faizabad passed an order over some objections of Kalab Hussain on 28 April 1947. These objections were for raising the platform to 12 inches, a court case over pakadand neem trees of Ganjshahida and a banyan tree being planted on the north side. Magistrate ordered that platform will not be cemented, nor will any idols be placed under any of these trees. The iron gates on the eastern side will not be shut. On the north of the mosque's eastern and outer gate, the thatched roof will not be extended without the permission of the City Magistrate. Mutwalli or Muslims will not repair the perimeter wall in southern corner of courtyard without the consent of the City Magistrate. These walls had developed cracks by the peepal and neem tree roots.

Report regarding the Babri Masjid by Waqf Inspector Muhammad Ibrahim (10 December 1948) confirmed the existing tensions at the place. The inspection report of Faizabad city says that no one goes for namaz for the fear of Hindus and Sikhs. If a passenger stays back in the mosque, by chance, he is troubled by the Hindus. There is a temple in the mosque's porch, where many Pandas stay, they cause trouble whenever Muslims come in the mosque. He claimed to have visited the spot and examined it himself. He found the allegations to be true. According to his description, local people told him that the there is a big threat to the Mosque and Hindus can damage its walls.

Barely two weeks later, on 23 December 1948, Muhammad Ibrahim presented a second report, of his Ayodhya journey, done a day earlier. He said that Baba Sukhadas had visited Ayodhya three months ago. Addressing the bairagis and priests, he said that there should be *Ramayana* recital at the birthplace. This news spread in the surrounding areas and within a month, hundreds of priests and pundits gathered at the spot.

The *Ramayana* recital carried on for weeks, during which the front of the mosque had been dug and a flag was hoisted. Many graves had been dug. Muhammad Ibrahim reported—'There is always a lock on the mosque. No azaan or namaz takes place at any time. The keys of the mosque are with the Muslims. The police do not let the lock open. On Friday, there is cleaning of the mosque and Morning Prayer is done for two or three hours. After which it is again closed. There is a lot of noise during the morning prayers. When namazis' leave, stones and shoes are hurled towards them.'

The Allahabad High Court said in its verdict that this report establishes the fact that the Hindus have been entering the inner premises. They have been worshipping there. There was no restriction on their entry there. At the same time, at least three non-Muslim structures existed in the outer premises. Uninterrupted worship was also being done there. After independence, the Hindus submitted an application to the government for constructing Ram temple near the mosque.

On 20 July 1949 The Deputy Secretary of Government, Kehar Singh wrote to District Magistrate of Faizabad for his recommendations in this regard. A copy along with the prayer,was sent to Faizabad Commissioner S.S. Hassan that the District Magistrate's report be sent to the government along with his comments. The commissioner sought a report from the District Magistrate on 7 September. The City Magistrate submitted his report on 10 October 1949, which states—'This application has been made by the Hindus to build a better and large temple in place of the existing small one. Permission can be granted in this regard, because the Hindus are very keen to build a grand temple at that place, where Lord Ramchandra was born. The land on which the temple is proposed to be built is Nazool land.'

A letter written in this regard, by Faizabad SP Kripal Singh, to the DM and the Commissioner is very important. This letter of 29 November 1949, to the Faizabad's DM/ Deputy Commissioner, ICS K.K.K. Nayar, was on the conditions prevailing in Ayodhya. Kripal Singh wrote that he visited the Babri Masjid and Birthplace Complex at Ayodhya that evening and found that many havan-kunds have been constructed around the mosque. Many graves have been dug at Kuber mound at about two-furlong distance from the birthplace. A statue of Mahadev has been placed nearby. He saw bricks and lemon near the birthplace. There was also a proposal to make a big havan-kund, where a large scale kirtan and yagya was to be organized on the full moon. Thousands of Hindus, bairags and outstation sadhus were to take part in it. It seems as if the plan was to encircle the mosque so that it is difficult for the Muslims to even enter the mosque and they are eventually forced to leave the mosque.

There was a big rumour that on the full moon, Hindus would try to enter the mosque to forcibly install idols of god and goddesses.

This letter is from SP of Faizabad written on 29 November 1949, in which he writes, that circumstances were such that people could enter the mosque anytime. Only 23 days after this suspicion was raised, people entered the disputed premises. God appeared in the disputed structure.

On 23 December 1949, Senior Sub-Inspector Ramdev Dubey, in charge of the Ayodhya station, filed an FIR. According to this, a group of 50-60 people entered the Babri Masjid the night before and placed the statue of Shri Ram in the mosque. K.K.K. Nayar informed about this incident to Chief Minister, Chief Secretary and Home Secretary through a radio message. Interesting part was that no Muslim had come forward to lodge an FIR for forceful eviction or obstruction.

Nayar supported the purpose of the people gathered, in his letter dated 26 December 1949, to Chief Secretary, Bhagwan Sahai. He denied the possibility of removing idols, saying that it is not something which he and the police superintendent can agree upon or do something about. He also said—'Entry in the mosque can only be done through the temple complex and it is always possible. Also, the temple complex is also always full of people. The mosque always remains deserted, except for one hour for the Friday prayer. Whether forcefully or secretly, the mosque will have to be put under police control to prevent Hindus from entering the mosque.' Nayar claimed that placing a deserted and almost never used mosque in police control, is a tremendous burden on the taxpayers.

In another letter written to the Chief Secretary on 27 December 1949, Nayar said that the Commissioner had given the Superintendent of Police and him, a plan to remove the idols from the mosque. He described the idea of removing idols in this manner—'It is like creating a grave threat to the peace in the whole district, it will definitely cause panic, which will be unprecedented in the history of this dispute.' He further wrote 'Hindus are determined and unanimous in keeping idols in its place. They are ready to die or kill for this purpose. Without judging the emotional depth behind this movement and without understanding the resolve and determination behind its support, no hasty decision will be right.' Nayar also presented a solution to the government. He advised that the mosque should be attached and both Hindus and Muslims should be evicted from here, only some priests would remain, who would continue to worship the idols. This will continue. The concerned parties will be referred to the Civil Court to determine their rights.

Till the order of the Civil Court, no attempt should be made to transfer ownership to Muslims. Nayar's advice was also supported by the Divisional Commissioner, who proposed to keep the place under police control and allow one priest to perform pooja till situation becomes normal.

Nayar wrote details of events in his diary, from 7 a.m. onwards, on 23 December 1949. An entry of 30 December 1949, mentions visit of the spot by Chief Secretary, where he gets surrounded by a crowd that was shouting, 'Open the gate of God.' (Justice S. Khan, page 35-36)

On 29 December 1949, Additional City Magistrate Markandey Singh of Faizabad and Ayodhya filed a case under Act 145 of the CRPC and issued an order for the attachment of property and simultaneously appointed municipal board chairman Priya Dutt Ram as 'receiver' for the maintenance of the property. The receiver took charge on 5 January 1950 and immediately had the worshipping and rituals started.

These events of Ayodhya echoed in the national capital. Deputy Prime Minister Vallabhbhai Patel, in his letter to Chief Minister Govind Ballabh Pant, on 9 January 1950, expressed his view of resolving this issue cordially in the light of mutual tolerance and goodwill between the two communities. He wrote—'I feel that there are very deep feelings behind this move. Even then such matters should be resolved peacefully, if we are able to garner natural consent of the Muslim community with us.'

After independence, Congress governments took the first step towards handing over Ayodhya to Ram. The Congress government of Govind Ballabh Pant in UP ensured that the idol of Ram Lalla, which had been placed secretly at the disputed site, remained. The path the initial Congress governments of the country took, Ayodhya continued to tread in the same direction. It was a logical end that the foundation laying of the temple was done during Rajiv Gandhi's government and the disputed structure was demolished during Narasimha Rao's government. Ayodhya has always been mysterious. One thing has been showing on the surface and altogether something else has been brewing underneath. Exhausted from the long struggle, Ayodhya now demands a pause. But history does not let it rest. Whenever it tries to take two steps back, it pushes it four steps forward.

Chapter 9

CHRONOLOGY OF EVENTS

Ayodhya's story stands on a time period. This time period is a continuous struggle between devotion for Ram and aggression against him. Every date of the Ayodhya conflict included in this time period is important. Ayodhya reveals something new with each of these dates. And every such date is marked in this chapter. Reading these chronologically makes the story of Ayodhya clearer. The entire history of Ayodhya comes alive in front of you. This is the relevance of these dates.

IMPORTANT DATES RELATED TO THE AYODHYA CONFLICT

1528

One of Babur's commanders, Mir Baqi got a mosque built in Ayodhya, which is considered the birthplace of Hindu God, Lord Ram.

1528-1731

There were 64 conflicts between both communities to capture the structure.

1822

Faizabad court's employee Hafizullah said in a report sent to the government that Babur had built a mosque at Ram's birthplace.

1852

In the regime of Awadh's last nawab Wajid Ali Shah, an incidence of violence was reported. Nirmohi Panth's people claim that Babur demolished a temple and built a mosque there.

1855

A battle took place between hermits and Muslims in Hanuman Garhi. Wajid Ali Shah sent a notification to British resident Major Artem regarding the situation in Ayodhya. Five documents in this notification constantly said that there is often tension between Hindus and Muslims over the disputed structure.

1859

The British government put this holy place under siege. The inside area was designated for namaz and the outside area for prayers.

1860

Mosque's khatib (religious scholar), Mir Rajjan Ali filed an application in Faizabad deputy commissioner's court to remove a 'nishan sahib' or flag of the Sikhs installed by a Nihang Sikh and a platform created thereafter in the mosque's campus.

1877

Mosque's muezzin, Mohammed Asgar again filed a complaint in deputy commissioner's office that Mahant Baldev Das had kept a 'charan paduka' in the mosque campus which is being worshipped. They have even made a fire place for worship. This probably would have been the 'havankund'. The court did not get anything removed, but prohibited Mahant Baldev from doing anything further, and got a separate way made for Muslims to enter the mosque.

1885, 15 January

The demand to build a temple here reached the court. Mahant Raghubar Das filed the first case. He asked for permission to be granted to create a pavilion on Ram Chabootra or the platform, which was under them. Coincidently, it was this year that the Indian National Congress was formed.

1885, 24 February

Faizabad's district court dismissed Mahant Raghubar Das's plea citing that the place is very close to the mosque. This would lead to conflicts. Sub judge Harikishan agreed in his verdict that Raghubar Das has captured the platform there. He suggested that a wall be built to separate the platform, but also maintained that a temple cannot be built there.

1886, 17 March

Mahant Raghubar Das filed an appeal in District Judge Faizabad, Colonel F.E.A. Chamier's court. Chamier said in his verdict that the mosque is built in the holy place of Hindus. But it's late now. Correcting a mistake that was made 356 years ago after so long isn't right. All parties to maintain status quo.

1912, 20-21 November

The first riot broke out in Ayodhya on the occasion of Bakrid against cow slaughter. Cow slaughter was banned in Ayodhya since 1906 under the municipal law.

1934, March

Riots broke out against cow slaughter in Faizabad's Shahjahanpur. Angry Hindus damaged Babri mosque's wall and dome. The government later got it repaired.

1936

An enquiry by the commissioner was done to figure out if Babri mosque was built by Babur.

1944, 20 February

A report of the enquiry was published in an official gazette, which came to light in 1945 during a Shia-Sunni Waqf Board case in Faizabad's revenue court.

1949, 22-23 December

Lord Ram's statue appeared inside the mosque. Hindu groups were accused for placing the statue. Both parties filed cases. Government declared the area conflicted and ordered seizure of the building. But prayers and worship continued.

1949, 29 December

Faizabad's municipal board's chairman, Priya Dutt Ram was appointed as the receiver of the conflicted area.

1950

Hindu Mahasabha's Gopal Singh Visharad and Digamber Akhada's mahant, Paramhans Ramchandra Das filed a petition in Faizabad court and started a case to claim ownership of the birthplace. Both asked for permission to worship there. The civil judge gave interim orders for not removing the statues and allowing prayers and worship keeping the inside area closed.

1955, 26 April

High Court sealed this order by the civil judge on 3 March 1951.

1959

Nirmohi Akhada filed another petition claiming their right over the disputed site and called themselves guardian of Ram Janmabhoomi.

1961

Sunni Central Waqf Board filed a petition against idols being placed in the mosque and claimed that the mosque along with the land around it is a graveyard.

1964, 29 August

VHP was formed in Mumbai on the occasion of Janmashtmi. RSS chief Madhav Sadashiv Golwalkar, Gujarati author Kanhaiya Lal Maniklal Munshi, saint Tukoji Maharaj and Akali Dal's Master Tara Singh were present in the function.

1984, 7-8 April

Hindu organizations formed Ram Janmabhoomi Mukti Yagya Committee in New Delhi for building the temple on the Janmabhoomi. Mahant Avaidyanath became its president. 'Rath Yatras' or rallies on chariots were taken out throughout the country for freeing Ram Janmabhoomi. Ram Mandir movement gained momentum.

1986, 1 February

On the petition filed by Faizabad's lawyer Umesh Chandra Pandey, District Judge Faizabad K.M. Pandey ordered that the mosque be unlocked and Hindus be given the permission to worship there. Within forty minutes of this decision, the City Magistrate got Ram Janmabhoomi unlocked. Muslims protested against Hindus being allowed to worship there.

1986, 3 February

Mohammed Hashim Ansari appealed against the decision by the District Judge in High Court's Lucknow bench. Hashim said in his petition that in this case, the District Judge has given a one-sided verdict without hearing the other side.

1986, 5-6 February

Muslim leader Syed Shahabuddin appealed to observe mourning day on 14 February against unlocking of the mosque. All India Majlis-e-Mushawarat demanded that the Prime Minister intervene in the matter.

1986, 6 February

A conference of Muslims took place against opening the lock in Lucknow. Formation of Babri Masjid Action Committee was announced in this conference. Maulana Muzaffar Hussain Kachauchavi became the committee's president and Mohammed Azam Khan and Zafaryab Jilani became coordinators.

1986, 23-24 September

Babri Masjid Coordination Committee was formed under the leadership of Syed Shahabuddin in Delhi. The committee called for boycott of Republic Day celebration on 26 January 1987.

1989, June

BJP brought temple movement on their agenda for the first time. In Himachal Pradesh's Palampur, BJP's national working committee passed a resolution on building Ram Mandir in Ayodhya and pledged that they will make it happen. This resolution also said that it's a question of faith and devotion, and hence the court cannot decide.

1989, 1 April

Dharmsansad called by the VHP announced proposed shilanyas or laying foundation of the temple on 30 September.

1989, May

VHP planned to collect 25 crores for construction of the temple.

1988, July to 1989 November

Home minister Buta Singh consulted various parties on the Ram Janmabhoomi-Babri Masjid conflict.

1989

VHP's former chairman Justice Deoki Nandan Agarwal filed a petition in the High Court as Ram Lalla's friend demanding that the mosque be shifted to some other location. The government transferred the main case along with four other related pending cases in Faizabad's district court to High Court's special bench. The hearing of all these cases began together.

1989, 14 August

High court ordered that status quo be maintained at the site of conflict.

1989, October-November

Three and a half lakh Ram shilas or bricks reached Ayodhya for temple construction from all over the country. These bricks were worshipped in every village of the country.

1989, 9 November

With Rajiv Gandhi's approval at the centre and Narayan Dutt Tiwari led state government's support, foundation of Ram Mandir was laid in Ayodhya. Laying the foundation was supported by all parties without any conflicts. Foundation was laid at Singhdwar of the proposed temple. It was later known that foundation was laid at the conflicted area.

1990, 1 January

Court ordered for a survey commission to be made. It asked the Uttar Pradesh archaeological department to take pictures of the conflicted area.

1990, February

Kar Seva was announced once again at Ram Janmabhoomi.

1990, June

It was decided in VHP's meeting in Haridwar that construction work of the temple will begin from 30 October. To gather momentum BJP president Lal Krishna Advani announced a 'rath yatra' from Somnath to Ayodhya. The 'rath yatra' that started from Somnath on 25 September reached Faizabad on 30 October.

1990, July-October

During V.P. Singh's government, a phase of talks began to resolve the issue.

1990, 25 September

BJP leader Lal Krishna Advani's 'rath yatra' began from Somnath for Ayodhya.

1990, 17 October

BJP warned the Central government that if Advani's rath yatra was stopped, the party would withdraw its support from the government.

1990, 19 October

Centre issued a three-point ordinance to capture the conflicted land so that it could be handed over to the Ram Janmabhoomi Trust for temple construction.

1990, 23 October

Looking at the massive opposition, government rolled back the ordinance at that time, without taking BJP into confidence.

1990, 23 October

Lalu government stopped the rath yatra on Centre's instructions. Advani was arrested in Samastipur. BJP withdrew its support from the centre and V.P. Singh's government lost its majority.

1990, 30 October-2 November

Lakhs of VHP Kar Sevaks reached Ayodhya. Some of them caused damage to the disputed structure. They hoisted a saffron flag on the top of the building. Mulayam Singh Yadav's government ordered firing to control the situation. More than 40 Kar Sevaks died. Riots began as a reaction to this in many parts of the country. Curfew was imposed in more than 40 districts of UP.

1990, 7 November

V.P. Singh's government failed to prove majority in the parliament after BJP withdrew its support. Chandra Shekhar became the new prime minister with the support of Congress.

1990, 1 December

All India Babri Masjid Action Committee announced that they will hold a pan India conference on 22 December. There was a meeting to reach a settlement between VHP and Babri Masjid Action Committee as well. But VHP's stand was that of continuing with the Kar Seva. On 1 December and 4 December, Prime Minister Chandra Shekhar brought both parties together to hold talks and reach a compromise. Rajashthan's CM Bhairon Singh Shekhawat and Maharashtra's CM Sharad Pawar were also present in the meeting. In this very meeting, it was decided that both parties should present evidence for their claims.

1990, 9 December

Security forces averted an attempt to blow up the mosque. This was verbal threat by Shiv Sena's Suresh Chandra. This youth was arrested in the campus. He had tied dynamite to his body in an attempt to blow up the mosque.

1990, 23 December

VHP and Babri Masjid Action Committee submitted documents pertaining to their claims to the government.

1991, 18 January

UP's CM Mulayam Singh Yadav made a committee for enquiry into the killings in Ayodhya and the riots following these killings.

1991

General elections were held in the country. BJP made its government in Uttar Pradesh. P.V. Narasimha led Congress government took over at the centre. BJP became the chief opposition party in Lok Sabha. It won control over Uttar Pradesh due to the Ayodhya Ram Mandir movement. This brought more speed to the Ayodhya movement.

1991, 7-10 October

UP's Kalyan Singh government acquired 2.77 acres of conflicted land. Some houses and temples on the acquired land were demolished.

1991, 25 October

High Court ordered the UP government to take over the acquired land. But it prohibited any temporary construction on the acquired land.

1991, 2 November

Chief Minister Kalyan Singh gave assurance to the National Unity Council that their government will ensure security of the disputed structure. The council together passed resolution of the structure's protection.

1991, 15 November

The Supreme Court told Chief Minister Kalyan Singh, on the basis of assurance given to the National Unity Council and High Court, to follow the High Court's order given on 25 October 1991 that prohibited any kind of construction on the disputed site.

1992, February

UP government started construction of a Ram wall around Ayodhya's disputed site.

1992, March

The 42 acre land aquired by the state government in 1988-89 was handed over to the Ram Janmabhoomi Trust for Ramkatha park.

1992, March-May

All temples, ashrams and bhavans on the aquired land were demolished. Work on making the land even began.

1992, May - check

The high court refused to put a stop on the ongoing construction work at the disputed site.

1992, 9 July

VHP started Kar Seva again. They started constructing a concrete platform.

1992, 15 July

High Court gave orders to stop Kar Seva and the temporary construction being done at the disputed site.

1992, July

Supreme Court filed a contempt of court case against Kalyan Singh. But Kar Seva continued.

1992, 18 July

National Unity Council's meeting took place which failed to bring about a compromise. National Unity Council told the UP government to follow the High Court's order and stop construction.

1992, 23 July

SC banned any kind of construction in the conflicted area. Prime minister spoke to the religious leaders and asked them to stop Kar Seva.

1992, 26 July

VHP stopped the Kar Seva that had begun on 9 July.

1992, 27 July

Prime Minister gave a speech on Ayodhya's situation in the parliament.

1992, August-September

A cell on Ayodhya was formed at the Prime Minister's office. Former cabinet secretary, Naresh Chandra became its president.

1992, October

Talks between VHP and Babri Masjid Action Committee again started on the PM's initiative. Two meetings took place.

1992, 23 October

A meeting between leaders of VHP and Babri Masjid Action Committee for studying the archaeological remains found at the disputed site took place.

1992, 30-31 October

An announcement to start Kar Seva again on 6 December 1992 was made in a meeting between dharmsansad and central 'marg darshak mandal' or group of mentors.

1992, 23 November

BJP boycotted the National Unity Council meeting. In the meeting, a proposal was passed with full majority which said that the government must work according to the order given by Supreme Court on 20

November 1992. This meant no construction work should be done at the disputed site.

1992, 24 November

Central government sent a company of the central security forces to Ayodhya without keeping the state government in the loop.

1992, 27-28 November

UP government gave an affidavit in the Supreme Court for the structure's security. SC appointed a supervisor whose job was to ensure that no temporary construction was being done in the name of Kar Seva there. Moradabad's district judge Tej Shankar became Ayodhya's supervisor.

1992, 6 December

Kar Sevaks demolished the Babri Mosque with the support of VHP, BJP and Shiv Sena. There were riots all over the country in which over 2000 people lost lives. Central government dismissed the Kalyan Singh government in UP even though Chief Minister Kalyan Singh had given his resignation before the dismissal of his government. By evening, a temporary temple was built at the disputed site and idols of Ram were placed again. A wall and shed were constructed under the president's rule on 6 and 7 December.

1992, 6 December

Two FIRs were lodged against Babri Masjid demolition at the Ram Janmabhoomi Police Station. FIR 197 was filed against Kar Sevaks and FIR 198 against Lal Krishna Advani, Murli Manohar Joshi, Uma Bharti, and Ashok Singhal along with other BJP leaders.

1992, 7-8 December

Central security forces took over the Ram Janmabhoomi area under them.

1992, 10 December

Central government imposed a ban on RSS, Bajrang Dal, VHP and Jamaat-e-Islami.

1992, 15 December

Central government dismissed BJP led Rajasthan, Madhya Pradesh and Himachal Pradesh governments for keeping relations with banned organizations.

1992, 16 December

Six accused including Advani were arrested and sent to Lalitpur jail for the Babri demolition. UP government lodged an FIR, FIR 198, in which Advani and seven other people were accused. The case was handed over to the Lalitpur special court.

1992, 27 December

Central government decided to take control of Ayodhya's disputed site and the surrounding area.

1993, 7 January

Central government acquired 67.7 acres of Ayodhya Ram Janmabhoomi Babri campus. This also had the temporary temple. The same day, the president, according to Article 143 (A), gave a presidential reference to SC asking it if there was ever a temple in place of the disputed structure and if it was demolished to build a mosque there. SC, after a long hearing, returned the reference stating that it cannot give an opinion on the matter.

1993, 27 February

CBCID submitted charge sheet for FIR 198 in Lalitpur's special court. In the charge sheet Advani and others were accused under section 147, 149 (besides 153A, 153 Band 505).

1993, 11 March

As a reaction to the threat to demolish the Babri mosque, bomb blasts took place in Mumbai. Thousands of people died in these blasts and the communal riots that followed them.

1993, 6 June

The UP government transferred FIR 198 from Lalitpur to Raebareli's special court.

1993, 25 August

CBI replaced CBCID in Advani's case. The UP government issued two notifications and transferred the case to CBI. In the first notification, CBI was given permission to investigate FIR 198 and the other notification ordered CBI to investigate attacks on media.

1993, 8 September

After consulting Allahabad High Court, the UP government formed a special bench in Lucknow for hearing the Ayodhya demolition cases.

1993, 5 October

For the first time, CBI also filed a case of conspiracy under section

120B against all the accused. It submitted a joint supplementary charge sheet in all 49 cases.

1997, 9 September

Special Judge asked CBI to file charges against the 49 accused. Out of these 49, 33 filed a review petition in High Court's Lucknow bench. Advani did not file a review petition.

1998

BJP came to power at the centre.

2001, 12 February

High Court accepted the review petitions of the 33 accused.

2001, 24 July

Mohammed Aslam aka Bhure filed a petition in SC against High Court's order on 12 February.

2001, 20 August

SC asked the UP government and CBI to file a counter affidavit against Bhure's appeal.

2002

In February VHP decided 15 March to be the final date to start construction of the temple again. Kar Sevaks started collecting in Ayodhya from all over the country. Bogie S-6 of Sabarmati Express, carrying returning Kar Sevaks was attacked in Gujarat's Godhra. 58 Kar Sevaks were burnt alive in that attack. Riots spread in the whole of Gujarat after this incident. More than 1000 people were killed in these riots.

2002, April

Hearing began on who has right over the disputed site in Allahabad High Court's special bench of three judges.

2003

Allahabad High Court's special bench asked ASI to investigate if there was a temple at that place earlier. High court told ASI to dig the place and find out. ASI found evidence of an eleventh century temple under the mosque.

2004

After six years of BJP's rule, Congress returned to power at the centre. One court of Uttar Pradesh said that deliberation must be done on Advani being established as innocent.

2005, July

Some suspected Islamic militants attacked the disputed site. Security forces gunned down these five militants trying to enter the conflicted zone.

2009, June

Librahan Commission, that was formed to investigate the Babri demolition, submitted its report to the government. There was a lot of ruckus in the parliament because the report accused BJP leaders of being part of the demolition.

2010

Allahabad High Court announced its verdict on four petitions filed on the Ayodhya conflict. The High Court said in its order that the conflicted area be divided into three parts. One-third of it to be given to Ram Lalla, whose representation is with Hindu Mahasabha, one-third to be given to Sunni Central Waqf Board and one-third part to be given to Nirmohi Akhada. In December, Akhil Bhartiya Hindu Mahasabha and Sunni Waqf Board moved SC against this verdict.

2011, May

SC prohibited division of the land and said that the situation was to remain as it was.

2014

Narendra Modi led BJP registered a historic win in the Lok Sabha elections and came to power at the centre.

2015

VHP again called for collection of bricks for Ram Mandir's construction from Rajasthan. After six months, two trucks full of bricks reached the disputed site in December. Mahant Nritya Gopal Das claimed that the Modi government has given a go-ahead for temple construction. UP's Akhilesh Yadav government said that they will not allow bricks to be brought to Ayodhya.

2017, March

SC said that the charges against Advani and other leaders for the 1992 demolition cannot be dismissed and ordered for the case to be investigated again.

2017, March

BJP achieved great success in Uttar Pradesh state elections and it took charge under the leadership of Yogi Adityanath.

2017, 21 March

SC said that this matter is sensitive and its solution should be found outside court. SC asked all parties to form one opinion and look for a solution.

2017, 5 December

SC decided to speed up hearing on all the public interest litigations against Allahabad High Court's decision on Ram Janmabhoomi and Babri Masjid given on 8 February 2017.

2018, 8 February

SC ordered all parties to ready their documents in two weeks. It also said that no new party will be added to the case now. The Chief Justice said that he will see the case as a land dispute only.

2018, 14 March

Besides the main parties of the case, SC dismissed all 32 intervention applications filed by third parties to avoid unnecessary intervention. Now only those parties were left that were included in Allahabad High Court's decision. SC also said that if both parties reach a settlement, court may give permission. But it cannot force or pressurize a party for the same.

◆

Chapter 10

THIS TOO IS IMPORTANT

All were shocked after the demolition. No one could understand anything. Leaders could not comprehend what had happened? Why it happened? Government and BJP both were suffering from guilt. The guilt of Prime Minister Narasimha Rao had its roots in his 'miscalculation'. And Atal Bihari Vajpayee's guilt had it origin in failure to keep the promise by his party to the Parliament and judiciary. Due this this very guilt, Lal Krishna Advani had resigned from his position of leader of the opposition in Lok Sabha. First time both had put forth their views in Lok Sabha. No confidence motion debate in Lok Sabha on 17 December had been meaningful.

One

Certain characters are etched on every page of the Ayodhya dispute. But they are missing from the memory of the people. Big revolutionary names have pushed them into the oblivion of history. But Ayodhya knows them. It recognizes them at every step of its history. To understand this dispute, it's important for you to know them well. We are introducing such characters to you here; those who are in the foundation of the dispute but are invisible, just like the stones of the foundation. Those people, whose photographs were not available, we have had their portraits made.

First Mughal Badshah of Delhi (1526-30)—Babur. Babri Mosque was built during his reign. Babur's father, a descendent of Taimur Lang and mother Kultum Nigar was from the family of Genghis Khan. Born in 1483, Babur inherited his father's legacy at the young age of 11. His estate

Fergana is now in Chinese Turkistan. On 21 April 1526, Babur became the ruler of Delhi after killing Ibrahim Lodhi. He had started taking notes in his diary right after the murder of his father. After remaining lost for five hundred years, this same diary became the 'Babur Nama'. 18 years of records have been destroyed from the diary, so today it does not have any mention of Babri Mosque in it. Babur has mentioned an incident of 25 May 1529. 'One night when five hours have passed by, I was busy writing, a storm came, by the time I could gather my things, the tent caved in. My head was hurt. The pages of the book got drenched with water. I was able to save the rest of the pages with great difficulty.' His diary was written in Turkish language. Later, Akbar had it translated in Persian.

Baqi Tashqandi is known as Mir Baqi. He was the general of Babur. A Shia Muslim, Mir Baqi was from Tashkent (today it's the capital of Uzbekistan). Babur had sent him as the governor of Awadh region. Mir Baqi had constructed Babri Mosque between 1528 and 1529, at the birthplace of Lord Ram. Mir Baqi stayed at Ayodhya between March 1528 and June 1529. Mir Baqi died at the Sahnawa village of Faizabad. There is a shrine there in his name.

Naga ascetic Abhiram Das from Darbhanga Bihar was leader of the group that placed the idol of Ram Lalla at the disputed building, on the night of 22-23 December 1949. This Naga ascetic of Ramanandi sect was associated with Nirvani Akhada. Tall and strongly built Abhiram Das was not an educated man. He wrestled. He knew the tricks of the wrestling-ring. He was called a fighter sadhu in Ayodhya. He was the member of Hindu Maha Sabha, and so he was close to Mahant Digvijay Nath. He is known as the 'restrictor baba' of Ram Janmabhoomi. He was the main accused in the FIR that was lodged against placing the idols. He died in 1981.

Devraha Baba was a divine sadhu from the long tradition of Indian saints. He lived by Saryu at Lar in Devaria, Uttar Pradesh. He was an expert in Mahrishi Patanjali's Ashtanga Yoga. Where did he come from and where was he born? His life is still a mystery for the people. He wore no clothes. A Ram devotee, he lived on a high scaffolding in the waters of Ganga and Saryu. Well known personalities from India and abroad were his disciples. President Rajendra Prasad, Indira Gandhi, Rajiv Gandhi and Atal Bihari Vajpayee used to go to seek his blessings. Whenever Indira Gandhi faced any difficulty she went to Baba for its solution. He presided over the religious parliament held at Allahabad Kumbh in January 1984. 9 November 1989 was decided here for the foundation laying. While attempts and obstruction of foundation laying were going on, Rajiv Gandhi went to meet Baba. Devraha Baba said to Rajiv Gandhi, 'Child let it happen'. It was for Baba's desire that Rajiv Gandhi got the foundation laid, even while he faced opposition within the party.

Karpatri ji was a monk politician. Swami Karpatri ji's real name was Harnarayan Ojha. He was called 'Dharma Samrat'. He ate only what fit his palms, 'kar' and so he was named Karpatri. Swamiji was not among those sadhus who sat in silent prayers in caves or solitude. He ran a movement to save the Sanatana Dharma and to stop the impact of western culture. He created institutions, published a newspaper and led a procession of sadhus at the Parliament. He was the president of the committee that selected Shankaracharya. His book *Markswaad aur Ramrajya* became popular. To protect the ancient Indian ways of teaching he created 'Dharm Sangha Shiksha Mandal'. He published *Sanmarg* newspaper. After formally becoming a monk, he picked up his staff to establish 'Dharma' or the righteousness in politics. He formed a political party by the name of Ram Rajya Parishad. Once four members of this party were in the Lok Sabha and 24 members were in the Rajasthan Vidhan Sabha. In 1966 it was Karpatri ji who lead a procession at the Parliament, against the killing of cows. Security forces fired at the sadhus in the protest. Dozens of sadhus died. Karpatri ji had also initiated the Ram Janmabhoomi movement. King of Balrampur Pateshwari Prasad, Mahant Digvijay Nath and Collector of Gonda, K.K.K. Nayar made a vow to free Ram Janmabhoomi in the presence of Karpatri ji.

Mahant Digvijay Nath was a revolutionary sadhu. He was part of the group that placed the idol in the Babri structure. He was the main accused in the Chauri-Chaura incident during the freedom movement. He was the Mahant of the top peeth, Gau-raksha Peeth of Natha-panthi Kanphata Sadhus. Current Chief Minister of Uttar Pradesh Yogi Aditya Nath heads the same peeth. He was also the state president of Hindu Maha Sabha. Digvijay Nath hailed from the same family of Ranas that Bappa Rawal and Maharana Pratap were from. His name in childhood was Rana Nanhu Singh. Digvijay Nath was a well-read sadhu with political acumen. He was a good tennis player.

The strategy to free Ram Janmabhoomi at Ayodhya was formed in the palace of Maharaj Pateshwari Prasad Singh of 'Balrampur Estate' of Gonda. Because of his Hindu sentiments, Maharaj was close to Karpatri Maharaj and Mahant Digvijay Nath. Born on 1 January 1914, Pateshwari Prasad studied at Mayo Collage of Ajmer. He grew up in the care of British Officer Colonel Hanson. He travelled far and long for his love for horse riding and tennis. One basis of his friendship with K.K.K. Nayar and Digvijay Nath was their common interest in lawn tennis. Maharaj often performed yagya. These yagyas or religious events gave a reason for sadhus and saints to gather at his place. In the initial months of 1947, during one such yagya, the strategy for the Ayodhya movement was formed.

Moropant Pingle was the architect of the Ayodhya movement. Responsible for taking this movement to every house through the 'Rama-stones' (sanctified bricks with Ram engraving), Moropant ji was a Chittapawan Brahman from Maharashtra. Very simple and humble, Pingle, who was a graduate from Morris College, Nagpur, always worked from behind the scenes. He had three lakh bricks sanctified, for the proposed temple, from every village in the country. Then these bricks (Rama-stones) journeyed from village to tehseel and then to district to a district headquarter. Due to this programme about six crore people got directly and emotionally involved with the Ayodhya movement. In one sweep this movement reached every village and every home. Stone laying, foundation laying, charan paduka, Ram Jyoti processions—all these activities were the brainchild of Pingleji. But he always remained in the background. Pingleji was groomed under first sarsanghchalak

Doctor Hedgewar. To remain in the background and not take any credit was Moropant Pingle's working style. His name is embedded in history for evoking the idea of Ayodhya in the minds of Hindus.

Ashok Singhal was the strategist for the great Hindu unity after independence. Singhal remained head of VHP for twenty years. He became RSS pracharak in 1942. He was the main force behind organizing the first dharmsansad at Vigyan Bhawan against Meenakshipuram conversions. After this event he was given the responsibility of Virat Hindu Conventions. Congress MP Karan Singh used to be the president in these conventions. Agra born Singhal's father was in government service. Singhal was a studious and impressive orator. He graduated in Metal Engineering from Banaras Hindu University in 1950. Singhal was a Khayal singer of the Guru lineage. He learned singing from Pundit Onkar Nath Thakur. He sang in the first dharmsansad, 'Chandan hai is desh ki maati, tapo-bhumi hai har gram, har bala devi ki pratima, bachcha-bachcha ram hai'. Many CDs were made of his singing. From lock opening at Ayodhya to the demolition, he remained a central character in this movement.

ICS officer of 1930 batch, K.K.K. Nayar hailed from Alleppey in Kerala. Idols were placed in the Babri structure or it can also be said that he was the one to have them placed while he was the district magistrate at Ayodhya. He is one person associated with the Babri issue in whose tenure a big change took place that had far-reaching effects on the socio-political fabric of the country. Alumnus of Madras University Nayar knew Tamil, Malayalam, Hindi, Urdu, and English along with French, German and Spanish. Nayar became the Collector of Faizabad on 1 June 1949. When idols of Lord Ram were placed in the mosque on 23 December 1949, Prime Minister Jawahar Lal Nehru asked UP Chief Minister Govind Vallabh Pant to have them removed immediately. UP government also ordered to have the idols removed, but district magistrate K.K.K. Nayar expressed his inability on the pretext of riots and fear of provoking Hindu sentiments. Also, the premises was locked down to prevent Muslims from entering it. When Nehru wrote again to have the idols removed then K.K.K. Nayar wrote back requesting for his own removal before removal of the idols. Sensing communal sentiment, the government backed down. DM K.K.K. Nayar took voluntary retirement in 1952. He became a member of the fourth Lok Sabha from Jan Sangh party from Bahraich seat of UP. Nayar had become such a big icon of Hindutva that his wife Shakuntala Nayar also got elected three times for parliament from Kaisarganj constituency on Jan Sangh ticket. His driver also became a member of UP Vidhan Sabha.

Hanuman Poddar was the facilitator of the group that placed the idols in the Babri structure on the night of 22-23 December 1949. Friends lovingly called him 'Bhai ji'. On that night Bhai ji was in charge of installation and ritualistic invocation of the idols. Simple, humble and ready to do anything for faith, Bhai ji was a staunch supporter of Hindutva. Hanuman Prasad Poddar Bhai ji's name was synonymous to Gita Press or religious books. Seth Jaidayal Goenka had established Gita press which grew in size like a large banyan tree under Hanuman Prasad Poddar. Born in 1892 in Shillong, Hanuman Prasad Poddar's parents were devotees of Hanuman, so they named the boy Hanuman Prasad. Hanuman Prasad was a friend of Digvijay Nath who was the head of Goraksh Peeth. In 1914, after meeting Mahamana Madan Mohan Malviya, he became active with Hindu Maha Sabha. That's why he was emotionally closer to Digvijay Nath. He was also in contact with revolutionaries like Arvind, Surendra Nath Banerjee, Bipin Chandra Pal and Chittaranjan Das. That was the reason Hanuman Prasad was jailed for 21 months by the British in Shimlapal village in Bankura district. He flamed the fires of the movement by publishing Ram Janmabhoomi edition of *Kalyan* magazine.

Ramchandra Paramhans is the only personality in the Ayodhya movement who has been a prominent person from the placement of idols to the demolition. When Bhageran Tiwari's son Chandreshwar Tiwari of Chapra (Bihar) came to Ayodhya in 1930, he was an Ayurvedacharya. When he met Paramhansa Ramkinkar Das of Digambar Akhada he was given a new name 'Ramchandra Das' and was given the task of freeing the Ram Janmabhoomi. He became a monk at the age of fifteen. He got associated with this movement in 1934. He was also the City-president of Hindu Maha Sabha. He became the Mahant of Panch Ramanandiya Akhada in 1975 and president of Ram Janmabhoomi Nyas in 1989. He had good knowledge of Sanskrit. He also had a good command on the vedas and classical Indian text. He was a straightforward, aggressive, strong-willed and stubborn ascetic. He was a junior member of the group that placed the idols in 1949. On 1 January 1950 he lodged a case in Faizabad court over the ownership and worshipping rights at the disputed structure. Shri Ram Janmabhoomi Yagya Samiti was constituted in April 1984 in the first dharmsansad held in Delhi. Paramhans Ramchandra Das was the President of this dharmsansad. The programme of Ram-Janki Rath Yatra between Sitamadhi and Ayodhya was decided in this meeting. He had announced in 1985 that if the locks were not opened, he would immolate himself. Digambar Akhada was the main akhada of Ramananda sect. The procession of Kar Sevaks which was fired upon in 1990 was also being led by Paramhans Ramchandra Das. He continued fighting for Ram Janmabhoomi till his last breath on 31 July 2003.

Born on 11 October 1916, in Kadoli town of Hingoli district in Maharashtra, Chandika Das Amrit Rao Deshmukh is known as Nanaji Deshmukh. Nanaji was also present in Ayodhya when the idols were being installed. Nanaji lived a long and eventful life riddled with scarcity and struggle. But despite paucity, he received high education at the Birla Institute of Pilani. He joined RSS in 1930. For work he chose the regions of Uttar Pradesh and Rajasthan. In 1940 he left his home and stayed unmarried to remain engaged in public service. Sarsanghchalak Guruji appointed him state pracharak of Uttar Pradesh. Saraswati Shishu Mandir, which is a strong chain for imparting education, was first established by Nanaji in Gorakhpur. In April 1974 during Sampoorna Kranti movement at Patna's Gandhi Ground, Nanaji fell over Jayprakash Narayan to cover him and save him from lathi charge. He broke his pelvis during this incident. In 1977 when Janata government was formed Nanji refused to become a minister saying, people who are above sixty should leave politics. Leaving active politics, in 1978 Nanaji started working for village upliftment at Gonda, Nagpur, Beed and Ahmedabad through 'Deendayal

Research Institute'. Nanaji Deshmukh was an astute Ram devotee; he chose Ram's penitentiary land Chitrakoot as the centre for his work. After the demolition of the disputed structure on 6 December 1992, Nanaji said that Babri demolition was unfortunate, it was not part of the proposed Kar Seva, but there was no need to be apologetic about it.

Despite being a Congress follower, Baba Raghav Das had an unshaking belief in the Ram Janmabhoomi Movement. He was among the five people who placed the idol at the disputed structure. Raghavendra Sheshappa Pachapuchkar of Pune is known for his Congress politics and as Baba Raghav Das in Ram Janmabhoomi movement. He was a Chittapavan Brahmin. After losing his entire family to plague in year 1891, Raghavendra Sheshappa Pachapuchkar reached Ghazipur through Allahabad and Banaras. In Ghazipur he met the famous saint Mauni Baba. After his initiation by Mauni Baba he reached Yogiraj Anant Mahaprabhu of Barhaj (Devaria). His guru died after one year. It was then that Raghavendra Baba became Raghav Das and he overtook the responsibility of his guru's ashram. He then joined the freedom movement. He quickly became popular because of his aggressiveness, Hindutva-centric outlook and Satyagraha. He joined congress in 1920, and in 1948 Ayodhya Vidhan Sabha by-polls were held. Pundit Govind Vallabh Pant had to get even with Acharya Narendra Dev. Baba Raghav Das was Congress's political sadhu. Congress fielded Baba Raghav Das against Acharya Narendra Dev. Baba Raghav Das had already taken up the issue of freeing Ram Janmabhoomi. In these elections Govind Vallabh Pant also aggressively campaigned in favour of Ram Janmabhoomi issue because Acharya Narendra Dev had the support of Muslims from Ayodhya and Faizabad. By now Congress had constructed Somnath temple in Gujarat's Junagarh. Closeness with Hindu Nationalism in Congress was evident. Congress propagated that Narendra Dev was against the temple. Acharya Narendra Dev lost elections to Baba Raghav Das. This was the first test of Ram Janmabhoomi issue in Indian politics.

Gopal Singh Visharad from Faizabad was a Hindutva-centric lawyer. Visharad was his degree. One gets visharad degree after accomplishing excellence in any one subject. He was the secretary of Faizabad unit of Hindu Mahasabha. After associating directly with Ayodhya movement, Hindu Mahasabha had created an organization – All India Ramayana Mahasabha, Visharad was its joint secretary. It was Visharad who got the Faizabad court to order the government on 5 January 1950, to not remove idols from the disputed structure. He was the original party to the Ayodhya dispute. While the idols were being placed, that night, pamphlets were being printed in one press at Faizabad, with an appeal, 'Lord has appeared, let's go to Janmabhoomi'. Visharad was very close to District Magistrate K.K.K. Nayar and City Magistrate Gurudutt Singh.

Gurudutt Singh was City Magistrate of Faizabad in 1949. A tall, resolute man with a thin moustache, this state Civil Service Officer was close to Hindu Mahasabha. A graduate from Allahabad, Gurudutt Singh never wore a hat in his entire career. He always wore a turban. A vegetarian, Gurudutt Singh had so much devotion towards Ram that he visited Ram Janmabhoomi every year when he was a student. Like District Magistrate Nayar, Gurudutt Singh was facilitating those who placed the idols in the disputed structure. Actually he was also the writer of the narrative that claimed that the idols appeared inside the structure. As a city magistrate, Gurudutt Singh lived in Lorpur House, built by the British. According to his son Guru Basant Singh, this was the place where District Magistrate Nayar and Abhiram Das often met at night to plan the strategy of placing the idols. Guru Basant was fifteen years old at the time. According to him, the morning that the idols were placed, his father was praying in front of god with folded hands, 'Lord, whatever is happening, let it happen.' The sanctum-sanctorum of the structure that was demolished had a picture of Gurudutt Singh along with that of Ram Lalla. After this incident, Singh resigned and became District President of Jan Sangh. Later he was elected as a legislative member of Jan Sangh from Faizabad.

Abdul Barkat was the gentleman who was on guard duty on the night of 22 and 23 December 1949 at the disputed structure. His duty was from 12 midnight onwards, but this man reached there at one o'clock at night. After reaching there, as he said himself, the miracle had already occurred. Sher Singh, the duty guard before him, had already helped finish the plan. To save his job, because he was late, he narrated the same story to the police, as was told to him by those who had placed the idols there. Abdul Barkat told the police, 'Suddenly I saw a flash of light inside the mosque. My eyes were blinded with it. I could not understand anything. When the light dimmed, I saw a miracle; Ram had appeared there along with three of his brothers.'

Ismail was the muezzin of Babri mosque at the time idols were placed there. Muezzins are supposed to give azan for namaz, but because no namaz was read here, he didn't have to do this task. He used to clean the mosque. On the night of 22nd December 1949 when Abhiram Das and other Naga Bahubali Vairagi went inside the building carrying the idol, they had a scuffle with Ismail. When Ismail tried to stop them, the monks beat him up. Finding himself alone he ran away from the spot. After running for two kilometres Ismail reached Ghosiyana locality of Faizabad. He did not return out of fear. He started working as a muezzin in a mosque in the same locality. He never returned to that road again.

Priya Dutt Ram was Ayodhya Municipal Board President from 1949 to 1950. After the placement of idols, fearing dispute, the District Magistrate took over the control of Babri structure. Priya Dutt Ram was made the 'receiver' of this property. On 5 January 1950 Priya Dutt Ram overtook the responsibility of the structure. He submitted a plan to the District Magistrate for its upkeep and prayers. Priya Dutt Ram said in his report that because Ram Lalla was a deity, who needs to be fed, bathed and clothed, a priest and storekeeper should be appointed and lock of one gate should be opened. One small door of the structure was opened, so that they can go inside and pray. Temple supporters have his picture hanging in the Ram Janmabhoomi workshop.

Mahant Avaidyanath was the first president of the Ram Janmabhoomi Yagya Samiti. He was one among the people who held the most talks from the government's side. He was a Lok Sabha member five times. He was close to Chandra Shekhar and Vishwanath Pratap Singh. Kripal Singh Bisht, born 1969, in Paudi district of Uttarakhand, became Avaidyanath and in 1942 he was appointed successor of Digvijay Nath. After the demise of Digvijay Nath in 1969 he inherited the seat of Athpanthi Kanphata sect. Avaidyanath also remained the president of a high-powered committee, Ram Janmabhoomi Nyas. Mahant Avaidyanath was also among the main accused for the demolition. He was elected for the fourth Lok Sabha from Hindu Maha Sabha for the first time, after which he became MP for three more terms from here. Mahant ji was also an MLA from the Maniram seat of Gorakhpur.

A prominent and sharp Hindutva centric leader, primarily a lawyer, renowned writer and educationist K.M. Munshi was Public Distribution Minister in Nehru's cabinet. Later he became the governor of Uttar Pradesh. When VHP was constituted in Mumbai for the resurgence of Hindutva, Munshi was among its founding members. He was known for his fierce Hindutvaite ideology. He left Congress in 1941 and became close to Hindu Maha Sabha. He again returned to Congress in 1946 and was among those who were close to Sardar Patel. After independence, along with Sardar Patel, Munshi got involved in the restoration of Somnath temple. He was sympathetic towards the Ram Janmabhoomi movement. That's why Nehru called him to be a Hindu revivalist. He was also a renowned literator.

Nritya Gopal Das is the Mahant of Mani Ramdas Chhawani of Ayodhya. After the demise of Paramhans Ramchandra Das he became the president of Ram Janmabhoomi Nyas. Chhawani is the residence of sadhus in the akhada tradition. He is also a criminal accused of the demolition of the disputed structure. He named 6 December 1992 as the 'Hindu Shaurya Diwas'. He was born on 11 June 1938 in Mathura. Nritya Gopal Das is the sixth Mahant of Maniram Chhawani. This is the temple of Vaishnav sects's Ramananda Akhada. Polite, soft-spoken and learned, Nritya Gopal Das's Char Dham temple was the control room of Kar Seva movement. This is where the arrangements of stay and food for Kar Sevaks were made. Nritya Gopal Das said about the demolition that there was neither conspiracy of demolition nor provocation, it happened through the prudence of Kar Sevaks.

Chemist by education H.V. Sheshadri was an active face of Sangh in the Ram Janmabhoomi movement. Sangh had given him the responsibility of figuring out the social chemistry on the Ram Janmabhoomi issue. To lend traction to Ram Janmabhoomi movement the first 'Ekatmata' march was done in 1983. He was made in-charge of it. Sheshadriji was present in Ayodhya along with other leaders on 6 December 1992. A dais was made at 200 meters and Sheshadriji was on it along with Lal Krishna Advani and VHP president Ashok Singhal. At the start of the Ram Janmabhoomi movement, it was Sheshadriji who was leading it from the spot as a Sangh representative. He knew many languages. When the situation started to get out of control and Kar Sevaks climbed the structure and started vandalising it, Sheshadriji made an appeal in Hindi, English, Kannada, Tamil, Telugu and Malayalam to Kar Sevaks to stop. But Kar Sevaks didn't listen to him. In 1998 Sheshadri coined the term 'Ram Janmabhoomi movement', a Hindu renaissance movement. Hongasandra Venkatramaiah Sheshadri was born in 1926 in Bangalore. He joined RSS after getting a post graduate degree in Chemistry from Bangalore University. He became Sarkaryavahak in 1987 and remained so until year 2000.

K.S. Sudarshan was the first Sangh chief from southern India. He ran Ram temple construction movement to the best of his ability. As a chief of RSS he was always against appeasement. He was in favour of Indianisation of Muslims. Rashtriya Muslim Manch was created during his tenure. It was K.S. Sudarshan who brought forth the aspect of nationalism in Ram temple movement, instead of a religious one. Sudarshanji wrote—'Laying foundation brick for Ram Janmabhoomi temple was not just a matter of a temple, it was a symbol of laying foundation of a nation.'

Kuppalli Sitaramayya Sudarshan was the fifth sarsanghchalak of RSS. Born in a Brahmin family from Raipur, Sudarshan came to RSS shakha for the first time at the age of 9 years. After completing Engineering from Sagar University, he became full time pracharak for Sangh. There is a tradition that full time pracharaks remain unmarried. Following this tradition, he dedicated his entire life to the country and the organization. When the fourth sarsanghchalak felt that he could not remain active due to his failing health, he handed the responsibility to Sudarshanji on 10 March 2000 at Akhil Bharatiya Pratinidhi Sabha.

When Babri mosque was demolished in 1992, R.N. Srivastava was the district magistrate. Srivastava was accused of being part of the conspiracy to demolish the mosque. According to the accusation, under his leadership the local administration made no attempt to prevent the demolition of the disputed structure. Even after repeated reminders he did not take help of central security forces stationed at Ayodhya-Faizabad. In his report to the state government he made baseless allegations against the central forces. In his statement given to Librahan Commission on 26 March 2002 he said that he had intelligence input that ISI agents were present at Ayodhya with explosives. In his statement he also told that VHP and BJP leaders were not given permission to address the Kar Sevaks from Ram Katha Kunj Manch. On 7 December 1992, the day after the Babri mosque demolition, he was suspended. He retired in the year 1996.

When Babri mosque was demolished in 1992, Devendra Bahadur Rai was the SSP of Faizabad. He had also been the PSO of UP Chief Minister Vir Bahadur Singh. The journey that he started with a khaki uniform, he ended with a uniform of RSS. On 7 December 1992, the day after the Babri mosque demolition, he was also suspended along with the DM Faizabad R.N. Srivastava. Srivastava and D.B. Rai were tried for being part of the conspiracy of demolishing the mosque. D.B. Rai was close to Bajrang Dal chief Vinay Katiyaar. Rai was the police officer of regional police service of 1971 batch. Soft towards the Kar Sevaks, Rai refused to act on the second day of the president's rule when it was decided to vacate the premises from Kar Sevaks. Nine years of his service were still remaining when D.B. Rai resigned and joined the BJP. He was elected from Sultanpur for Lok Sabha in 1996 and 1998 with a BJP ticket. D.B. Rai also wrote a book titled *Ayodhya: 6 December Ka Sach*. He made a claim that the Prime Minister at the time, P.V. Narasimha Rao was also responsible for the demolition of Babri mosque.

A living example of harmony between two cultures known as 'Ganga-Jamuni-tehseeb', Mohammed Hashim Ansari was the prime advocate of

Ayodhya dispute. He was advocating for the Babri mosque since 1949. He led a simple life. Earlier he had a bicycle repair shop and then he opened a tailoring shop. When Sunni Waqf Board filed a case for Babri mosque in 1961, he was also a party in it. Hashim Ansari also challenged the verdict of unlocking in 1986 in Allahabad High Court.

On this petition High Court ordered to maintain status quo on 3 February 1986. Hashim Ansari's family has been living in Ayodhya for many generations now. Ansari always took the view of Hindu-Muslim unity. He was the prime party in the Ayodhya issue. But he never held any bitterness. He was friends with all the sadhus and saints of Ayodhya. Hashim Ansari never missed greeting sadhus and saints and Hindus on any of the Hindu festivals. Although there were ideological differences between Paramhans Ramchandra Das and Babri mosque proponent Hashim Ansari, their friendship was unbreakable. Often, they both took a ride on an ekka or the horse carriage to go to Faizabad on the dates of the court case. 95-year-old Hashim Ansari died on 20 July 2016.

Karingamannu Kuzhiyil Muhammed was the first Muslim archaeologist who announced that there was a Hindu temple under the Babri structure. Born in Kerala's Calicut, K.K. Muhammed did MA in history from Aligarh Muslim University. As a student of School of Archaeology, he participated in the excavation at Ayodhya in the year 1976-77. In this excavation he found twelve pillars of an ancient temple, upon which the Babri mosque structure was built. A base made of bricks was found under the pillars, in excavation done under the leadership of Director General of Indian Archaeological Survey of India, Professor B.B. Lal. This was in 1990, when the dispute worsened about whether the site had first been a temple or a mosque. At that time, based on his study, K.K. Muhammed said that Babri mosque stands on the debris of an ancient Hindu temple. Pillars of an ancient temple and other symbols have been used in this mosque. Fourteen such pillars had been found at this disputed site upon which the domes were present. These domes were like the ones found in 11th and 12th century temples. K.K. Muhammed says that after the High Court ordered ASI to excavate, fifty such base-platforms for pillars were found. Other than this, an 'Amlaka' of the stone disk of the main tower and a water passage for the deity were also found. Muhammed believes that a solution to this dispute could have been found much earlier. Muslim society was also in agreement, but the leftist historians who were associated with Babri Action Committee, provoked the people saying that nothing was found there and that it was all false propaganda. K.K. Muhammed was of the view that other than Doctor Surajbhan, there was no other specialist in that group, including Professor Irfan Habib, who understood Archaeology.

Swami Vasudevananda Saraswati was the same Shankaracharya, under whose presidentship of fifth dharmsansad, 6th December was decided for Kar Seva. He became the Shankaracharya of Jyotish peeth Badrik ashrama in 1989. Swami Vasudevananda Saraswati was a strong proponent of Ram Lalla being the owner of that place. He thought that all parties should agree to this. He believed that only an impressive temple of Ram Lalla should be built at that spot. Fourth dharmsansad was organized in Swami Vasudevananda Saraswati's presidentship in April 1991 at Delhi's Talkatora Stadium, where a demand for a handover of disputed structure to Shriram Janmabhoomi Nyas was made. He kept fighting with Swaroopananda over control of Jyotish Peeth. This was the reason Swaroopananda was always against the Ram Janmabhoomi movement. He never supported the movement. On September 2017, Allahabad High Court, in its decision, refused to consider him a Shankaracharya.

Swami Vamdev was a simple and polite saint. Four feet tall, Vamdev had all the qualities of being a saint. Vamdevji dedicated his entire life to stop cow slaughter and to instead construct Ram temple at Ayodhya. Ex-Prime Minister Narasimha Rao tried his best to pull him away from VHP but failed. Under the presidentship of Swami, in the year 1984, All India saint conference was organised at Jaipur. In it, for 15 days 400 sadhus and saints intensely discussed the future path for the Ram Janmabhoomi movement. VHP appealed for Kar Seva in Ayodhya on 30 October 1990. Despite his old age Swami Vamdev crossed all obstacles and somehow managed to reach Ayodhya. On 2 November 1990, after the firing on the Kar Sevaks, Swamiji got so angry that he warned the administration of bloodshed. He said that if the administration didn't remove curfew and allowed Kar Sevaks to see Ram Lalla, there would be a big bloodshed. When the structure was being demolished on 6 December 1992, Swamiji was present at the Kar Sevakpuram. On March 1993 Swamiji mentioned the issues of Kashi and Mathura after Ayodhya in the conference of saints. On the Ram Navmi of April 1993 there was a nine-day worshipping ritual. Swami Vamdev who fought for the Ram temple died on 20 March 1997.

An arms dealer in the guise of a saint, a specialist of mediation for power, one who claimed to possess tantric powers to read minds—the true identity of Chandraswami remained hidden in many layers of his attire. He was a saint who always had business with the government. He was a Congress person in the disguise of a saint. Not many people would know that he mediated on the Ram temple issue as well. He was the initiator of a decisive dialogue with the Narasimha Rao government on the issue of Kar Seva. Even though he was controversial he enjoyed a certain acceptance among all the political parties. From swamis to politicians, actors and criminals all were in touch with him. He had nothing to do with religious philosophy. While mediating for the Ram temple construction, all were paying attention to him, including Mulayam Singh Yadav, Narasimha Rao and Bhairon Singh Shekhawat from the BJP. He had made a deep impression on Narasimha Rao. In April 1993 Chandraswami organized a conference of 300 sadhus and religious heads in Delhi. In this conference it was announced that Ram temple should be constructed in place of the Babri mosque. Also, the mosque should be outside the five-kilometre periphery of the temple. Chandraswami was trying to end the hold of VHP on Ram temple issue. Central government was behind these attempts of Chandraswami. In this chain of events, after two months, on June 1993, Chandraswami organized Som-Yagya at Ayodhya. Even when there was president's rule imposed, Chandraswami was permitted to enter the disputed premises. Chandrswami was born in 1948 in Alwar, Rajasthan. His real name was Namichandra Jain. Before Chandraswami became a tantric, he was active in politics. He joined Youth Congress in Hyderabad at 17 years of age. But after few days he became disciple of a sadhu Amar Muni at Bihar-Nepal boarder for tantric practices. He had close association with many actors and big politicians from India and abroad.

Justice Harinath Tilhari and Justice A.N. Gupta were the judges at Allahabad High Court in the year 1992. When State and Central governments had imposed a temporary ban on viewing and worship of Ram Lalla, bench comprising both these judges on 1 January 1993 ordered to resume worshipping of Ram Lalla. A curfew was imposed in Ayodhya after the incident of 6 December 1992. People could not worship or pray to the deity. In this situation, Harishankar Jain filed a petition at Allahabad High Court to resume the prayer. Justice Tilhari and Justice Gupta had given their verdict on this petition. The bench in its decision said, 'A system should be put in place for proper viewing of the Lord. Also, an arrangement should be made to protect the Lord from storm, rain, cold and wind.' After this order, prayers were started again and continue till today.

Special bench of Allahabad High Court had heard the case of ownership of Ayodhya's disputed land thirteen times in twenty-one years. From year 1989 to 2010 a total of eighteen judges heard the case. Members of the second bench hearing case of ownership of the disputed land in the year 1990 were; Justice Satish Chandra Mathur, Justice Brijesh Kumar and Justice Syed Abbas Raza. Among them Justice Raza had also been part of the first bench. When Mulayam Singh government acquired 2.77 acres of land in October 1991, it was challenged by the second bench. After the arguments that took place on 4 November 1992 in the court, it was decided that the verdict would be given on 11 December 1992. But the disputed structure was demolished on 6 December, i.e. before it could happen. In his order given on 11 December, Justice Satish Chandra Mathur wrote, 'This bench is accused of delay in making the decision and contributing in the demolition of the structure. We had to give decision on acquiring of 2.77-acre land and not on the structure. There was no dearth of security for the structure from the verdict of the courts. All had vouched for its safety. Courts don't have any executive powers to implement their verdict. This is the responsibility of the executive, meaning the government. It is easy to bring the genie out of the bottle but not easy to put it back.'

A saint by nature, Maulana Abul Hassan Ali Nadvi alias Ali Miyan was the chairman of All India Muslim Personal Law Board. There was an unwritten agreement between Ali Miyan and former Prime Minister Rajiv Gandhi regarding Ayodhya. Under pressure from Ali Miyan, Rajiv Gandhi reversed the decision of the Supreme Court in Shah Bano case by bringing legislation into parliament. In return, Ali Miyan remained silent on Rajiv Gandhi's decision to the opening of Ram Janmabhoomi. It was a mutual agreement between Rajiv Gandhi and him. This was the reason that till Rajiv Gandhi was alive, the Muslim Personal Law Board was not very aggressive. A meeting took place between Maulana Nadvi and VHP on the Ayodhya dispute. Many attempts were made to find a way out but failed. His translated book created quite a stir in the Ram Janmabhoomi Mukti Movement.

Maulana Abdul Hai, father of Maulana Nadvi, wrote an Arabic book *Hindustan Islamic Ahadme*. In 1973, Ali Miyan translated it in Urdu. In its chapter, 'Mosque of Hindustan', it was said that Ayodhya's Babri Masjid was constructed by Babur. Hindus call it the birthplace of Ramchandraji. Babur constructed the mosque exactly at the same spot. Later this book was removed from all the libraries of India. Ali Miyan was a scholar of international fame in the Islamic tradition. He was born on 5 December 1913 in Raebareli, Uttar Pradesh. His father Maulana Hakim Syed Abdul Hai was a great Islamic scholar. He wrote several books on Islam. After his father's death, Ali Miyan was involved with Darul Uloom Nadwa. Maulana Abul Hasan Nadvi was also the founding member of Muslim World League, which is the supreme council of mosques around the world.

Zafaryab Jilani is a senior advocate and member of the All India Muslim Personal Law Board. In the case related to the disputed structure, he has represented Babri Masjid Action Committee in Ayodhya. He has also been the Additional Advocate General of UP government. Since 1978, young lawyer Zafaryab Jilani had started active participation on Muslim issues. In 1985, he joined the All India Muslim Personal Law Board. When Faizabad district court ordered to open the temple premises on 1 February 1986, Zafaryab Jilani had strongly opposed it. On 15 February

1986, along with many other Muslim leaders he constituted Babri Action Committee and became its convener. Jilani is opposed to the out of court settlement of the Ayodhya issue.

Prof. Rajendra Singh was the fourth Sarsanghchalak of Rashtriya Swayamsevak Sangh. For the first time during the tenure of Rajju Bhaiya, a swayamsevak became Prime Minister. For the first time, under the leadership of Atal Bihari Vajpayee, the NDA government was formed. All his life, Rajju Bhaiya struggled for the construction of Ram temple in Ayodhya. In 1983, Rajju Bhaiya met with some senior Congress leaders who had been sidelined from the Congress party. They together, wrote a letter to Indira Gandhi and asked her to restore the three places of Hindus – Kashi, Mathura and Ayodhya. However, Indira Gandhi ignored this insistence. Rajju Bhaiya was the first non-Maharashtrian and the first non-Brahmin Sarsanghchalak. He was RSS chief from the year 1994 to 2000. Born in Shahjahanpur, Uttar Pradesh, people at home affectionately called Rajendra Singh, Rajju. After studying at Allahabad University, he was a professor of physics department. He came in contact with the RSS in 1942, during Quit India Movement. In 1966 he left professorship of Allahabad University and joined RSS full time.

Syed Shahabuddin was a politician, social worker and an officer of the Indian Foreign Service. Syed Shahabuddin is known to advocate the Muslim side firmly in the Shah Bano case. Shahabuddin organized a Central Action Committee and observed a day of national mourning on 1 February 1986, when the locks of the Babri building were opened in Ayodhya. He met the Prime Minister with all 41 Muslim MPs of the Lok Sabha and Rajya Sabha and demanded the handover of the Babri Masjid to the Muslims. Later, Shahabuddin made a Babri Masjid coordination committee by joining all the existing committees on Babri issue of which he himself became the convenor. This committee announced the 'boycott' of the Republic Day of 1987. Syed Shahabuddin was also a member of the All India Muslim Personal Law Board. Shahabuddin used to say that the Babri Masjid issue was not a religious but a legal issue. Born in Ranchi in 1935, Shahabuddin was selected for the Indian Foreign Service in 1958. In 1978, he resigned from the IFS and joined politics. Chandra Shekhar is credited for bringing him into politics and Janata party. He was elected three times for the parliament between 1979 and 1996.

Shrish Chandra Dikshit, a frontline leader of Ram Janmabhoomi movement, was DGP of Uttar Pradesh. He was in this position from 1982 to 1984. After retiring in 1984, Shrish Chandra Dikshit became the central vice president of VHP. He was also a member of the Shri Ram Janmabhoomi Nyas. Shrish Chandra Dikshit was considered as the confidante of VHP International President Ashok Singhal. He had a special role in taking the movement to the masses. Whether Kar Sevaks were to be quietly smuggled into Ayodhya or Kar Seva was to be done dodging all the law and order, he had the sharp mind to accomplish it. He was also one of those who laid the foundation of Ram temple in Ayodhya. In 1989, at the dharmsansad at Prayag-Kumbh, foundation laying of the temple was announced. After this, Shrish Chandra Dikshit travelled all over the country carrying the brick given by Devaraha Baba on his head. He was also arrested during the Kar Seva in Ayodhya in October-November 1990. Before Prime Minister Narendra Modi, he was the one who hoisted the saffron flag of victory over Varanasi Lok Sabha seat. In 1991, he was elected to the Lok Sabha from Varanasi. Earlier, no other BJP candidate had ever won this seat.

Madhukar Gupta was the Divisional Commissioner of Faizabad during the Ram Janmabhoomi movement. He was an IAS officer of 1971 batch from Uttar Pradesh and later from Uttarakhand cadre. In 1980, when he was the District Magistrate of Moradabad, he effectively controlled a large-scale riot. For this reason, on 7 October 1990, the then Chief Minister, Mulayam Singh Yadav, made him the Divisional Commissioner of Faizabad. On 30 October 1990, one lakh Kar Sevaks gathered in Ayodhya. At that time Madhukar Gupta had the responsibility of maintaining law and order, so he ordered to fire at the Kar Sevaks. He was the son of the real maternal uncle of VHP leader Ashok Singhal. When Kar Sevaks were fired upon in Ayodhya in October 1990, he said that not much loss of life had happened. Madhukar Gupta became the Union Home Secretary in June 2007. Gupta comes from a family of bureaucrats. His grandfather, father and brother were all associated with the Indian Administrative Service and the Indian Police Service.

The Kothari brothers, Ram Kumar Kothari (23) and Sharad Kumar Kothari (20) were real brothers. Both were from Kolkata and volunteers of Bajarang Dal. They were part of the first lot of Kar Seva held at Ayodhya on 30 October 1990. Both had hoisted the saffron flag on the disputed building. Government was agitated with the incident of destruction of things and climbing on the domes by the mob on 30 October. It decided to fire if Kar Sevaks violated the rule of law. On 2 November Kar Sevaks were determined to march towards the disputed premises. The Kothari brothers were in front in this mob. Police first dragged the younger brother from the procession and aimed at his head. Seeing this, the older brother came forward and challenged the policemen, 'leave my brother and if you have to kill then kill me.' This emotional call had no effect. They shot both the brothers. Both died on the spot. Hiralal Kothari had only these two sons.

Vishnu Hari Dalmia had been the president of VHP. Born in 1924, Vishnu Hari Dalmia was an industrialist and a Hindu leader. VHP was established in 1964. He remained its president from the year 1992 to 2005. When Shriram Janmabhoomi Nyas was established in 1964, Vishnu Hari Dalmia was appointed its treasurer. The interesting this was that when Dalmia was leading the temple movement, his son Sanjay Dalmia was a member of parliament from Samajwadi Party. On 8 December i.e. two days after the demolition of the disputed structure, he was taken into custody along with Lal Krishna Advani, Dr Murli Manohar Joshi, and Ashok Singhal. He is the son of founder of Dalmia group, Jai Dayal Dalmia and nephew of Ramkishan Dalmia. Dalmia Nagar was established by the Dalmia brothers in the 40s.

Ram Janmabhoomi Mukti Yagya Samiti's senior minister Dau Dayal Khanna was a Congress member of the Third Legislative Assembly of Uttar Pradesh. In the 1962 assembly elections, he won the election on Congress ticket from the Kanth seat of Moradabad district. Dau Dayal Khanna was the Health Minister of Uttar Pradesh Chief Minister Chandrabhanu

Gupta's cabinet. In 1983, Dau Dayal Khanna had come close to the VHP. In that same year, Dau Dayal Khanna was isolated from the Congress at the Hindu Convention held in Muzaffarnagar. Sarsanghchalak Rajju Bhaiya also participated in this meeting. In the meeting, a letter was written to Indira Gandhi, in which it was demanded that the three religious places—Mathura, Kashi and Ayodhya should be handed over to the Hindus. On 18 June 1984, the Shriram-Janmabhoomi Mukti Yagya Samiti was formed. Mahant Avaidyanath of the Goraksh Peeth became its president and Dau Dayal Khanna was made the senior minister of the committee. Rath Yatra was taken from Sitamarhi in Bihar to Ayodhya under the leadership of Dau Dayal Khanna on 25 September 1984.

Deoki Nandan Agarwal was Allahabad High Court judge. After he retired he filed a court case as a friend of Ram Lalla (minor), telling the court that Ram Lalla should be a party; because Ram Lalla resides in the building. That he is the current occupant. After which High court made Ram Lalla (idol) a party in the case. Related to Ayodhya issue, a total of five cases were filed. Among them the last one; (no. 236/1989) Bhagwan Ram Lalla present, was filed by Deoki Nandan Agarwal on behalf of Ram Lalla on 1 July 1989. Deoki Nandan Agarwal had been a judge at Allahabad High Court from 1977 to 1983. A law expert, Deoki Nandan Agarwal presented himself as a close friend of lord Ram. According to Hindu beliefs an invoked idol of a god is a living entity, and can fight its own case. But the worship-idol is considered a minor, so another person is expected to fight the case on its behalf. To fight the case, court appointed Deoki Nandan Agarwal as a close friend of Ram Lalla. Section 32 of the code of justice jurisprudence considers presence of god (idol) as a living person. It can be considered a person and party in a case. On this basis, court accepted his appeal. In the case filed by Deoki Nandan Agarwal it was demanded that the entire perimeter belonged to the appealing party (the residing-lord), so the parties opposing construction of a new temple or those causing any opposition or objection should be stopped from doing so. After the demise of Deoki Nandan Agarwal, Triloki Nath Pandey from VHP is acting as a friend advocate of Ram Lalla.

IPS officer of 1975 batch, Officer Karmvir Singh was the Faizabad SSP during the opening of temple premises in 1986. On 1 February 1986 Faizabad District and Sessions Judge Krishna Mohan Pandey summoned District Magistrate Indu Kumar Pandey and SSP Karmvir Singh. Court asked Karmvir Singh if opening the gates of the temple could spoil law and order. At this Karmvir told the court that there was no fear of deterioration of law and order because of the opening of the gates. He had no objection to the unlocking. Judge Krishna Mohan Pandey ordered to open the locks on that very evening by 4.40 p.m. Barely forty minutes after the order being given by the judge, District Magistrate Indu Kumar Pandey and SSP Karmvir Singh reached Ram Janmabhoomi temple and removed the gate locks. In 2009 Karmvir Singh became the UP DGP and retired in 2011. It was the first time that a court order had been complied within forty minutes.

In 1986 Indu Kumar Pandey was the District Magistrate of Faizabad when the temple premises was unlocked. He was a 1975 batch IAS officer from UP Cadre. The responsibility of executing the order of opening temple premises on the 1 February 1986 was upon Indu Kumar Pandey. During the hearing of appeal on temple door opening, Faizabad District and Sessions Judge Krishna Mohan Pandey had summoned District Magistrate Indu Kumar Pandey along with the SSP Karmvir Singh. Indu Kumar Pandey told the court—'to maintain law and order and to protect the idols there is no need to keep the gates locked. There is also no need to create a false disruption between the idols and the devotees. Someone must have showed his judiciousness and put a lock on the gate but since then no one has looked into whether there is any need to keep the gate locked or not.' Barely forty minutes after the order given by the judge, District Magistrate Indu Kumar Pandey and SSP Karmvir Singh reached Ram Janmabhoomi temple and removed the gate locks. Later Indu Kumar Pandey became the chief secretary of Uttarakhand.

In 1990 during the firing on Kar Sevaks, Subhash Joshi was the SSP of Faizabad. Subhash Joshi was the 1976 batch IPS of Uttar Pradesh Cadre. On 30 October 1990 on the occasion of Kartik Poornima, one lakh Kar

Sevaks gathered at Ayodhya. Lead by Swami Vamdev and Mahant Nritya Gopal Das Kar Sevaks left towards the disputed structure. To stop Kar Sevaks police fired at them, the force was being led by SSP Subhash Joshi. Five Kar Sevaks died in the firing. Ayodhya was quiet for one day. Then the anger among Kar Sevaks exploded, police fired again and twenty-five Kar Sevaks died in this second firing. Atal Bihari Vajpayee recounted incidents of brutality in the Lok Sabha. Later Subhash Joshi became the Director General of BSF. He was also the DG of NSG. After retirement Modi government appointed him the director of NTPC.

A brother to ex-Prime Minister Rajiv Gandhi through family relations, Arun Nehru had been State Minister for Home Affairs. It was Arun Nehru who was behind the opening of the Ram Temple. Arun Nehru and the chief minister of UP at the time, Vir Bahadur Singh had advised Rajiv Gandhi to unlock the disputed premises. Rajiv Gandhi had had a compromise with the Muslim hardliners in the Shah Bano issueand because of this he was being attacked for it from all quarters. The unlocking of the gates was Arun Nehru's advice to have attention diverted from the Shah Bano case. Born in Lucknow on 24 April 1944, Arun Nehru was the great grandson of Jawahar Lal Nehru's cousin Nand Lal Nehru. Indira Gandhi brought Arun Nehru into politics. He fought the 1980 by-election from Raebareli. Arun Nehru represented Raebareli in 1984 as well, in the Lok Sabha. Differences cropped up between Arun Nehru and Rajiv Gandhi on Bofors issue. After which he joined Janata Dal. He became an MP from UP's Billhor on Janata Dal ticket. He also became a minister in the V.P. Singh government. In 1990, he too was a part of the talks that sought solution during the movement for the Kar Seva.

A strong Congress leader Vir Bahadur Singh remained UP Chief Minister between 1985 and 1988. It was during his tenure that the doors of Ram Temple at Ayodhya were opened. Ram Janmabhoomi movement was at its peak in 1985. VHP was leading it. An appeal was filed at Faizabad district court on 31 January 1986 for unlocking the birthplace. Vir Bahadur Singh didn't want the credit to go to the VHP, so Arun Nehru and Vir Bahadur Singh advised Rajiv Gandhi to open the disputed premises and the lock was opened immediately, barely forty minutes after the court's verdict. Through Mahant Avaidyanath, Vir Bahadur Singh was also talking to the people involved in Ram Janmabhoomi movement. He was the only link that Congress had to talk to this party in the dispute. The reason was his close association with Mahant Avaidyanath, because like him, Mahant ji was also from Gorakhpur. Vir Bahadur Singh was born in Gorakhpur in 1935. He won Paniyara Lok Sabha seat in 1967 on Congress ticket. After that he was elected for five terms for UP Vidhan Sabha namely 1967,1969, 1974, 1980 and 1985. Being a close confidante of Sanjay Gandhi, Vir bahadur Singh was also close to Arun Nehru. He enjoyed the confidence of the Gandhi family to the maximum. It was then that an incident occurred. The Prime Minister at the time came to see the damage caused due to floods in Barabanki district. He made Narayan Dutt Tiwari resign for not managing the flood relief properly. Vir Bahadur Singh was made the new UP Chief Minister. Later when Arun Nehru left the Congress, Rajiv Gandhi removed Vir Bahadur Singh from UP chief ministership and made him the Communications Minister at the centre.

Buta Singh was the Home Minister in the Rajiv Gandhi government between 1986 and 1989. During the Ram Temple Movement Buta Singh was the link between the Central government and the UP state government. During Buta Singh's tenure UP saw two Chief Ministers— Vir Bahadur Singh and Narayan Dutt Tiwari. During the tenure of Vir Bahadur Singh, in 1986, the temple locks were opened and during Narayan Dutt Tiwari's tenure, in 1989, temple foundation was laid. Buta Singh made decisions with the help of few officers he was close to in the Lucknow secretariat. Chief Minister's office was completely sidelined on the Ayodhya issue. It was merely being used as a post office for relaying of information. It was Buta Singh who made Rajiv Gandhi agree to the laying of the foundation in 1989. Exactly one week before the foundation laying he arranged a meeting between Rajiv Gandhi and Devraha Baba at Gorakhpur. Buta Singh had also been Agriculture Minister in the Rajiv Gandhi government (1984-86).

EPILOGUE

The struggle for the Ram Janmabhoomi at Ayodhya has completed an entire journey around the circumference of democracy. The building of the grand Ram temple which has commenced with the Bhoomi Pujan will impact the generations to come and has changed the functioning of the Indian democracy. The Supreme Court judgement, the allocation of land for both the mandir and a masjid and the subsequent BhoomiPujan. The Bhoomi Pujan is an epoch in India's civilizational history and a paradigm shift in the working of the Indian democracy. The building of the grand Ram temple at Ayodhya, the birthplace of Ram marks the resurrection of India's cultural identity which stood besmirched for 491 years since its destruction by Mir Baqi in 1528. The Hindus of India have waited for hundreds of years to see their beloved Lord Ram to have a home of his own. The ideals of Lord Ram are not for the Hindus alone but epitomize the Indian civilization and the Indian nationhood and are so deeply intertwined that one cannot exist without the other. The temple at Ram Janmabhoomi at Ayodhya is the ultimate manifestation of the idea of India which is beyond a mere nation state and a continuous living civilization of 3000 years. Prabhu Shree Ram belongs to all Indians.

The running down of the Ram temple in Ayodhya was not a one-off incident in the cultural history of India but a systematic assault on the Indian civilization from the Islamic invasion which started in Seventh Century with the capture of Sindh by Mohammad Bin Qasim. The breaking of the temples from Kashi to Mathura to Somnath over the years has been a religiously ordained duty on the invading rulers and served as a mark of their commitment to the tenants of Islam being against idol worship. These invasions and destructions hurt the pride of India, humiliated its inhabitants and left a deep wound in their psyche. The Bhoomi Pujan is the initiation of the process to restore dignity and pride in a wounded civilization, the one that has been longing for justice.

The ethos of the Sanatan Dharma which are embedded in the Constitution of India are finally finding their rightful place. Indian ethos is essentially Hindu in character and this idea was being demolished since the dawn of Indian secularism making the Indian secularism anti Hindu. Instead of religious brotherhoods, the Hindu idea of Vasudhaiv Kutumbakam is a living testimony to the Hindu values of embracing all.

Dharmic thought which is essentially all embracing and much wider in its scope than secularism is the true concept of the interplay of governance and the religion. There are different paths to achieve truth and salvation but no path negates the other and every path is true in its own way. This idea of the running of the Indian state has been seen with contempt due to its Hindu roots is back in the reckoning post the Bhoomi Pujan. The secular narrative has been to the effect that appealing to the Imam for Muslim votes or the Church for Christian votes was considered to be secular but engaging with Hindu sadhus and seers was anti secular. This narrative has certainly been buried for the commencement of the construction of the Ram temple.

The building of the Ram temple is certainly an end of a certain politics which dismissed all the calls for Hindu pride under the garb of secularism, the ones who viewed the uprising of the Hindu samaj as a majoritarian act, not being able to move past the colonial baggage, who failed to understand the intricate connection of Raghuvansh and Bharatvarsha. It was truly sad when the existence of lord Ram was questioned by the government of the day before the Supreme Court of India in 2007. We have indeed moved a long way from that low to the point where the running of country's governance is imbibed with Dharmic value embedded in the Constitution that Lord Ram espouses of which the Bhoomi Pujan marks the seminal point.

The issue going on for centuries will finally end. But will the wound of the ongoing struggles between two civilizations heal? Ayodhya is a wound inflicted by the pangs of faith and division after independence. Changing the present is still easy. But is getting over the past equally easy?

History is a compilation of memories. And wounds etched in the memory of a civilization don't heal easily. Especially, when the wound of Ayodhya is a constant reminder of the stabs inflicted in the name of religion, civilization and honour. The faith which Babur wished to destroy by a sword, could not forget this laceration even after four hundred and fifty years. The community remained committed to build the temple there throughout history, at costs unforeseen. The grievances of this wounded civilization have got a soothing balm through the Supreme Court verdict and Bhoomi Pujan. The history in India has been whitewashed to suit a particular political bend to maintain peace and create an India, but the Hindu grievances were never addressed to and this Bhoomi Pujan marks the start of Hindu revivalism which is the underlying binding glue of the civilization and culture. Despite the fact that none of the current generation of Hindus were actually present when their culture and symbols of worship were being dishonoured but they carry with themselves the collective memories of victimhood which the Bhoomi Pujan and the temple construction finally is addressing.

Supreme Court's verdict is way above the ground of majority or minority. This decision has been given keeping in mind the merit of law as well as the higher ideal of equality. Behind the verdict is the tradition of actual worship that has been going on for centuries and the scientific evidence given by the Department of Archeology. It is clearly written in the judgment that this case was going on, on the basis of archaeological remains. The Ayodhya verdict is a testimony to the fact that our judicial system is dependent on the concept of multicultural society. Equality has always been empowered at the heart of the Constitution. This decision also made it clear that the law does not give preference to the faith of any particular religious community. Both the logic and the facts behind the Ayodhya verdict exist. In this, the old travelogues of foreign travellers have been considered as evidence. The verdict mentions William Finch from 1607 to 1611 and Father Joseph Tiefenthaler's travelogue between 1766 and 1771, according to which the disputed site is the birthplace of Lord Ram. There has always been worship here. The judgment also cites a report by the Archaeological Department which states that the remains of the Twelfth Century structure were found under the structure of Babri Masjid, which are of Hindu civilization. On the other hand, the Muslim side failed to provide evidence as to who owned the mosque for the three centuries after 1528. On this basis, this place was considered the birthplace of Lord Rama. The Hindu side proved that Lord Ram was worshiped even before the mosque at that place. At the same time, the Hindu side also proved heritage of the Ram chabutra in the outer porch.

The proposed design of the temple as of now is 360-feet long, 235 feet wide and 161 feet high. There is a proposed plan for redevelopment of entire Ayodhya as one of the most significant spiritual centres of the world. The proposed design shall have its soul in the traditional temple architecture but at the same time will be graced by the most modern technology. It will also address the issues of Environmental Sustainability. The design proposes the area of temple to be 2.7 acres whereas the area of the site is 67.3 acres. The foundation stone of the temple was built there in November 1989. The total stone requirement for the temple would be 3,75,000 CFT approximately of which 70,000 CFT is already available and carved. The foundation stone was laid at the Singh Dwar of the proposed temple. What has been proposed is that the entire complex will have a light and sound show, Musical fountain, satsang hall, yagyashala, gaushala, Sitarasoi, bhogbhawan interactive I.T. enabled museum and immersive galleries with themes based on the Ramayana for educating visitors and pilgrims, staff residences, residences for priests, souvenir shop, library, research center, 10 bed hospital , 360 degree theatre, fire station and the administrative building. The entire complex will ensure the ease of pilgrims and maximizing opportunities for a seamless darshan. It will also contribute greatly towards uplifting the local economy. The minimum time the construction of the temple would take will be nothing less than 40 months.

Ayodhya means that which cannot be won, and the Supreme Court verdict once again proved that Ayodhya is invincible. It cannot be won. With this, some complex questions were also fixed forever. Ram Janmabhoomi is where Ramlala is sitting today. That land cannot be divided. But Ayodhya did approve both, the temple and the mosque. Saryu has happily agreed that its water is for both pooja and wuzu. The true substance of Ram is engraved in the principles of Ramrajya, and the real Ramrajya emanates from dignity, harmony and dialogue. We have to stand by it. Only when we respect it, will Ayodhya's centuries-old wound be transformed into pleasant memories of the present. There will be no anger, no pain. Ayodhya has come in the form of a golden opportunity. This opportunity can be banked upon to ensure the unity of this country, like never before. Harmony and brotherhood can turn the poison of social acrimony and estrangement into elixir of love and oneness. Eradicating the temple-mosque dispute can herald a new resolve for the country's economic progress. A return of the mainstream issues necessary for life, society and the nation may become the norm. We should not let go this opportunity. This is the test of history. We have to confront this with full honesty and good intentions. This is the biggest lesson of Ayodhya.

ACKNOWLEDGEMENTS

To my ancestors, who instilled the culture of Ayodhya in me.

To the memories, that stayed alive in me without any notes even after such a long period .

To my father Manu Sharma, who taught me how to write.

To my master, teacher and guide Prabhash Joshi, who let my imagination take flight in the free skies of Ayodhya.

To my guru and the renowned critic Dr. Namwar Singh, who pushed me into writing this book every time we met.

To the constant pillar by my side, Shri Nripendra Misra, head of the temple construction committee of the Shri Ram Janmabhoomi tirth Kshetra trust for his valuable input on the structure and design of the mandir.

To the trilogy of editors—Ram Bahadur Rai, Hari Shankar Vyas and Rahul Dev for reading the script and guiding me.

To Shivendra Kumar Singh, Abhishek Upadhyay, Sopan Joshi and Amit Prakash Singh for crafting the content.

To my friend, M.P. Bhupendra Yadav for sending me three books on the Ayodhya verdict and pressurizing me to start working on the book.

To Professor Pushpesh Pant for a giving me a dose on ideologies.

To my brother Tushar Mehta who made documents related to Ayodhya available to me.

To Dr. Sandeep Kumar for the research and context.

To Abhimanyu Jindal from the Nehru Memorial Museum, Teen Murti and Rajkumar Srivastav from Indian Express Archives, Chandigarh who made thirty years old notes of mine available to me.

To IPS officer Rakesh Pandey who helped me with information ranging from the gazetteer of Faizabad to the accounts of foreign tourists who visited Faizabad.

To Rajendra Kumar, Manmohan Sharma, Praveen Jain, Kishan Seth, Satyanarayan Goyal, Pawan Kumar and Mahendra Tripathi for the precious and rare photographs that make this book lively. Rajendra

Kumar had even had his jaw broken when he was beaten up by Kar Sevaks while taking these pictures.

To Sharad Kapoor, whose hospitality made me feel at home in Ayodhya for twenty years!

To my peers and fellow journalists from Faizabad, Triyug Narayan Tiwari, V.N. Das and Gyan Prakash Pandey.

To my intellectual and writing partners Dayashankar Shukla 'Sagar', Yateendra Mishra, AlokSrivastav, Pranay Yadav, Yogesh Singh, Ajay Singh (Varanasi), Pramod Shukla, Yashwant Deshmukh, Yashwant Vyas and Mukesh Bharadwaj.

To Sushil Dwivedi, Rohit Sahay, Rahul Chowdhry and Shamsher Singh for encouraging me by quietly sitting by my side everyday while I was writing the book.

To Aashi (Swarna) for finding newspaper cuttings.

To Sandhu (Sandeep) for taking printouts till late at night and for finding books.

To my biggest critic Naveen Tiwari who after reading the manuscript for the first time appreciated it and said, 'Good work'.

To the Rupa Team for showing interest in the content and releasing the book with full gusto.

To the Captain, Sachin Sharma, for making me understand the police side of the story during the movement.

To 'Jerry' who sat beside my table all through the writing.

To Ishanee, whose insistence made me write the book.

To Parth, who made my work easy by lending me his computer.

To Veena, for the endless debates on Ayodhya.

And last but not the least, much gratitude to all you readers for placing your trust in me and picking up this book to read.